STRANGE FLORIDA II

MORE WEIRD AND UNUSUAL STUFF

CHARLIE CARLSON

LUTHERS
NEW SMYRNA BEACH
FLORIDA

FIRST EDITION
SECOND IN A SERIES
COPYRIGHT © 2007 BY CHARLIE CARLSON
ALL RIGHTS RESERVED

ISBN-13: 978-1-877633-80-5
ISBN-10: 1-877633-80-1

No part of this book may be reproduced or transmitted in any
form or by any means—graphic, electronic or mechanical—
including photocopying, recording or by any information
storage or retrieval system without written permission
from the publisher, except for brief quotations used
in reviews as provided by the "fair use" doctrine.

PRINTED IN THE UNITED STATES OF AMERICA

Published by
LUTHERS PUBLISHING
1009 North Dixie Freeway
New Smyrna Beach, FL 32168-6221
www.lutherspublishing.com

Original cover art by Mike Halen
Edited by Erika Leah Carlson
Associate Researcher Christine Kinlaw-Best

LIBRARY OF CONGRESS
CATALOGING-IN-PUBLICATION DATA

Carlson, Charlie, 1943–
Strange Florida: the unexplained and unusual/
Charlie Carlson.
1st ed.   p.   cm.
ISBN 1-877633-39-9 (pbk.)
1. Florida—Miscellanea.
2. Curiosities and wonders—Florida.
1. Title

F311.6.C37 1997   97-39306
975.9—dc21   CIP

STRANGE FLORIDA II

An Introduction to Strangeness

During the second century, Chinese seafarers brought home stories about dragons, with orange serpent-like tongues, living on an Indonesian island. For centuries, tales about these mythical creatures were passed down from one storyteller to the next. A few folks actually believed the dragons really existed, even though there was no proof except for outdated seafarer tales. The farfetched stories were laughed at by skeptics, at least until 1912, when scientists discovered the Komodo Dragon, the world's largest and most ferocious monitor lizard.

The Komodo Dragon is an example of how we often restrict ourselves to a box surrounded by walls of what we believe is possible, or impossible. We humans should realize that our knowledge about the infinite universe, and everything in it, will fit neatly on the point of a pin. Just a mere hundred years ago, skeptics would have scoffed at the idea of computers, microwaves, and toasters. In earlier times, such technology would have been considered the devil's work and I would have been burned at the stake for writing about weird stuff. We can easily see how today's "supernatural" can become tomorrow's "natural."

With millions of unexplained sightings and encounters spanning centuries, I am convinced that, at some point, somebody has experienced something which cannot be readily explained by our present knowledge and technology. It would be ridiculous to think that this many people are under a spell, hallucinating, or are misidentifying something; of course that would be a little weird, too.

We have to admire open-minded folks who risk ridicule to continue searching through haystacks of strange phenomena for a needle of truth. Even the staunchest skeptic must admit that such persistence has often paid off in new discoveries. We can only wonder what will be next, extraterrestrials and sasquatch? Inquisitive minds want to know about this stuff because most of us have a curious urge to make sense of the world we live in, which includes trying to explain the unexplained. Oddities and unusual people are easy to accept because we can go see them. On the other hand, we can't just jump in our car and go visit bigfoot or see a water monster. Such elusive mysteries require being in the right place at the wrong time or wrong place at the right time.

The definition of 'strange' means anything bizarre, unusual, odd, peculiar, puzzling, paranormal, weird, or just plain out of the ordinary. In other words, anything that isn't normal. I used to be 'normal,' I wrote history books, until 1997 when I published my first *Strange Florida*. It out sold all my history books combined. In April 2005, my first hardback, *Weird Florida*, [Barnes and Noble] was released and quickly became a regional best seller. It was immediately obvious to me that people like reading about weird stuff. Needless to say, I haven't written a history book since. However, within my strange books you'll find a healthy dose of Florida history and folklore. What you will read in this book has been dredged up by my research and interviews with people and through my personal network of ufologists, cryptozoologists, parapsychologists, and ghost hunters. I must also mention my many readers, bless their weird hearts, for providing me with countless tales and first hand encounters. Of course, if we solve any of these mysteries we will take the fun out of it and I'll have to find a new line of work.

Charlie Carlson

STRANGE FLORIDA II

FLORIDA'S SWAMP THING
Is a human-like creature lurking in Florida's Wilderness?

If there was ever a candidate for Florida's mascot of the paranormal, it would be the mysterious skunk ape. Described as an eight foot tall, shaggy-haired, human-like thing, eye-witnesses claim it weighs in excess of six hundred pounds and stinks to the high heavens. This big, smelly creature is Florida's equivalent to the bigfoot, or sasquatch, of the Pacific Northwest.

Alleged encounters with Florida's skunk ape go back hundreds of years. Pioneer and Indian legends speak of giants called the Mangrove People and the Sand People living along the Kissimmee River. Some folklorists believe these legends may possibly refer to tribes of skunk apes.

In the late 1800s, a pioneer of east Orange County, John Tanner, wrote in his journal about *"finding Indian graves on the St. John's banks with skeletons as big as giants. The knee cap of the leg was as long and tall as our hip bone, and the skull bone was so large it would fit over our heads."*

In 1935, workers excavating a shell mound near Lake Monroe dug up what was reported to be *"a human thigh bone as long as a normal man's entire leg."* Could these ancient bones have been the remains of what people today call the skunk ape, or just super-sized Timucuan Indians? Who knows? It's certainly an intriguing mystery that keeps on ticking.

A skeptic once asked me, "If there's such a thing, then why ain't somebody seen one?" Well, considering the thousands of reported sightings on record for the past hundred years, we must conclude that somebody has seen something they could not explain. Certainly a good portion of these sightings can be explained as misinterpretations or hoaxes, but what about the others? Could it be hallucinations? I really doubt that many folks have been hallucinating. If so, then we have another weird story to write about.

Since 2005, I have offered a ten thousand dollar reward for a live skunk ape, preferably a big 600 pound male, unwashed of course to retain his trademark stench. (I've also offered five grand for a live chupacabra, but that's another story.) So far, I'm still waiting for somebody to bring me one of these things. Does this mean these critters don't exist? The answer is no; it may just mean my reward is too cheap.

Florida's hairy hominid has many names, among which are, *Swamp Monkey, Swamp Ape, Everglades Ape, Abominable Swamp Man, Weeden Island Monster, Old Harry*, and *Holopaw Monster*. While a photo-hoax was called the *Okeechobee Ogre*, in Bardin, Florida, it goes by *Bardin Booger* and in a northwest Orlando suburb you can still hear stories about the *Fairvilla Gorilla*. It seems every section of the state has a nickname for the creature. However, witness reports and newspaper articles over the past twenty-years,

STRANGE FLORIDA II

show sightings to be a little more concentrated in the Everglades, the Withlacoochee State Forest, East Osceola County, West Brevard County, Blackwater River State Forest, and the Ocala National Forest.

If you want to know anything about researching Florida's hairy hominid, your best bet is Scott Marlowe, a cryptozoologist with the Pangea Institute, which maintains a data base of over 200 sightings. Having instructed courses in cryptozoology for the Florida Keys Community College, Marlowe has spent decades researching what he prefers to call the "Swamp Ape." His interest in the elusive critter began in 1975 with his own sighting of a 7 foot human-like creature standing beneath a street light in the parking lot of his Lakeland apartment complex. Marlowe said, "When you see something like that, it becomes burned in your mind, you don't forget it."

I have to agree with Scott Marlowe since I can relate to my own sighting at age 14 while camping with friends off State Road 46 near the Wekiva River. Many moons have passed since that night, but as I recall, we saw a silhouetted figure in the moonlight that looked like a very tall, husky, human-like thing with long arms, standing about 50 yards to our front, in the middle of the road. Whatever it was seemed to watch us for a couple of minutes before leaping over a barbed wire fence and tearing off through a thick swamp. We could hear it crashing through the tangled swamp, which is something no sane human would do at night. Having never heard at that time, of a skunk ape, or any references to sasquatch stories, we called it a "wild man." We returned to our campsite, built a blazing fire, and sat up the rest of the night. The next morning, we inspected the spot where we had seen the thing and found orange peelings scattered on the road. Apparently, the creature had been eating oranges from a citrus grove on the opposite side of the road from the swamp.

No one believed our story, but thankfully, we were vindicated a few years later when local newspapers reported several sightings of hairy man-apes in the same area of the Wekiva basin. Other people had seen the beast. One person claimed to have encountered an "ape-like thing" inside a greenhouse at an Apopka plant nursery. It was suggested that the witness had seen a bear. The Wekiva is a known habitat for black bear, but there's a big difference between a bear and a large primate. What we saw was definitely not a bear, a gorilla maybe, but certainly not a bear.

Based on years of study and dozens of field expeditions, Scott Marlowe believes Florida's hairy anthropoid differs from the standard sasquatch or bigfoot. One major difference, based on Marlowe's study of witness descriptions, is the human-like neck of the Florida creature. In the case of the sasquatch, or bigfoot, the head sits closer on the shoulders giving the appearance of not having a neck. The swamp ape can turn its head to look behind, where the sasquatch must turn its torso completely around. Marlowe suggests the Florida variety is more muscular and may possess a higher, human-like, intelligence. He theorizes that intelligence is involved with the creature's tendency to organize in family troupes and to migrate in search of food sources or in response to weather conditions. As for the gagging odor from which the skunk ape derives its name, Marlowe says, "it's really not a distinguishing feature since the same stench is frequently associated with hairy hominid sightings in regions other than Florida."

In November 1977, a 67-year old Baptist preacher from Fort McCoy came face-to-

STRANGE FLORIDA II

face with the huge hairy beast in the Ocala Forest. While cutting firewood, the man claimed to have seen a man-ape standing in the palmetto bushes. He described the creature as "standing seven to eight feet tall, with dark hair covering its chest and head but not much on the arms. The face was flat and hairless, with a wide nose and deep-set eye sockets." Fearing a physical threat from the beast, the preacher quickly retreated to his truck to get an ax. When he returned to where he had seen the creature, it had disappeared into the forest. He estimated the sighting to have lasted about half a minute, but long enough to realize it was not a known animal. During this same time frame, three miles away near the Big Scrub Campground, another person reported seeing an ape-like, seven foot tall animal at 9:30 at night "that weighed at least 800 pounds." A hunter allegedly fired several rounds at the beast but said he must have missed it since no blood was found. One of the most frightening encounters to make the news happened in 1959, when three boy scouts claimed they were chased from their campsite in the Ocala National Forest by a "big, hairy monster with a human-like face and the body of an ape."

One of the most curious accounts comes from 1971 and involved a five member archaeological team excavating an aboriginal site deep in the Everglades. They described how an 8 foot tall, shaggy-haired, man-ape came tromping into their camp at 2:30 in the morning, threw things around, and then ran off into the swamp. The thing left behind an obnoxious stench and 17 ½ inch tracks. It's safe to say this was no prankster; after all, what fool would be rambling around the Everglades in the middle of the night wearing a gorilla suit? In a separate sighting, also in the Everglades, the creature was described as having long, shaggy, *whitish* or *grayish* hair. Certainly no creative hoaxer would use a "white" hairy suit if he intended to look like the stereotypical bigfoot.

Several intriguing reports have come from the remote regions of Yeehaw Junction, Kennansville, and Holopaw. It was in this section of the state, at the Three Lakes Wildlife Management Area, where several deer hunters witnessed two hairy hominids crossing a rural road. One creature, referred to as a male, was described as a bi-pedal ape-like beast covered with dark brown fur and about six and a half feet tall. The first one was followed about 15 yards behind by a slightly smaller, darker creature which appeared to have breasts and was assumed to be a female. The witnesses believed the smaller one was carrying something at waist level which may have been a youngster.

The Three Lakes case is significant because *multiple* witnesses allegedly observed *multiple* creatures, with possibly a youngster. Let's face it, if there are adult skunk apes, then there has to be baby ones, too. However, only a few reports on record have mentioned juveniles. I wonder if "littlefoot" would be a better term for a young bigfoot? Following a lecture about Florida folklore at a historical society meeting, I was cornered by Gerald Keeling, 72, who related, in almost a whispering tone, how he was driving with his sister through the Pumpkin Swamp on Route 358, northwest of Cross City, when they spotted a small, shaggy-haired thing standing in the edge of the woods. Gerald stopped his car, shifted into reverse, and backed-up for a better look just in time to see the thing casually amble off into the thick woods. "It was only about four feet tall and looked like a cross between an orangutan and a human," Gerald explained. "I have no idea what the hell it was but it definitely had a human face to it. It was just standing there, on the other side of a small ditch. I think it was a young one. We didn't mess around in case the momma was nearby. I told a few close friends about it, but that was all."

In 2001, bigfoot enthusiasts were thrown into a high pitched frenzy when an elderly

STRANGE FLORIDA II

woman living in Myakka submitted several photographs of an anthropoid to the Sarasota County sheriff's department. The unidentified woman, being concerned about a large animal roaming around her property at night, placed some apples on her porch hoping to attract the creature. For two nights the creature came up to her porch and took the apples. On the third night she had her camera ready and snapped several pictures of what looks remarkably like an orangutan. In my opinion, *it was an orangutan*, and Scott Marlowe also believes it was an orangutan. Of course, this hatches another strange mystery, did someone lose their orangutan? If so, he's running loose in Myakka and stealing apples. I wonder why no one else has seen this apple thief. The woman who took the photographs of the hairy primate described it as having a putrid odor and six to seven feet tall when kneeling, and ten feet high when standing. I examined the photographs and, in my opinion, the size was greatly exaggerated. Although most agree it's an orangutan, a few diehards still think it's a *skunk ape*. Hey, I know a skunk ape when I see one and the animal in those photographs *is an orangutan* and *not a skunk ape*.

The first publicized photographs of a skunk ape were taken in Collier County by David Shealy, who put Florida's bigfoot into the national spotlight on several television shows, including *Inside Edition* and *Unsolved Mysteries*. Shealy has described the creature as smaller than bigfoot, having only four toes, and claims it likes to eat lima beans. I don't know how he figured that out, but maybe it's the beans causing the obnoxious odor that's emitted by the beast. Shealy established the first *Skunk Ape Research Center* in Ochopee where Florida's annual Skunk Ape Festival is held each June. In addition to being a lot of down home fun, the event is a gathering spot where folks can freely exchange stories about their skunk ape encounters. I've visited there and can tell you that Shealy's place is about as far as you can get from civilization in Florida.

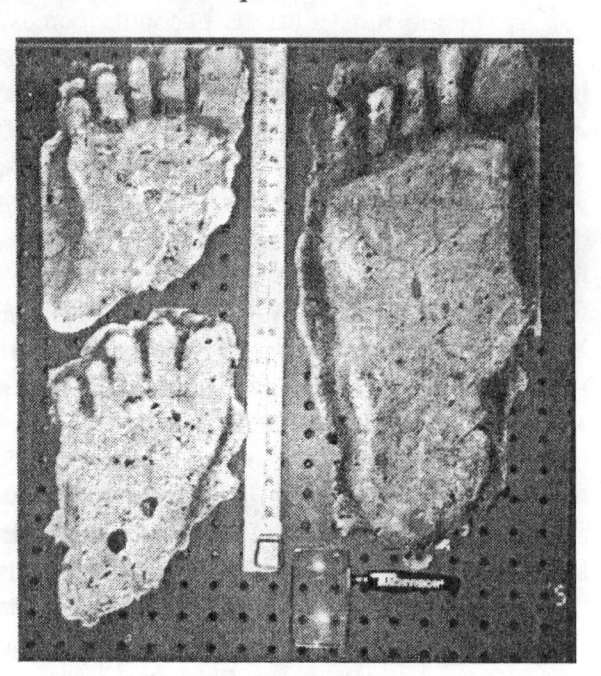

THE FIFTEEN INCH HUMANOID FOOT PRINT CASTS MADE BY JACK SIMMONS IN 1992.

In the wake of Hurricane Charley, in 2004, a woman was driving on a rural road and saw something crouched over in a ditch. As she slowed her car almost to a stop, a hairy beast stood up and looked at her. Although a bit shocked, she was able to get a good look and described it as standing 6 to 8 feet tall and covered with hair. It took the witness in this case a considerable length of time to go public with her sighting.

As with any other weird experience, the fear of ridicule keeps most skunk ape encounters out of the news. If you saw a big hairy monster would you report it? One cryptozoologist estimated for every reported skunk ape encounter, there are twenty that will never be known. The most intriguing accounts come from rural oldtimers who have never heard of a skunkape, but have told me stories about seeing a "wildman" or "ape."

In November 1966, a woman motorist met with a scary situation at the edge of dark,

STRANGE FLORIDA II

when she had a flat tire on a desolate county road near Brooksville. While changing her tire, she became aware of a strange odor and noise coming from the opposite side of the road. She glanced around and saw a human-like creature, about seven feet tall, standing in the road. According to her account, which appeared in a newspaper, the hairy monster weighed around 400 pounds and squatted beside the road as if curious about what she was doing. Fortunately, for the terrified lady, another car came along and whatever it was disappeared into the woods.

One of the most bizarre stories comes from a long distance trucker who had pulled into an I-75 rest plaza near Wildwood to catch a few winks. He alleged, according to a newspaper article, that he was awakened by a bigfoot pulling him from the truck cab. According to the report, the shaggy-haired monster carried him, kicking and yelling, under one arm for several yards. "My face was pressed into the thing's hair," stated the trucker, "and it had an awful odor." He finally broke free and made a mad dash for the safety of his truck cab. Once inside, he rolled up the windows and locked the doors while the creature pounded its fists against the truck. The driver responded with several loud blasts of his air horn which sent the ape-man high-tailing it into a nearby swamp.

In 1971, another truck driver had a close encounter one night on Highway 27 near Bellglade with a hairy beast. At first he thought it was a hitchhiker in his headlights. He pulled off the road and reached over and opened the passenger door for the hitchhiker. When he caught a whiff of an awful stench, he sensed something was wrong and tried to close the door. As he reached to shut the door, a huge hairy beast with a man-like face tried to climb into the cab. The driver jumped out and ran as fast as he could away from his truck. He waited, scared and out of breath, until the thing climbed down from the cab and disappeared into the swamp. Cautiously, he returned to his truck and climbed inside and locked all the doors. The cab was filled with a putrid smell. Once back on the highway, the driver said he had to roll down the windows to rid the cab of the odor.

Violent behavior is rare in stories about the Skunk Ape; however, one chiropractic doctor related how a patient came into his office complaining of an injury caused by being attacked by a giant swamp ape. Being a good doctor, he treated the patient for a neck sprain, and asked, "Are you sure you want me to put this in your report, because it will be submitted to your insurance company." The patient replied, "I don't care who knows about it. It was a 7-foot tall stinky swamp ape." The report was submitted to the insurance company, and they accepted it.

The skunk ape phenomenon has even found its way into government conspiracy stories. Although such stories have little support, according to a tale circulated in the 1970's, the military captured a live skunk ape and was keeping it in a secret vault hidden within the Everglades National Park, that is, until the creature beat its way through a concrete wall and escaped. In another story, skunk ape hair samples were confiscated from a researcher's home by *men-in-black* agents of the government. As an investigative writer of weird stuff, I've always been under the impression that the *men-in-black*, if they really do exist, were more interested in harassing witnesses of alien spaceship landings. Okay, I might as well mention that a few UFO enthusiasts have attempted to connect bigfoot encounters to alien spacecraft sightings. It is amazing how one unexplained phenomenon can sometimes get sidetracked with another unexplained mystery. If there is a government conspiracy regarding the skunk ape, then what would be the motive of keeping the lid on it? I recall asking a similar question about that alleged UFO recovery in Roswell, New Mexico. My inquiry resulted in a form letter from the air force denying it happened. If the government is keeping a secret it certainly is not going to tell someone like me…or you.

Physical evidence, such as fecal matter, hair samples, blood samples, etc., has been scarce. The few hair samples which have been analyzed in the lab have produced only inconclusive results. A few Florida folks have offered for examination plaster casts of big foot prints. I don't know many people who run around carrying a box of Plaster of Paris, but in 1992, Jack Simmons made plaster casts of large humanoid prints near the Volusia-Brevard county line, a couple of miles from the Merritt Island Wildlife Refuge. These casts are dubious at best, although at the time Mr. Simmons made them, there were two skunk ape sightings within a radius of ten miles. One of those involved Paul Schmidt, of New Smyrna, who claimed that while delivering newspapers before sunrise one morning in nearby Oak Hill, he saw the mid-section of a giant hairy biped in the headlights of his truck. In an interview with the author, he described the creature as having long, shaggy, grey hair and walking upright. When asked to describe any other characteristics, Schmidt related, "A terrible smell, like rotten cabbage, so bad that I gagged, I almost vomited."

According to varying estimates, in order to sustain a breeding population there would have to be between 500 and 2000 of these elusive creatures. Scott Marlowe gets a little more specific with his speculation that if migration is involved, reproduction could probably be sustained with 750 to 1000. Marlowe's data suggests a migration pattern with the creature staying within particular quadrants of the state. In November 2005, based on the hypothesis of migration patterns, Scott Marlowe led an expedition into the Green Swamp where, after braving snakes and skeeters, they discovered what appeared to be several nests, made from saplings, in a circular arrangement. Could these have been swamp ape nests? Marlowe thinks it is highly possible if consideration is given to the arrangement and transportation of the saplings forming the nests which could have only been done by an intelligent animal with an opposing thumb.

The skunk ape is not unknown to the Florida Fish and Wildlife Commission which frequently receives requests from people for permits to hunt the creature. Of course, the Commission does not issue such permits, but I'm told their office of information does keep a file of newspaper articles about the skunk ape. The U.S. Fish and Wildlife Service once issued a news release stating that bigfoots [or is bigfeet the plural?] would be listed on the endangered species list if proven to be real. Obviously, with so many sightings, government agencies are willing to consider the possibilities. In April 1977 the Florida State Legislature introduced a bill (H.B.1664) to protect the elusive creature. The bill specifically stated, "Any person taking, possessing, harming or molesting any anthropoid or humanoid animal which is native to Florida, popularly known as the Skunk Ape, or doing any act reasonably capable of harming or molesting such animals" would be punished in accordance with the law. State Representative Paul Nuckolls, remarked, "I would hate to see someone catch one and put it in a circus or zoo." The bill was never passed into law, but the interesting point is that the possibility of such a creature existing was real enough for the state lawmakers to consider protecting it.

I think it's time for state lawmakers to pass a bill making the skunk ape the official mascot of Florida's weirdness. With more natural habitat being lost to development, the skunk ape will soon have no place to hide. We can expect sightings to increase, along with our chances toward proving, one way or another, the existence of Florida's ape-man.

STRANGE FLORIDA II

Florida's Apparitions, Specters, & Spirits...

A haint by any other name is still a ghost.

The Biltmore Hotel in Coral Gables has received its share of publicity from ghost-hunters for being Florida's most haunted hotel. Built in 1925, the Biltmore was closed during the 1970s and that's when the spirits checked in, according to local witnesses have seen strange lights inside the vacant hotel. One group of ghost hunters explored the building using a variety of spirit-detecting devices, including digital recorders that picked up unexplainable sounds, "like people talking." Since the re-opening of the hotel, guests have told of mysterious messages appearing in the steam on bathroom mirrors, and doors that open on their own, and some claim to have seen the apparition of "a little old man with a cane." Another story has a ghost-guest residing on the thirteenth floor, where elevators often stop even when the button has been pressed for another floor. The *thirteenth floor*, give me a break, how cliché can a ghost story get?

Okay, here's the scoop on the Biltmore as I heard it. During the Prohibition era, a gangster by the name of Thomas "Fatty" Walsh was involved in an illegal whiskey business with a partner who was staying in a room on the thirteenth floor. A heated argument erupted between the two gangsters and Fatty was shot dead in the thirteenth floor room. I guess "Fatty the Gangster" became "Fatty the Ghost" and is still hanging around pulling pranks on guests.

In St. Petersburg, the Don Cesar Beach Resort, built in 1925, is haunted by its former owner, Thomas Rowe, who died in 1940. According to ghost busters who have investigated the place, Mr. Rowe can be seen decked-out in white and wearing a Panama hat, roaming the halls and grounds. Current management discredits the stories, but I think having a ghost would be an attraction for business, like Ashley's Restaurant in Rockledge, where the management even puts their ghost story on the back of the menu. Ashley's haunting has appeared in all kinds of publications and in television documentaries. A few years ago I participated in a TV documentary that was filmed there and in 2003, accompanied the Spookhunters, based in Orlando, on a field investigation of the place. I later used Ashley's as a backdrop to my novel *Ashley's Shadow*, published in 2005, which is based on a dead girl who supposedly haunts the restaurant.

I have a fondness for Ashley's Restaurant for two reasons; first, it has great food at reasonable prices, and second, it has a great ghost story which goes back several decades. Employees and patrons tell of being touched, shoved, goosed, or having their hair yanked by invisible entities. Kitchenware moves about, lights flicker, and apparitions have been seen in the mirror of the ladies' room. Some have experienced a "choking sensation" in the corridor leading to the restroom.

The cause of Ashley's haunting is blamed on an assortment of spirits. One story has the Tudor-style building sitting atop an Indian burial mound, another claims it used to be the railroad station that burned down and killed some people. Then there's the one about a girl killed on the highway out front, or the boy killed out back on the Florida East Coast railroad tracks. Sorry to say, historical research does not substantiate any of these claims. However, another account can be documented by census records and microfilm of old newspapers and police files. It's the story of Ethel Allen, a 19 year old girl murdered in 1934. Her mutilated, nude, body was found dumped in the Indian River between Rockledge and Eau Gallie. According to the ghost legend, she was killed in the storeroom, which today is the ladies restroom, and has come back to haunt the place. The part about the storeroom murder is not supported by historical facts, but there is a clue linking Ethel to Ashley's eatery. A 1934 newspaper article about the murder, states that Ethel Allen was "employed at Jack's Tavern." My research indicates that in the 1930s, Ashley's was called *Jack's Tavern*, owned by a Jack Allen. He may have been related to Ethel, however, according to the census, he was not her father or brother. Whatever the case, it certainly makes Ethel Allen a prime suspect in the haunting of Ashley's.

Many wannabee ghost hunters literally operate in the dark because they fail to search through records for evidence that will support a haunting. Before striking out as a ghost buster you need a little proof that a spirit really existed as a living person or that an event actually happened, otherwise, you'll be on a wild goose chase instead of a ghost chase. In the case of Ashley's resident ghost, historical research led me to Merritt Island where I found Ethel's simple grave in the Crooked Mile Road cemetery. A little research can make haunting stories more intriguing, or in other cases, dismiss them as something that never existed in the first place.

The Kingsley Plantation on St. George Island north of Jacksonville can lay claim to several resident specters. The plantation was established in 1813 by Zephaniah Kingsley, who owned it until 1839. Today, it is a historical site consisting of the original planter's house and the ruins of 25 slave-quarters. Compared to other slave masters, Kingsley was a nice guy and allowed his slaves to work at their own crafts and tend their own gardens once the plantation work was done. His slaves were allowed to keep any profits from the sale of their crafts and produce. Kingsley liked his slaves, so much that he married one, Anna Madgigine Jai. As Mrs. Kingsley, Anna became quite active in the plantation's management. When the United States passed laws discriminating against freed slaves, Kingsley moved his family and slaves to Haiti. Many descendants of Zephaniah and Anna Kingsley still live in Haiti today. Meanwhile, back in Florida, a few ghosts from the past still roam the grounds of the Kingsley plantation on St. George Island.

A former tour guide for the historic Kingsley Plantation recalled how people frequently heard a child's cries coming from a well near the plantation house. Although historical evidence is absent, a slave child supposedly fell into the well and drowned. The eeriest claim has to do with Old Red Eyes, the ghost of a slave that murdered and mutilated several slave girls. According to the story, he was hanged for his evil deed from an oak tree beside the road leading to the plantation. Witnesses tell me that if you drive along this palmetto-lined road at night you'll see Old Red Eyes following your car. As an experiment, I drove the road late one night and saw two "glowing red eyes" up ahead. It turned out to be the taillights of a car, loaded with teenagers, looking for Old Red Eyes.

STRANGE FLORIDA II

In Key West, my ghost pick is *Robert*, a malevolent doll. Exhibited in the Artist House at 534 Eaton Street, this life size doll, made in 1904, has been heard giggling and laughing and on several occasions, has been seen moving. Obviously this thing must be possessed and should be exercised...or is that exorcised? The spooky doll often turns up in other places inside the house, apparently relocated by unexplainable means. Robert the doll is believed to be the likeness of an artist named Gene Otto when he was a child. Otto died in 1974 and was followed in death by his wife in 1977. Mrs. Otto's spirit allegedly occupies one of the second story bedrooms. Visitors often remark about feeling the presence of a small spirit girl on the stairs in the rear of the house. A photo taken by one visitor near the stairs shows a swirling white mass of "something." Maybe spirit energy?

Another Key West haunted place is the Audubon House, on the corner of Whitehead and Greene streets, where a tall entity wearing a ruffled shirt and a long dark coat has been seen on the porch. Witnesses believe it's the apparition of John James Audubon, the famous naturalist and artist. If you don't encounter Audubon's ghost, just go down the street to Ernest Hemingway's house, preferably around midnight when the famous author can be heard pecking away at his typewriter or seen looking at you from a second-story window. Since his demise in 1961 from a self-inflicted gunshot, people say Hemingway's spirit has continued to occupy his former home.

You'll need a boat to get to the Cabbage Key Inn where Indian spirits have been seen in the rooms and kitchen area. The Inn, built in 1930, sits on a Calusa Indian burial mound on Cabbage Key, off Florida's southwest coast. One person claimed to have seen two Indians arguing in the kitchen as if they were unaware they were dead. The main spirit at the Inn seems to be a brown-haired woman in a blue dress that frequently appears in the guest rooms. There are stories about her sitting on beds and wandering from room to room. After she scares the daylights out of you, she walks through the door without opening it. Another odd sight at the Inn, unrelated to ghosts, are the thirty-thousand one dollar bills plastered and stapled to the walls inside the bar. This wallpaper is genuine currency put there over the years by patrons of the Inn and you can see it for yourself.

There is an urban legend in Lake City about a building occupied by the Columbia Board of Education that has to do with an annual manifestation of a murdered girl. Allegedly, each year around Valentine's Day, the dead girl is seen in the hallway. The legend is based on a twelve year old girl murdered by serial killer Ted Bundy. On another ghostly note, Lake City is also host to the annual reenactment of the Civil War battle at Olustee. Floating orbs of light have been captured by cameras on the battlefield and during the annual Blue and Gray Ball. Speculation is that the orbs are the spirit energy of soldiers killed during the Battle of Olustee, Florida's only major Civil War battle.

Watch out if you drive on Highway 98, near Lakeland, for a phantom semi-truck that tailgates motorists. I wonder if this is the same ghostly 18-wheeler people have seen on Interstate-four between Orlando and Daytona? The traffic is so congested and crazy on these stretches of asphalt that it's a wonder anyone would even notice a phantom truck.

If you're easily excited by poltergeist shenanigans, then you'll be intrigued by a poltergeist case involving a novelty storage warehouse in Miami. In my opinion this has to be America's best documented proof of poltergeist activity. Go back to December 1966 through January 1967, when the Tropication Arts warehouse, a distribution center for Florida souvenirs, experienced 225 unexplainable incidents of merchandise flying or rolling off shelves. Workers frantically tried to figure out what was going on. There was so much breakage that the owners called in the police to investigate. The first officer on the scene witnessed so much strange stuff that he called for backup. The unexplainable activity was actually witnessed first-hand by the police, a detective, a journalist, insurance investigators, and eventually a team from the American Society for Psychical Research joined the investigation.

During a ten day period, the ASPR team documented 150 incidents and narrowed the cause down to Julio Vasquez, a 19 year old Cuban worker. Vasquez was the only worker present during all of the incidents. Researchers concluded that Vasquez, who was experiencing personal turmoil in his life, was subconsciously projecting some kind of psychical kinetic energy. He was tested in a controlled laboratory experiment, which found he could produce a high level of psychic energy. Researchers wanted to do more experiments and even offered Vasquez money, but he refused, saying he didn't like being a guinea pig. On January 30, 1967, Vasquez was fired for stealing from the warehouse and the poltergeist activity ceased. The extent of Julio Vasquez' psychic ability will never be known, because in 1969, while working at a Miami gas station, he was shot and killed in a holdup by two robbers.

The Villa Paula, built in 1925, is a historic mansion in Miami that was originally used as the Cuban Consulate. The first consul, Domingo Milord, named the place in honor of his wife, Paula, who passed away in 1931 in an upstairs bedroom after her leg was amputated. The building was closed in the late 1930s and sold to a private owner who later witnessed an entity described as a one-legged woman. It was believed to be the spirit of Paula Milord who had lived there for thirty years. The mansion has gone through several owners and, for a brief period beginning in 1970, it was owned by the U.S. Department of Housing and Urban Renewal as a residence for senior citizens. It was abandoned in 1974 and became a hangout for derelicts and drug addicts. In 1975 an investor restored the classic old home to its original charm. New floors, chandeliers, woodwork, and furniture brought the Villa Paula back to life. It was put up for sale, but ten years went by without a buyer. Some believe prospective buyers were kept away by the location, but others thought it was because the place was haunted. It seems most of the ghostly antics began after the building was restored. First, it was a swinging iron gate that kept slamming shut on cats, killing them one by one. The cats were only the first to encounter the unknown at the Villa Paula. Rapping sounds were heard emanating from the walls, while kitchen utensils and china flew from cabinets. People reported seeing the manifestation of a one-legged woman in the house. Doors would shut without cause while the aroma of Cuban coffee drifted through the rooms, although no coffee was brewing in the house. Later, there were reports of a dark haired woman-spirit wearing a Spanish-style dress. It is believed that both apparitions were the ghost of Paula. In 1989, the Villa Paula was sold in an auction and converted into an office building.

In Tallahassee, the Old Leon County Jail, which was closed in 1960, has a spiritual presence. Since closing, the building has been used for records storage and as a temporary office facility. Workers there have reported strange sounds, mysteriously opening doors, and of being touched, pushed, and yanked by unseen hands. Skeptics, ignoring the air-tight construction of the old jail, have blamed the wind. One account, which I have been unable to verify, claims that during renovation in the mid-1960s, a human skeleton was found in the elevator shaft and two others found between the walls. A group of mediums were inspired by the bizarre tale and conducted a séance in the jail,

STRANGE FLORIDA II

which they claimed, *"produced such intense spiritual energy that the participants immediately ended the session."* Having read first-hand stories from people who have worked there, I must conclude that the Old Jail does have some unexplainable weirdness.

In Alachua County, there's an old two-story country house that past owners claim is haunted. The last residents, Buz and Pat, no last names please, sold the place after seeing an apparition dressed like an old baseball player. Baseballs would mysteriously appear inside the house and, on one occasion, a ball crashed through the window. It seemed to come out of nowhere. The former owner, Buz, told me, *"The weird stuff started about a month after we were settled. The worst was when the sounds started. It was spooky, I mean at night when we were asleep there would be loud moaning, like a man in pain, then when we got up the sound would stop."* They would find kitchen drawers pulled out with all the utensils dumped in the floor. My informant described his frustrations as a former resident, *"I would be working with a hammer or tool of some kind, lay it down, go back for it and it would be gone. Then later I would find it in some place I knew full well I hadn't put it. Now you figure that out."* After a little bit of research, the former owner discovered that, in 1930, a woodworker had lived in the house. He made baseball bats for well-known ball players! Well, that certainly fit the ghostly experiences of the residents. At this writing, the house is on the market again. I called the realtor in Gainesville and asked if the place was haunted. She replied, *"No comment."* She then requested that I not identify the property location or the real estate agency in this story. Needless to say, this request put a strain on my paranormal conscience but since I'd rather avoid a legal wrangle over a haunted house, the secret is safe with me.

There's an urban legend in Rockledge about a man in a cocked hat. This is a yarn from history, so take it for what it's worth. Along the river road where a little piece of land juts out into the Indian River, people claim to have seen a man dressed in Colonial clothing and wearing a cocked hat. He appears to be floating as nothing is seen below his knees. Those who believe the story say it's the apparition of Henry Jennings, a pirate who supposedly had his headquarters along the Indian River. Okay, if one ghost is not enough for this location, hold-on to your cocked hats for another one. People have also seen a pretty, blonde, female hitchhiker in the same spot. She appears on rainy nights and catches rides with passing cars. After hearing the story, I drove that stretch of road twenty times looking for the blonde. No luck. I didn't even see the fellow in the cocked hat. Those who have picked up the rain-soaked blonde lady say she left no water in their car when she got out. Variations of the *woman hitchhiker* story can be found throughout American paranormal lore. I suspect the two stories from the same spot are concocted from the same basis, or maybe the guy in the cocked hat is impersonating a blonde girl just to get a ride. I mean, people are more likely to pick up a pretty blonde than a weird, legless guy wearing a cocked hat.

Workers at a building on the Pensacola Naval Air Station tell stories of objects flying about rooms, office machines turning on and off, doors slamming, and hearing strange sounds, including an unseen entity operating a floor buffer. Personally, I would not complain if a ghost was buffing my floors. The building, constructed in 1926, was used as a hospital until 1986 when it was converted into offices. This same military installation claims another haunted structure, the Pensacola Lighthouse where the former keeper died. The footsteps and other noises made by the dead keeper can be heard inside the lighthouse.

STRANGE FLORIDA II

St. Augustine wins the prize for the most haunted city in Florida, which is not surprising since it is America's oldest city, with more ghost tours than you can stir with a stick. Sandy Craig was first when she opened the *Original St. Augustine Ghost Tour*, now there are five tours, all trying to keep pace with the spirits of the Ancient City.

St. Augustine's paranormal centerpiece has to be the Castillo de San Marcos. In 2003, through special arrangement with the National Park Service, I spent the night in this old Spanish fort with the Spookhunters, a paranormal investigative team. They were successful in capturing several orbs of light with digital video equipment and several unexplainable high readings on electro-magnetic field detectors. In one room, our noses sensed the definite presence of a sweet aroma, like cheap perfume. This supported a 1784 story we had heard about the love affair of Senora Delores Marti and Captain Manuel Abela. She was the wife of Colonel Garcia Marti who was garrisoned at the fort at the beginning of Florida's second Spanish period.

When Colonel Marti discovered that his wife was fooling around with Captain Abela, he ordered both of them chained to the dungeon wall and then, while they were still alive, he sealed up the two lovers behind a coquina rock wall, like a tomb.

Fast forward to 1938, or 1833, depending on the source, a false wall was discovered in the fort, behind which was found human bones. Were these the bones of Senora Delores Marti and Captain Abela? Who the heck knows, but after the discovery of the bones people began smelling perfume in the fort and seeing the apparition of a woman floating across the grounds.

There are so many ghost stories about St. Augustine that you could fill a big book, which several writers have done, including one of my favorites, David Lapham's *Ghosts of St. Augustine,* [1997, Pineapple Press]. There are two haunted places that I want to highlight here, Catalina's Garden and the St. Francis Inn. Catalina's Garden is a restaurant, located at 46 Avenida Menedez, which has changed hands and names many times, so just look it up by the address. The place is full of weird stuff, like candles lighting themselves, lights that turn on and off, and other typical poltergeist-type stuff that seems more active during cold or rainy weather. I had my own encounter in this establishment one rainy evening while enjoying a nice meal. The lights began to flicker, then went out leaving the dining room in blackness. Then, all of a sudden, they came back on. In case you're wondering, I wasn't about to give up my meal for a ghost, so I just kept eating in the dark. My experience may not sound like much, but what about customers who have seen the apparition of a man in a 1880s-style black suit on the stairs or standing in the corner of the dining room? On the second floor, usually in the ladies' restroom, people have had a vision of a woman wearing a white bridal dress. It may have been the spirit of Catalina, the youngest child of Francisco and Juana de Porras. She was born there in 1753, when her family lived in a house on the same spot where the restaurant now stands. When Spain turned Florida over to the British in 1763, the Porras family moved to Cuba. Catalina grew up and married Joseph Xavier Ponce de Leon in Cuba but, having a strong attachment with her childhood home, she longed to return to St. Augustine. When Spain regained control of Florida in 1783, Catalina, with her husband, moved back to St. Augustine to reclaim her childhood home. During the twenty year British period, the house had been unoccupied and used for storage. It took until 1789 before Catalina could gain ownership of the place. Sadly, she only lived six years after moving into her home. The Great Fire of 1887, which destroyed a large portion of the city also burned Catalina's house. One account states that a man living in the house lost his life in the fire. Could he be the man in the suit seen in the restaurant? In 1888 the house was rebuilt on the original foundation to exact specifications based on an artist's sketches. It remained a dwelling until 1976 when it became the Puerto Verde restaurant.

The St. Francis Inn is a charming bed and breakfast near the Oldest House on St. Francis Street. It's been operating under various innkeepers since 1845, when it was a boarding house run by Anna Dummett. In 1855, the house became the property of Major William Hardee, later known in Civil War history as General Hardee. Yep, it's got a resident ghost, Lily, a black slave girl. Legend has it that Lily fell in love with Hardee's nephew, certainly a forbidden affair in those days. To avoid detection, the two lovers had to meet in secret. The hopeless relationship ended with Hardee's nephew taking his own life and leaving Lily grief-stricken. Whether or not 'Lily' is her real name, no one really knows, but she wanders the place turning on and off electrical appliances and lights, moving things, making sounds, and frequently showing her ebony-brown arm and hand on the railing of the back stairs. If you make reservations there hoping to experience something, try to get a room on the third floor, that's where stuff happens.

Sanford's former Mayfair Inn Hotel, overlooking Lake Monroe in Sanford, is partially haunted, at least the east wing. The hotel was built in the 1930s and was used to house naval officers during World War II. Later, it was the southern home to the New York Giants baseball team before becoming a Naval Academy for boys. Today, it is a missionary training facility owned by the New Tribes Mission. So any number of spirits could be haunting the place especially since the east wing may be sitting over part of the 1836 battleground where Seminoles attacked Fort Mellon. It may also be sitting on unmarked soldier graves of Fort Mellon's lost cemetery.

There's another haunted place in Sanford, down the street on Palmetto Avenue. It's the city's old firehouse, built in 1887. Local realtor and renown Florida artist, Barbara Farrell, owns the old firehouse and has converted it into a studio apartment. Unexplained footsteps are frequently heard on the stairs, pebbles drop out of nowhere, and sounds are heard above the ceiling, where a third floor was used as a courtroom. In 1928, the structure became a two-story building when the third floor was removed.

Barbara thinks some of the strangeness may be attributed to spirits of deceased firemen. She has good reason, since the fire department's history shows several firemen losing their lives in the line of duty. At one time, the firehouse was connected to the city jail which adds another haunting prospect. On March 30, 1923, Percy Bayless, convicted of shooting a deputy sheriff, was hanged in the walled-in courtyard out back. Maybe Percy's ghost is pulling off paranormal pranks.

Drop by the Museum of Seminole County History between Sanford and Orlando and look for the little red rocking chair. This child's rocker has been known to rock back and forth on its own, which I have witnessed. The little chair is the only surviving piece of furniture from the Albert Hawkins' home that, in the 1920s, burned to the ground.

I've found that you can go to just about anyplace in Florida and ask around about ghost stuff and you'll soon be directed to a haunted house or will hear a ghost story. We enjoy ghost stories because they stir our curiosity, give us goose bumps, and entertain us, but most importantly, spirits give us a little hope beyond the grave. Just remember to be kind to the dead, you can't always see them, plus, they far out number the living. My own advice to you, is that *some things are best left alone.*

STRANGE FLORIDA II

TITANIC
Hunting the spirits of the ill-fated ship in Florida.

Tour guide and medium, Susan Thompson used to begin her nightly ghost tour of the Titanic exhibition in Orlando by telling guests about a magnificent British luxury liner. The big ship was the largest and fastest of the time and carried the wealthiest of passengers, 2,000 to be exact. When the huge ocean liner struck an ice berg in the North Atlantic, she sank in a matter of hours, taking over 1200 passengers to a watery grave. You're probably thinking of the Titanic that sank in April 1912, but in this case it never happened, except in a story written by American author, Morgan Robinson, 14 years before the Titanic sank. The name of the ship in Robinson's story was the "Titan." The uncanny parallel between Robinson's prophetic story and what actually happened to the Titanic is enough to raise goose bumps on the staunchest of skeptics.

According to what Thompson says, the Orlando attraction may be haunted by spirits of the ship. "It wasn't just me," she said, "all the tour guides and even many of our tour guests experienced things that can only be explained as spirits." Indeed, other tour guides have confirmed the sightings inside the seventeen room attraction. "The ghost tours were always at night after the regular crowd had left," explained Thompson, who recalled the after-hours ghost tour was as popular with tourists as the main exhibit tour.

Okay, so what are Titanic ghosts doing in Florida? My guess is that they came attached to some of the artifacts displayed in the museum-like exhibition. But the former tour guide says that's not it. "They're most likely attracted to the actors at the exhibit who portray personalities that went down with the ship." In its realistic scenes, the attraction uses professional actors, many of whom have an uncanny resemblance to certain passengers and known crew members.

"Have you ever felt you were being watched?" asked Thompson. "That was a common feeling for the tour guides." She recalled how on several tours, guests and staff members had seen a lady in a long brown dress standing up on the gangway waving at the guests. On other occasions various poltergeist-like phenomena was observed, like feelings of being touched, lights that would act up, sounds of footsteps, and objects being moved by unseen forces. One example happened inside the gift shop when several people witnessed a glass vase float off the shelf and allegedly hang suspended in mid-air. "It was an expensive piece of glassware," recalled Thompson. "I didn't want it to break so I grabbed it. The guests could see it floating, but could not see the little spirit girl who was playing with it. We called her, Catherine, and she became well-known around the exhibit. Several people actually saw her." One actress at the exhibit remembers sitting on a couch in one of the scenes and having a small child's hand reach out from behind. At first she thought it was a child from the tour group, only to find out that there were no children, unless perhaps, it was Catherine, the little spirit girl. A check of Titanic's 3rd class passenger list shows a Catherine Johnston, a little girl who went down with the ship.

Several paranormal investigative teams have checked the place out, including Orlando's famed Spook Hunters group who made a film of their visit. A paranormal team, from Jacksonville, left a recorder in one of the rooms while they checked out other areas. Later, when the recording was played back, they heard distinct footsteps and voices on the tape, yet no one had been in the room during the recording.

One former tour guide told about seeing a dark shadow in the shape of a man, moving back and forth on an overhead gang plank. Susan confirmed that a moving shadow was often seen in the location by both tour guides and guests. "No doubt, a restless ghost," she said, adding, that when some managers closed down the exhibit at night they often had a feeling of being watched, and frequently reported sounds of footsteps that seemed to be chasing them out of the room.

Tour guests would often see a green light shaped like a cross next to a picture of Bruce Ismay, president of the White Star Line. "Actually, the green light turned out to be the reflections of a lighted exit sign," explained Thompson, "but even after I told them what it was, many refused to believe it." Bruce Ismay was faulted for reducing the number of life boats on the Titanic, he survived to regret his ill-fated decision. His spirit has made an appearance a few times. One gentleman on the tour, using a cell phone camera, captured the image of an apparition in two pictures. The pictures were examined by staff members who confirmed the image was indeed, that of *Bruce Ismay*.

In one room, known as the Harland and Wolfe shipyard room, where guests can experience Titanic's construction period, the apparition of a young boy has been seen. "At first I thought he was one of the actors portraying a crew member," remarked Thompson. Several other former staff members claim to have seen this same apparition. "For the lack of a name, we called him, Danny," said Thompson, "But here is what's so strange, at the Harland and Wolf shipyard in Ireland there are allegedly two spirits of workers who were killed during the building of Titanic. One of their names is, Danny."

The Titanic exhibit in Orlando has changed names and ownership since Thompson worked there, but is it still haunted? Who knows, you'll have to find out for yourself by visiting the attraction. Even if you fail to see a spirit, you'll step back in time to experience a realistic history lesson about one of the world's greatest human tragedies.

STRANGE FLORIDA II

The sky is falling!
Strange Stuff Falling from the Sky
Where was Chicken Little when we needed him?

All kinds of crazy things have fallen out of the skies over Florida. Of course, this isn't so unusual, considering scientists estimate that 1000 tons of stuff falls to earth each day. That makes me want to stay inside. Most of this sky-falling stuff is too tiny to be seen...unless it's a meteorite, or a kitchen sink, money, bricks, chains, ice, frogs, eggs, beans, or starfish, all of which gets into the weird area. All of these things have mysteriously dropped from the sky in the United States. As an example, on May 11, 1911, a Florida alligator fell out of the sky into the backyard of an Evansville, Indiana, home. Neighbors grabbed bed slats and beat the daylights out of the poor critter. In December 1877, according to a newspaper article, Dr. J.L. Smith observed six alligators, averaging about twelve inches, fall from the sky over Silvertown, South Carolina. In 1890, a farmer in Georgia reported that a small alligator had fallen out of the sky and landed in his tobacco field. Strangely, there are no records of gators dropping out of the clouds over Florida, which is where you'd expect one to fall.

On September 10, 1892, a heavy cloud drifted over Gainesville and unloaded some welcomed rain and some strange white strands of a thread-like substance. It fell for an hour all over Gainesville; an estimated fifty pounds of it. Children were offered ten dollars a pound to clean it up. "It almost looked like falling Angel hair," said one girl about the event which appeared in several newspapers. Reverend R.F. Miller sent a bundle of the stuff to the Smithsonian Institute for scientific study. A few weeks later, he received a report from Dr. George Marx, of the U.S. Agricultural Department, who determined that Gainesville had been covered with spider webs.

Sky falls have been reported for centuries as seen in this 1557 drawing of falling fish.

Dr. Marx explained how the strange material had been spun out of the glands of thousands of spiders, although not a single spider had been found. Marx said the phenomenon had occurred in other parts of the United States, but this was the first time it had been reported in the Southeast.

On May 19, 1959, an Orlando resident reported that a frozen egg fell out of the sky. It was a common hen's egg, frozen hard, and where it came from is anybody's guess. It's a good thing it didn't hit someone in the head. Perhaps it had been dispatched by a high flying chicken or maybe it rolled out the back door of a cargo plane hauling eggs.

Golfers in Punta Gorda must have been happy on September 3, 1969, when new golf balls rained down from the clouds. An eye-witness to the event, estimated, "there must have been hundreds of golf balls." Some people speculated that a tornado had sucked up the balls from one of the many golf courses in the area. Maybe the balls were knocked there by some heavy swinging golfers. At least golf balls are smaller than the twenty

STRANGE FLORIDA II

pound geode that, in 1955, was found in the middle of a Seminole County celery field. Since the field had been freshly plowed the day before without encountering any foreign objects, it was presumed the big rock, a type normally found in the Appalachian mountain range, fell from the sky.

In Port Richey, hundreds of small flopping fish came out of the sky in September, 1971. There are many reports of small fish and frogs falling during rains in Florida. The explanation offered by experts is that eggs are evaporated up in moisture and then, somehow, are suspended in the atmosphere until they hatch. One answer for falling fish is that tornadoes carry them aloft, which is as good as any other explanation.

Ice cubes fell on a woman's Lake Worth house in September, 1977. This was a lasting event with ice cubes pelting the woman's aluminum roof for three or four days. Try to sleep with that kind of racket going on. She was lucky it was only ice cubes and not the huge block of greenish-colored ice that narrowly missed a Dade County house and crashed into the yard. Experts suggested the ice had fallen from an airplane. According to their theory, treated waste water drained from the lavatories often freezes at high altitudes and then thaws and falls off when the aircraft descends to lower levels which are warmer. In case you're wondering, getting hit by a chunk of frozen toilet water is not a supernatural event.

There are such things as large ice balls, called megacryometeors, that on rare occasions plunge from the sky. Megacryometeors resemble super-size hailstones, although these objects share textural, isotopic, and hydrochemical features of hailstones, they are not true hailstones. The name megacryometeors is a name used to describe a conglomeration of atmospheric ice formed at high altitudes.

In 2001, the Polk County Health Department checked out icky brown goo that landed on Lakeland and, years earlier, a wad of glue-like mess fell out of the sky over Dade County. It was a blob of greenish, sticky substance which, after a short time, melted away leaving no residue to analyze. If it fell from an aircraft, I don't think it was lime Jello.

On February 28, 1958, a glittering object fell in the backyard of a Miami home. Upon close inspection, the glittering sphere appeared to be composed of thousands of individual cells, sort of like a honeycomb. What was really strange is that this glittering globe was pulsating, as if alive. The homeowner, a former police officer, decided to stick his finger into the sphere but said he could not feel anything. I don't know if that means his finger went numb or he could not feel anything inside the hole. Here's what I do know, if something falls out of the sky and pulsates, I'm not sticking my finger in it. When the man pulled his finger out, he said it left a hole in the sphere.

When the object appeared to be expanding or spreading on the lawn, the man collected samples of it in a jar. Eventually, the strange mass dissolved or evaporated until nothing was left. Strangely, the sample concealed air-tight in the jar had dried up and disappeared, too. There were several witnesses to the unusual object but no one offered an explanation as to what had landed in their neighborhood.

DEATH FROM THE SKY
On August 11, 1944, in a tragic miscalculation, an Army-Air Corps bomber accidentally dropped a bomb on the Cosson family home in Alaqua, Florida. Four family members were killed and five others wounded.

Strange Tracks on the Beach
Was it a hoax, or did something crawl out of the sea?

In February 1948, Clearwater, on Florida's gulf coast, had a population of about 15,000 people and one monster that created a frightening stir for beachcombers. Whatever it was crawled, or waded out, of the unknown depths of the Gulf of Mexico at night to leave hundreds of birdlike tracks on the beach. These were no regular bird tracks; they were 14 inches long and 11 inches wide, with three toes.

The tracks were reported in the newspaper and on a local radio station. People began calling in about seeing something weird on the beach at night. One report has the thing knocking over a lifeguard chair. Sightings of the tracks spread all up and down the coast, from Clearwater to Sarasota. Then, for almost a year, no tracks were seen, instead similar tracks were discovered over a hundred miles to the north, near the mouth of the Suwannee River.

The "monster experts" were contacted to examine plaster casts of the tracks and one investigator estimated the prints had been made by a creature weighing 2000 pounds. Another suggested the tracks were those of a giant salamander. The famed cryptozoologist, Ivan Sanderson, was called in and quickly determined it was no hoax because the tracks had been made by something too heavy and tall to be man-made. He even flew over the Suwannee River looking for the creature, and in some accounts it is reported that he had seen a giant bird on the shore. He theorized the tracks were made by a giant penguin. *Whoa there, Jo Jo, did he say "giant penguin?"* What was he talking about? There were no feathers or giant bird droppings found, and what was a penguin was doing this far north. There have been no really big birds in Florida since the great auk became extinct. The auk is often referred to as a "penguin," although it was not an ancestor of today's penguins. Skeletal remains of the great auk were found in the late 1950s, during an archaeological survey at Castle Windy, south of New Smyrna.

It wasn't long before people began seeing big birds swimming in the Gulf. A report came in from a boater, sailing off the coast, claiming to have seen a big penguin swimming in the Gulf. The boater's claim sort of validated Sanderson's theory and, probably helped launched the Giant Penguin legend.

The mystery was never solved, well at least until sixty years later when the monster surfaced in a confession from an 85 year old man. The man claimed he and a prankster friend had made the giant bird-like tracks on the beach. According to his claim, they had made the tracks at a local blacksmith shop out of lead, each weighing about thirty pounds. The tracks were fixed to a pair of gym shoes. The two pranksters would go out late at night and put on their monster tracks and walk all over the beach. The next day they would wait for the excitement, which was usually reported in the newspaper.

Okay, maybe these pranksters really did perpetrate a hoax on Clearwater Beach, but what about the tracks along the Suwannee River? Or the prints later seen on the beach farther down from Clearwater? It seems that only part of this old monster mystery has been solved, but, if a creature does exist, don't expect it to return. Today's over-crowded beach would certainly keep any monster away.

STRANGE FLORIDA II

THE LIVING DEAD...
Is it true? Does Orange Park have a walking zombie?

Zombies are usually associated with Voodoo, a cult religious practice common in a few South Florida Haitian neighborhoods. However, zombies are not something you would expect to find in a Northeast Florida trailer park so, out of desperation for a good zombie tale, I grabbed the only one I could find; which became more intriguing after I heard it from two different sources. My inside source, Billy Ryan, was first with this story about Jacksonville's walking dead. It sounded like a legend worth looking into, and after an email from another contact, Fran Wiggins, I set out to find the origin of the story.

Actually, our subject zombie roams a trailer park in Orange Park, on Jacksonville's southwest side. Those in the know, say the zombie is usually seen on full moon nights in and around a particular trailer park or in the adjacent woods. Described as gruesome, with thin, bronze-tinted skin, he slowly walks between the mobile homes of the trailer park. The park manager has heard about a strange image seen prowling about, looking into sheds, hanging out around some orange trees, and basically acting like your standard zombie. On at least one occasion, the cops responded to the park to check out a complaint about a prowler. My inside source tells me they "saw something very unexplainable."

Zombie (zom'be), *n., pl. -bis,* **1.** A corpse brought back to life by the power of voodoo power. **2.** A walking dead person. **3.** An alcoholic drink made of several kinds of rum.

The zombie story goes back a few years in this area. However, some folks believe it is actually "a handicap man with a bone disease or one of the street people." My inside source, Ryan, described the situation for me, "Some of the elderly people, the ones who drink a lot, holler at the zombie when they see him moving throughout the trailer park looking into sheds. One of the old timers, named Clarence, tried to talk to him. He asked his name and the zombie said something that sounded like 'Emmett'." Since then, this living dead man has been called "Emmett the Zombie." Most of the longtime residents at the trailer park have heard about the "walking dead man" but are quick to point out that he has never hurt anyone or damaged any property.

Now for a bit of a twist, I have learned that Emmett is a real person, but not a real zombie. Actually, the zombie legend is kept alive by certain pranksters who have been dressing-up like the walking dead to scare the local drunks.

STRANGE FLORIDA II

Weird Prophesy...
Did Jules Verne Foresee Florida as *America's Space Center*?

The French science fiction novelist, Jules Verne, seems to have had strange ways of seeing into the future, even when it came to Florida. In 1865, he wrote *From the Earth to the Moon*, one of his most celebrated novels. Although it was written a century ahead of the Apollo moon mission, Verne's story was about man's first trip to the moon, a fictional journey launched from, you guessed it, Florida!

In the Jules Verne novel, the launch site was at "Tampa Town," only about a hundred miles from today's Kennedy Space Center, the location of the real moon shot. In his story, as with the actual Apollo moon mission, there were three men inside a space capsule. Verne referred to his three characters as "crewmen" as the word "astronaut" had not been coined yet.

The author described the space vehicle in his novel as "cylindrical, conical projectile", an uncanny close match to NASA's early space capsules. The great French writer also realized that the best method of changing course of a space vehicle is by firing small rockets, like those used to steer later spacecraft. The space vehicle in *From the Earth to the Moon* was launched from a big, 900 foot long cannon called the "Columbiad." The name is very similar to NASA's first space shuttle, *Columbia*, launched in 1981. He described a multi-stage rocket too, referring to it as a "moon train." There was even a dog on board Verne's imaginary spacecraft, long before the Soviet's launched their cosmonaut-canine, Laika, *involuntarily*, into orbit aboard Sputnik II.

The prophetic Verne also accurately calculated the distance from the Earth to the Moon. His space ship took 73 hours and 13 minutes to reach the moon. The actual Apollo journey took 73 hours and 10 minutes to reach orbit. For Jules Verne to have selected Florida out of all places for his story is a bit strange. The similarities between Verne's fictitious moon mission and the real Apollo mission is down right uncanny.

...Then there was *Florida's Celestial Railroad*

Jules Verne's novel was not the only possible predictor of Florida's future as the Space Center. In 1891, the Jacksonville and Lake Worth Transportation Company opened a narrow gauge railroad line on Florida's east coast, called "The Celestial Railroad." With only seven miles of track it was known as the "World's Smallest Railroad." For 75 cents, passengers were transported from Jupiter to Juno, with stops along the way at Venus and Mars. It sounds like it was a ride through the solar system. Actually, the planetary names along the Celestial line were names of rural settlements. Venus and Mars, as place names, have long since faded from maps; however, Jupiter is still a town.

ONE OF FEW REMAINING PHOTOGRAPHS OF THE CELESTIAL RAILROAD. [*FLORIDA STATE ARCHIVES*]

STRANGE FLORIDA II

That strange I-4 DEAD ZONE
Where there's a haunting secret beneath the asphalt!

Located half way between Daytona Beach and Orlando, on busy Interstate-four, you'll find a sinister spot called the Dead Zone. I was the first author to bring this eerie story to the public in 1997 when I included it in my first *Strange Florida* book. Since then, the I-4 Dead Zone has become one of Central's Florida's most talked about haunted places in addition to being featured in several books, including national publications, and in Florida newspapers. My intrigue for this story comes from first-hand knowledge. The land where the Dead Zone is located once belonged to my maternal grandfather, Albert Hawkins, until it was claimed under eminent domain for building the interstate highway. Several books have featured the I-4 Dead Zone and referenced me as their informational source. Actually only two other writers have ever consulted me about the subject, with the others getting the entire history wrong. As a historian specializing in this part of the state, I owe it to my readers to provide accurate history of the Dead Zone.

The Dead Zone is a quarter mile stretch of the interstate just before it crosses the double bridge over the St. John's River. Since the highway was opened in 1962, there have been more traffic accidents, some with fatalities, in this short span of highway than in all other sections from Daytona to Tampa. People have reported that cell phones will not work while driving through this area. Several motorists have told about unusual static on their car radios. One woman says that her car radio mysteriously changes stations when she drives through the Dead Zone. One driver claimed to have picked up "spirits talking" on his radio. A few local motorists refuse to drive through the Dead Zone, even if it means a detour of twenty miles. Each day thousands of tourists, bound for Orlando's theme parks, travel this road unaware of the Dead Zone.

If paranormal forces are responsible for what happens in the Dead Zone, then it must be related to what lies beneath this stretch of highway. Until recently, few people knew anything about the history of this area until my associate researcher, Christine Kinlaw-Best, and I began digging into old records for our co-authored book, *The History of Monroe*. What we discovered certainly suggested the high possibility of a supernatural cause for all the strange experiences in the area.

In 1887, this area was surveyed by the Florida Land and Colonization Company for a Roman Catholic settlement to be called "St. Joseph's Colony." A priest, Father Felix Swembergh, was to oversee the colony once it was established. In reality, it was a real estate scheme, cooked up by Henry Shelton Sanford, cloaked in religion and aimed at attracting German immigrants. However, only four immigrant families came to settle in the colony. The families were still in the process of building their homesteads when they were hit with a yellow fever epidemic that covered the entire state. Four members of one family succumbed to the dreaded sickness and were buried in a remote spot on the edge of the settlement. They were never given last rites because the colony priest, Father Swembergh had been called to assist with the sick in Tampa where he died of yellow fever only a week after arriving. The graves of the colonists, believed to be two children and their parents, are now under Interstate-four.

By 1890, the area had become Monroe Station on the Orange Belt Railroad. It eventually became the Lake Monroe community, so named after the nearby lake. In 1900, D. V. Warren bought from the Thrasher family the land where the graves were located and carefully cleared around them for farming. The tiny cemetery sat like an island in the middle of Mr. Warren's field. In 1905, Albert S. Hawkins purchased the property from Mr. Warren and was told about the little burial plot.

The graves were always respected by the Hawkins family, although no one could make out the names on the weather-worn, wooden markers. In 1920, a local spiritualist named Maggie Bell, warned folks against *"tampering with the dead."* This probably reinforced the effort not to disturb the graves. Local children were told, *"Don't mess with the graves."* As late as 1930, flowers were still being placed on the four graves, usually by children who referred to the place as *"The field of the dead."* By the 1940's the site was surrounded by a rusting wire fence and a stand of banana trees. The markers had rotted away at the head of each grave. Local tradition explained the graves to be the resting places of a *"Dutch family who had died from the fever."* Through generations of retelling the story "Deutsch" [German] had been misinterpreted as "Dutch.".

In 1960, the Hawkins homestead was claimed by the government for constructing Interstate-four. Surveyors were informed about the four graves and the sacred spot was well marked with yellow ribbons, but the interred were never removed. The first sign of strangeness occurred after trucks began dumping fill dirt on the burial site to elevate the new highway.

In the very week that the first load of dirt covered the graves, hurricane Donna hit the area. The storm had already crossed South Florida and was heading out into the Gulf of Mexico, and then it made a sudden turn on a northeast course that carried its eye right across the graves. Strangely, the storm actually crossed the Florida peninsula twice.

The wrath of Hurricane Donna shut down all work on the new interstate for over a month. Several pieces of heavy equipment sank in the mud and a dragline was washed down the embankment of the new right-of-way. Donna was rated as the worst hurricane of modern times to hit the interior of Central Florida. While it may only be coincidental, the hurricane's abrupt change in direction, and its path, happened exactly at the time the graves were disturbed. It does give us reason to wonder if there was a paranormal connection. Adding to this weirdness in 2004 was Hurricane Charley. When highway construction again disturbed the graves, Charley made an unexpected northeastward turn and followed Interstate-four right across the dead zone. The TV weather reporters referred to it as, "the Interstate-four hurricane." Old timers remained silent, but had their own opinions of what had caused the storm to turn; they had seen Hurricane Donna do the same thing, forty-four years before, when the graves were first disturbed.

Depending on the source, there have been between 1,048 to 1,740 traffic accidents in the Dead Zone since the highway opened in 1962. State Highway Department records show that, in a twenty-four month period from 1995 through 1996, there were 44 accidents that injured 65 people. I don't know if it means anything, but the sum of these two figures adds up to 109, the exact age of the graves during the period of the accidents. Perhaps the spirits are sending a message to remind us that the Dead Zone is a sacred place of rest. Maybe the dead are seeking revenge for disturbing their resting place. While we are left to wonder about this mystery, there is one fact we cannot ignore, if you drive through this area on Interstate-four, you'll be driving over the dead.

STRANGE FLORIDA II

Florida's Last Great *Mastodon* Hunt...

Believe it or not, herds of mammoth and mastodon once roamed throughout the marshes of prehistoric Florida. Their skeletal remains have been found all over the state, especially in phosphate pits and springs. In the 1950s, Buck Hawkins, a commercial fisherman, was digging worms along the St. John's River when his potato rake unearthed a tooth from a prehistoric mammoth elephant. Unable to identify the object, it became a door stop for twenty years until it fell into the possession of the author. Paleontologists believe Florida's ancient elephants died out about 9000 years ago. However, a humorous piece of folklore claims the last great mastodon hunt actually took place in 1860 near Silver Springs where for years fossilized bones of prehistoric animals had been plowed up in fields or found in the springs.

A visiting newspaper journalist in the mid-1800s, theorized that Silver Springs may have been a watering hole for extinct mammoth, mastodon, camels, giant sloth, and bison. Being somewhat schooled in prehistoric stuff, he was able to identify many of the bones found by local farmers.

Local folks, having little knowledge of paleontology, thought the bones were from beasts still roaming the swamp. One backwoods fellow, Matthew Driggers, declared in 1860, that he was "goin' to hunt down one of those big varmints and kill it." One morning, just before daybreak, Mr. Driggers was awakened by a shrill bellowing coming from deep in the swamp. He quickly sat up in bed, his ears perked up and his eyes widened as he heard the beastly cry again. The sound kept on coming, again and again, penetrating the woods and upsetting the whole neighborhood. Driggers grabbed his shotgun and with a team of hounds in tow, made haste to his nearest neighbor, Patrick Kennedy. Upon reaching the Kennedy homestead, Driggers pounded his fist on the door, "Git up in there, Pat, thar's a beast aloose in the woods. Hark, you kin hear him!"

Kennedy, brushing sleep from his eyes, unlatched the door and opened it. "Yep, I hear him. That thar's one of them old masterdons...we done seen the bones of his kin in the springs." He reached behind the door for his gun and proceeded to stuff his pockets with shotgun shells. "Well, sah, I'll tell you one thing, he's a big 'un cause his voice is curioser than anything I ever heard before. There's one thing for sertin, if'n he's out thar my dogs kin find him." The two backwoodsmen headed in the direction of the swamp and were soon joined by a posse of neighbors, all bent on hunting down the beastly mastodon. The early morning hunt had mustered just about every settler for miles around, some wearing only their long drawers and boots. They pushed through the palmettos and slogged through swamps trying to keep up with their squadron of hounds. The awful sound came again, this time closer than ever, sending the dogs cowering back to their masters. "That thar old masterdon is just ahead," exclaimed one hunter, "...and I ain't so certain I wanna git any closer."

Mathew Driggers, being somewhat more courageous, said, "Not me boys, I'm bound and determined to see what that thar ol' masterdon looks like...then I'm goin' to bring him down with this here gun." With Driggers taking the lead, the rest soon followed. Before long, the assortment of characters stumbled out of the woods near the basin of Silver Springs where they saw a steamboat unloading freight at the dock. This was one of the first paddle wheel steamboats to make it up river to Silver Springs landing. The hunters approached the boat's captain and inquired if he had heard the sound or seen any *masterdons* along the river that morning. Driggers stepped forward and attempted, to the best of his ability, to imitate the wildly call.

The Captain laughed, reached up and yanked a rope, sounding the boat's steam whistle. "Is that what you boys heard? This is my first trip up this river and I've been blowing that whistle all morning at every bend."

Satisfied that there was no great mastodon running loose in the swamp, the exhausted hunters gathered their panting dogs and returned to their homes. And that, folks, believe it or not, is the story of Florida's last great mastodon hunt.

Source credit: Sunshine, Sylvia, {Abbie M. Brooks} Petals Plucked From Sunny Climes, Nashville, 1880, pp 84-86.

STRANGE FLORIDA II

Those Mysterious Strange Sounds From out of nowhere

On several occasions over the past hundred years or so, people of sound minds have reported hearing strange noises that seem to have no explanation. The earliest acoustical mystery was reported in the 1882 journal of Elijah McLean, who wrote "There were sounds coming from the far side of the woods like something blowing up. I went over there but there weren't nothing or nobody seen. I thought war had done come." It is not certain where Elijah experienced his weird sounds but in 1887, people living in Marion, Putnam, and Colulmbia counties heard "cannon booms that could not be explained."

There are various references world-wide describing a phenomenon called "acoustical mirages" which sometimes sound like "double-booms" that shake the ground and rattle windows. While scientists can only guess at what causes these sounds, some believe it has to do with electrical disturbances in the atmosphere. An unexplained phenomenon called the Barisal Guns of India has been heard for centuries. This acoustical mystery is usually heard in the Ganges Delta during heavy rains. A similar phenomenon in New York is the Lake Guns of Seneca. In both cases no guns are involved, the sound just seems to happen.

Residents living along the Gulf coast have heard cannon-like detonations on clear mornings. One boater twenty miles out from Cedar Key claimed to have experienced "booming sounds like distant cannons." The sounds were heard shortly after sunrise and were repeated in five minute intervals and seem to come from no specific direction. Hmmm, I've heard of "day breaking" but did not know it made a sound. In these cases there was no military testing, no aircraft-type sonic booms, and the weather was calm. Some scientist suggested that the phenomenon was related to undersea natural gas eruptions. The only problem with this explanation, unless it was coincidental, is that the sounds were heard at the same time on different days.

During the 1950s, sonic booms were frequent in the Ocala region because of military exercises at a bombing range in the Ocala National Forest. On January 25 and 26, 1994, several sonic booms were heard across Central Florida, with reports coming from Leesburg, Ocala, Gainesville, Dunnellon, and Deland. This was not related to military activities and sensitive seismographic equipment at the University of Florida showed no registration of the strange sounds. The sounds were described as "like what a supersonic jet makes when it breaks the sound barrier." A thorough check with McDill AFB, the Jacksonville Naval Air Station, and the Federal Aviation Authority indicated no aircraft had caused the mystery. NASA confirmed that the space shuttle had not caused it. But one scientist speculated, without data, that the sound could have originated somewhere other than Florida, a sort of acoustical mirage caused by the inversion of air and made audible over Central Florida. Maybe I'm ignorant, I don't understand how this inversion of air thing would work, but it sounds good when there's nothing else to blame.

STRANGE FLORIDA II

On May 7, 1996, sonic booms shook windows across Central Florida in Flagler, Marion, Volusia, Brevard, Orange, and Seminole counties. Dull vibrations from the same phenomenon were felt in Palm Beach and Alachua counties. The unexplained sound was similar to what you hear when the space shuttle makes its re-entry. However, Kennedy Space Center said the sounds had nothing to do with their operations, and certainly not the shuttle which had been in the hangar since March. Many folks thought the booms had been caused by an earthquake but the seismographic station in Gainesville had not registered any earth tremors. Checks were made with the FAA, the Coast Guard, and with the Ocala Bombing Range, yet none of these could offer any explanations. One possibility offered by geologists, was that the sound was caused by a collapse of a subterranean aquifer. These are the super-huge underground chambers in which Florida's drinking water is stored. If the ceiling of one of these fell it would no doubt create a big echoing rumble. Still scientists could offer no definite explanation.

Mysterious booming acoustics are not Florida's only unexplained sounds. In 1954, two well-drillers in Alachua County were doing what they do, drilling a well. They had reached the 200 foot level without striking water. Instead, they said cold air started blowing out of the drilling shaft like an air conditioner. Thinking they had penetrated an underground limestone cavern, the men removed their drill and prepared to cap off the dry shaft. Then they noticed a faint sound, like a voice, coming from the 200 foot deep hole. They claimed that upon putting their ear to the hole they could hear sounds of human voices. *"It was like somebody was talking underground,"* said one of the men. They admitted the sounds to be very faint and could not make out any language or specific words. They were so convinced of voices coming from underground that they began yelling down the hole, *"Hello, can you hear me?"* There was no response from the subterranean talkers, so the men packed up and left. A few weeks later they returned to the site to prove their claim to some skeptical friends, however, the mysterious voices and cold air had stopped. An amateur geologist checked out the story and speculated, *"They had probably drilled through the ceiling of a limestone cavern which released a pocket of cold air and thus created an unusual sound which was misinterpreted as voices. Once the air was expended the sounds stopped."* That was the only explanation offered.

In the summer of 1959, Robert Oswald recalled being on a deep sea fishing trip five miles east of Flagler Beach when he heard a constant tinkling sound. *"There were five in our party,"* he recalled in 2004, while fishing from a dock in New Smyrna. *"The sea was very still with almost a glass-smooth surface and our engine was not running. The sound seemed to be all around us and sounded like the sound metal wind chimes make. It went on for nearly an hour before becoming faint and eventually we couldn't hear it anymore. It was pretty loud. We didn't report it, didn't see any need, but we thought about how strange it was. I don't have no idea what the hell was causing it, but five of us heard it."*

In February 1969, people on Jacksonville Beach reported hearing "strange rattling sounds coming from two overhead clouds." One woman described the sound as *"like constant crumpling of cellophane."* Exactly one week later, the same phenomenon was reported by people in Miami. Was it a freakish weather phenomenon? No one really knows and, like all the other mysterious acoustics, it remains a mystery.

STRANGE FLORIDA II

JAGUARUNDI SIGHTINGS IN FLORIDA
Could this account for stories about black panthers?

Displaced animals are creatures that are indigenous to one place but are mysteriously seen in another. Florida is well-known for sightings of displaced animals, usually an exotic species that has escaped captivity or that has been released by its keeper. Tropical species can survive quite well in Florida's subtropical environment. Eyewitnesses have reported strange sightings of everything from monkeys to monitor lizards. The strangest was a road kill in 2005 of a grey kangaroo on Interstate-95 in Brevard County. We can only wonder about where it came from. Such reports are usually limited to a single animal in a particular area and not widespread sightings across the state.

One morning, while driving on Route 3 through the Merritt Island Wildlife Refuge, I saw a strange animal dart across the road in front of my vehicle. At first it appeared to be a large otter, but a second glance told me it was a jaguarundi. Having spent time in Central American jungles, I was familiar with this animal, at least enough to identify it. I reported my sighting to the local wildlife biologist who acknowledged a history of jaguarundi sightings in the wildlife areas of Merritt Island. The Federal Wildlife Service, using trip-cameras, had even tried unsuccessfully to get a picture of a jaguarundi.

The jaguarundi is a small cat indigenous to South and Central America but is known to range as far north as the Arizona and Texas borders. It is often referred to as the "otter cat" because of its otter-like characteristics. Measuring from its head to the tip of its long thick tail, the animal has a low, elongated body which can reach a length of 50 inches and weigh 20 pounds, making it larger than domestic cats but smaller than a jaguar or panther. It is a solitary, secretive creature that is difficult to track and, usually, only seen by being in the right place at the right time. The mystery for Floridians is the numerous sightings of this species from Pensacola to the Keys.

Florida's leading jaguarundi researcher is award winning cryptozoologist Lisa Wojcik, an associate of the Pangea Institute. While government wildlife agencies have officially denied the presence of this species in Florida, Wojcik's extensive research and field work strongly suggest that the jaguarundi is alive and well in Florida. Venturing beyond attempted proof of the jaguarundi's existence in Florida, Wojcik may be close to cracking the case of how the strange cat got here.

Could the Jaguarundi have existed in Florida since prehistoric times?
Some years ago, the late paleontologist H. James Gut, a mentor of the author, had a fossilized cat jawbone in his collection that he attributed to the jaguarundi. The question is, did this species continue to survive or did it die out only to be reintroduced later? "It would be extremely difficult to prove they were here since the Pleistocene," says Wojcik. "So far there has been only a single jawbone for study." Originally the jawbone was presumed to be jaguarundi, however more recent speculations suggests it belonged to another prehistoric cat. According to Wojcik, "This leaves only theory based on the analogy of other species, such as the burrowing owl, scrub jay, and indigo snake that migrated to and have remained in Florida since the Ice Age." Other prehistoric migrants that once extended their range to Florida, like the coyote, peccary, California condor, and most notably the jaguar and ocelot, later pulled back to their present day ranges in Latin America and the western states. Fossil beds along the Ichetucknee River in Columbia

STRANGE FLORIDA II

County and Rock Springs in Orange County have yielded fossilized cat bones that suspiciously appear to be jaguarundi. Other fossils, suggestive of jaguarundi, have been found in Brevard and Marion counties. These have fueled debates between scientists over whether they belonged to jaguarundi or some other cat. Wojcik remarks, "I am intrigued by the possibility that jaguarundi could have migrated here during the Ice Age and survived, but I am highly doubtful." She said that if survival were proven, then the jaguarundi would be a native species qualifying for endangered species protection.

Is there another explanation for Jaguarundi in Florida?
Wojcik's research strongly suggests the jaguarundi presence in Florida is attributed to human introduction between 1934 and the 1940's. "There are three different storylines," she explained. "The first one being that they were escaped exotic pets let loose in the 1940's; and the second that, in 1934 or the early 1940's, a bankrupt circus let its animals go free." Dismissing these explanations and focusing on a third possibility, Lisa Wojcik has followed an intriguing trail of research to Chiefland, Florida where, in the 1940's, a writer may have introduced the jaguarundi from Mexico or Honduras by releasing them in state parks and wildlife refuges. This hypothesis is supported by a cluster of sightings around the Chiefland area and articles by the late Wilfred T. Neill, a Florida wildlife author and herpetologist, who wrote about an unnamed "Florida writer" releasing the species in Florida. This mysterious writer was said to have visited Central America and wrote about wildlife and Native Americans. Indeed, this certainly seems to add up to something. Unfortunately, identity of the mysterious writer is unknown; however, research has discovered a writer by the name of A. Hyatt Verrill, who lived in Chiefland in the 1940s. Verrill made several visits to Central America and Mexico and wrote about the Aztecs and Mayan cultures. He also wrote articles about the elusive jaguarundi and said he had seen several of the animals, to include two roadkills. Was Verrill the mystery writer written about by Neill? Or could it have been an associate of one of these men?

…And what about Florida's mysterious black panther sightings??
Native American legends even speak about the black panther or water panther, called Missipichu. Well, this gets us back to the jaguarundi. In the first place, according to Wojcik, "What people refer to as a "black panther" is actually a melanistic form of leopard." She points out that leopards are not known to inhabit Florida and are considerably larger than jaguarundi. "Very few people are aware of the jaguarundi, but most people seem familiar with what is commonly referred to as a 'black panther'." Therefore, Lisa Wojcik believes that eyewitness reports of black panthers in Florida are actually sightings of jaguarundi.

While hundreds of jaguarundi sightings have been reported, there is still no physical proof that the animal exists in Florida. Although, there have been claims of road kills and of people producing pelts, and even a skull. Wilfred T. Neill, in *Florida Wildlife* magazine, stated that he had found a jaguarundi road kill in Highlands County of which he had saved the pelt and skull. He also reported seeing a jaguarundi which had been trapped in Dixie County. Unfortunately for scientists like Wojcik, this evidence has been misplaced or lost. In spite of the absence of hard evidence, Wojcik has found enough anecdotal evidence and reliable sighting data to conclude that there are living, breeding populations of jaguarundi present in Florida. Just remember, the next otter or black panther you see darting across the road may really be a jaguarundi.

STRANGE FLORIDA II

What happened to Flight 19?
Were the pilots victims of the Bermuda Triangle?

On December 5, 1945 five TBM Avenger planes took off from the Opalocka Naval Air Station near Ft. Lauderdale on a routine training mission. They were to fly a triangular pattern 160 miles to the east, then 40 miles to the north, and back to home base. The flight time was calculated to take two hours. The five planes took off at 2 p.m in clear weather and were soon over the Atlantic when something very strange happened. At approximately 3:15 the tower at Ft. Lauderdale received an emergency call from the flight leader, Lt. Charles Taylor. Quote *"We cannot see land. We are not sure of our position. We seem to be lost. We don't know which way is west. Everything is wrong. Strange. We can't be sure of any direction. Even the ocean doesn't look as it should..."* Later he sent a second message. *"All of our compasses are out."* It became increasingly difficult to hear the fading communication due to static.

U.S. NAVY PHOTO

Although, the tower could vaguely hear talk between the planes, the pilots apparently could not hear transmissions from the tower. In one of the last transmissions, one of the pilots radioed, *"Every gyro and magnetic compasses were off...going crazy...with each showing a different reading."* In some accounts you will read how a ham radio operator picked up communications from Lt. Taylor allegedly saying, *"Don't come after us. They look like they're from outer space."* There is no evidence of this message and the official records make no mention of it. It is most likely a fabrication of urban mythmakers.

All communication was soon lost, as well as the five planes of Flight 19. This is when a massive air and sea search was launched to find the planes. One of the first planes to go looking for the missing aircraft was a twin engine Martin Mariner with thirteen crewmen on board dispatched from the Banana River Naval Air Station. Twenty-three minutes after takeoff the Martin Mariner vanished about 25 miles east of New Smyrna Beach. A blimp from Daytona and surface craft from the New Smyrna Coast Guard Station were immediately sent to search for the missing Martin Mariner.

All total, six planes with 23 crewmen had mysteriously vanished within two hours, an event that launched the largest search in U. S. Naval history involving hundreds of surface and air craft extending from Key West to Bermuda to the coast of Maine. Night and day the military searched for the missing planes but found no sign of the lost planes or crewmen.

STRANGE FLORIDA II

The following is a transcription pertaining to the missing Martin Mariner from official microfilm [serial 6330P21] of the Navy's 1946 Board of Inquiry investigation.

```
Dated 16 Sep 1946
From Chief of Naval Operations
Washingon D.C.
  [An extract from testimony taken during the inquiry]
"At 2112 information was received from the Joint
Operations Center, Miami, that an explosion was
observed by the SS Gaines Mills at a position 23
degrees, 59 minutes north, 80 degrees, 25 minutes west,
at 1950R. At 2122, after being unable to contact the
Daytona Beach Dumbo [blimp] they were directed to
proceed to the position of the explosion. This message
was sent blind. At 2125 New Smyrna surface craft were
dispatched to the position of the explosion. At 2135,
PBM Training No. 60 was dispatched to the position of
the explosion with instructions to guard the 3000
kilocycles by radio. At 2147, PBM training planes No.
32 and 60 were directed to conduct an expanding square
search beginning at 28 degrees at 80 degrees."
Item 55. The USS Solomons CVE67 dispatched 06127
reported as follows: "Our air search radar showed plane
[Martin Mariner] after takeoff from Banana River last
night joining with another plane then separating and
proceeding on course 045 degrees at exact time SS
Gaines Mills sighted flames and in exact spot the above
plane disappeared from radar screen and never
reappeared."
Item 56. The concentrated search operations from 6
December to 10 December 1945 inclusive, by surface and
aircraft in the area of the reported explosion failed
to reveal any debris of the missing PBM or evidence of
its crew.
Summary Note: It appears that all planes simply
vanished.
```

Note: In the opening scene of Steven Spielberg's movie *"Close Encounters of the Third Kind"* you will see scientists checking the engine numbers of five Avengers which were found in the Southwest desert....this fictional scene is based on the true disappcarance of Flight 19 it implies they were captured by a UFO. There's a whole menu of theories about what happened to these planes, among which includes Space Aliens, a force from Atlantis, undersea hydrates of methane gas, vortexes, a magnetic storm, water spouts, freak weather conditions, and, of course, the infamous Bermuda Triangle....the only thing known for sure, is that five TBM Avengers with 10 crewmen and a twin cngine Martin Mariner with a crew of 13 vanished from the face of the earth on the evening of December 5, 1945....never to be heard from again...not one piece of debris, life vests, or anything has ever been found.

STRANGE FLORIDA II

The Curse of Koresh's Tomb
10,000 faithfully awaited his resurrection from the dead!

The mystery begins with the strange theories of Dr. Cyrus R. Teed and his curious settlement of followers on the Estero River, near Fort Myers. In 1870, Dr. Teed was a doctor of eclectic medicine living in New York when he had a vision or prophetic message from an angel. He immediately struck out for Chicago to preach his theories and recruit a following to his new religious belief that we live, not on the outside surface of the earth, but on the inside of a "Cosmic Egg." Being a genuine doctor, we can surmise that he was not a person prone to far out fantasies. Of course, he may have experienced a few hallucinations along his career path or perhaps he was a schemer out to gain a following as a prophet for profit.

Dr. Cyrus R. Teed

According to Dr. Teed's science of "cellular cosmology," which he based on mathematical calculations, we live on the concave interior of the earth with the "golden orb of day" floating around in the center. He explained how the stars, comets, and planets were mere illusions. In other words, the earth is like a universal size chicken egg without the yolk. Here's the way it worked, if you're standing in Florida and looking up through a super-powerful telescope you should be able to see the other side of the earth.

Not only was Cyrus Teed turning astronomy upside down, he was preaching a progressive ideology on racial tolerance, sexual equality, ecological conservation, and a communistic lifestyle. All of this stuff sounded reasonable to 4000 people who quickly jumped on Teed's religious band wagon as it began to roll. Teed changed his name to Koresh, Hebrew for Cyrus, and became the Messiah of his new order, which he dubbed the Koreshans. However, not everyone was buying into this new religious movement with its communistic philosophies. Realizing that the mounting opposition was ready to run the Koreshans out of town, Koresh began looking for a place to establish a settlement for his followers. In 1894, he acquired a large tract of land near Fort Myers on the Estero River which he said had special magnetic qualities and had determined was the "center of the earth". That's right, the center of the earth is near Fort Myers according to the Koreshans. It's strange that some entrepreneur hasn't made a tourist attraction out of the place. It was on this spot where Koresh and 200 his followers established New Jerusalem, a self-supporting settlement complete with its own bakery, school, laundry, machine shop, electric generator plant, and wood-working shops. It was a tax-free Utopian colony; however Koresh spoiled everybody's fun by prohibiting drinking, smoking, gambling, swearing, and sex.

Koresh was the incarnation of the divinity, sinless and all-knowing. Therefore, he could not die. His body could only be changed by death and he would rise again, transfigured and glorified to inaugurate the rule of heaven on earth. The Koreshans, about

STRANGE FLORIDA II

ten thousand strong, believed all of this to be true, because that's what they had been told by Koresh. A Chicago newspaper in 1895 describes Cyrus Teed, a.k.a. Koresh, as "having a mesmerizing influence over his converts." In a 1905 commentary, he was said to be "a rascal using religion." In other words, with his ability to make people believe bizarre stuff, perhaps he should have become a politician.

In 1887, Koresh decided to prove his theory to pesky skeptics that we really do live on the inside of the earth. He called upon Professor Ulysses Grant Morrow of the Koreshan College of Life to develop an experiment to measure the inside curvature of the earth. Morrow designed a huge contraption called a rectilineator, which was constructed of ten big T-squares set horizontally on ten carefully balanced mounts.

PROFESSOR MORROW'S RECTILINEATOR ON THE BEACH NEAR NAPLES, FLORIDA, IN 1897

Professor Morrow, working the Koreshan Geodetic Survey, setup the rectilineator on a stretch of beach near Naples, Florida. The strange device was so large that it required a month to set up and calibrate. The idea was to demonstrate how the earth's surface curves upward, rising at the rate of eight inches a mile, thus proving we live on the inside of a big globe. Do not try this experiment at home; you won't have enough room and your neighbors will think you're nuts. Morrow's experiment took five months, as the big rectilineator had to be moved section by section to measure a distance of four and a half miles. The end part of the apparatus actually ran into the Gulf of Mexico where, on May 5, 1897, the device touched the water's surface. This was interpreted as indisputable evidence that the earth really curves upward. Immediately Cyrus Teed, oops, I mean, Koresh, announced that through mathematics and geometrics, Professor Morrow had successfully proven that we live on the inside of a big ball. Although the amazing revelation had no impact on conventional science it significantly increased Koreshan membership. As for claims that Koresh would rise from the dead, nothing was proven by Morrow's rectilineater experiment; his flock would just have to wait until his death.

On December 22, 1908, Cyrus Teed, a.k.a. Koresh, died of head injuries suffered two years earlier during a riot against the Koreshans at Fort Myers. Ten thousand followers waited faithfully for their messiah's body to transform, rise from the grave, resurrect itself, or whatever divine immortals do after death. While they waited in suspense, Henry D. Silverfriend, Vice-President of the Koreshan University made a statement that he "observed the body while unburied and could see the transformation in progress through the color in our Messiah's wrists." He went on to state that "several in our party doubted that Dr. Teed was dead, and that a local physician declared he was not dead but only in a trance." However, a Chicago physician examined the body and declared he *was* dead. Koreshan faithfuls were getting a little impatient; hey, it takes time to transform! In the meantime, Teed was getting a little ripe, so they decided to bury the body, not in the Koreshan settlement, but on Estero Island in the Gulf.

A tomb had been built on Estero Island for Teed from a pile of concrete blocks brought to the Island for another purpose. Teed's body was placed in a zinc box, which he had used for bathing. That's right, he was buried in his bath tub, which was conveniently shaped like a coffin complete with handles on the sides. The coffin was placed inside the tomb which was hermatically sealed. Hundreds of believers came to Estero Island to wait for their messiah to bust out of his tomb in a glorified transformation. And so they waited, and waited some more. Two years went by without any sign of resurrection and folks were about to give up their hope. Then, Emil Fisher, a German member of the Koreshans, decided it was time to check the tomb.

Things Get A Little Weird at Teed's Tomb

Emil Fisher, along with a few others, went to Estero Island and approached the tomb with the intentions of looking inside. As soon as he placed his hands on the concrete structure, Fisher began to shake and jerk as if possessed by something. As several of the group ran to help, he turned into a raving maniac and had to be subdued. He was bound with rope and, in the company of the sheriff, was immediately shuffled off to the state mental hospital in Chattahoochee. He never made it; while enroute between Jacksonville and Chattahoochee, Fisher went into a foaming fit and died in screaming agony.

Professor George Hussay, a teacher at the Koreshan colony, was not dismayed at Fisher's strange death and was determined to check the tomb. Hussay ignored warnings not to tamper with the tomb and went to the island where he began unsealing the tomb. Then, all of a sudden, he was stricken with madness and went into a raving fit. He shook violently and lashed out at those trying to calm him. "He was insane," remarked one observer to a newspaper reporter. Like Fisher, he was rushed off to the insane asylum at Chattahoochee where he died shortly after being admitted.

Was Koresh's tomb cursed? Or was it Koresh causing anyone who touched his tomb to go crazy? Maybe Emil Fisher and George Hussay ate some spoiled sushi that affected their brains. Hey, anything is possible; but whatever caused the madness remains unexplained to this day.

STRANGE FLORIDA II

Strange Skies: Florida's Aerial Phenomena
Hey y'all, what's that silver contraption hovering over the swamp??

Have aliens visited Florida? No, not the illegal earthling type, I mean the kind from outer space, the gray ones with big heads. 'Aerial phenomena' is a soft term for unidentified flying objects. However, not every light in the sky is a UFO and not every UFO is a space ship from Uranus or any other extraterrestrial place. If it is in our atmosphere and cannot be identified, then it is an unidentified flying object, which can include space junk, secret experimental aircraft, meteors, balloons, pelicans, sky rockets, or whatever, including extraterrestrial craft from other worlds.

Florida ranks third in the country for UFO sightings reported to the National UFO Reporting Center. Maybe the outer space folks are keeping tabs on what NASA is doing at Kennedy Space Center.

The following chronological sampling is proof that the Sunshine State has not been ignored by these things we call unidentified flying objects.

Circa 1871: This is possibly Florida's oldest UFO sighting on record. In his journal, Josiah Wilcox wrote, *"Coming down by Cedar Key we seen a big fire come down at night and sit on the shore of an island. We watched it. It [hovered or floated] over the shallows for a length of time, I would say ten minutes or better, then it shot like a gun straight up to the sky."*

July 15, 1944: A black cylinder-looking craft was seen moving over North Tampa with an undisclosed number of P-38 aircraft in pursuit.

December 1945: Eugene Denmark reported that he was flounder fishing from a small boat when he saw a glowing globe drift in from the Atlantic and lingered over Mosquito Lagoon. [This area later became part of the Kennedy Space Center].

May 1946: A Navy lieutenant reported an elliptical shaped object over LaGrange, Florida.

August 1, 1946: Capt. Jack Puckett reported a cigar shaped object at 4000 feet northeast of Tampa, maneuvering near his C-47 transport plane while enroute from Langley, Virginia to McDill AFB in Tampa. The strange craft was officially reported as "a long cylindrical shape, twice the size of a B-29 bomber, with luminous port holes."

February 20, 1950: [Ref: USAF Intelligence Report] Navy pilots, ground observers and radar at Key West Naval Air Station reported two glowing objects streaking across the sky at a very high altitude above the base.

June 15, 1952: A fast moving triangular craft with a single light on the rear was observed over Jacksonville. It made a sudden stop then accelerated out of sight.

July 18, 1952: Several personnel at Patrick AFB observed four amber lighted UFOs circling over the base. Included in the observers was a meteorologist. After playing over the base for a few minutes, the objects flew off toward the west.

July 22, 1952: A metallic disk hovered over New Smyrna Beach. [Source: NICAP report].

STRANGE FLORIDA II

July 29, 1952: In Miami, Ralph Mayer took 40 feet of 16mm film of a bowl-shaped object with small projections on the top and bottom. Analysis of the film by the University of Miami indicated the object was 27 feet in diameter and traveling in excess of 7000 mph. Mr. Mayer retained a few frames for himself and submitted the remaining film to the U.S. Air Force who never returned it or an analysis of their findings.

August 1952: A scout master, near West Palm Beach, was driving his scout troop home when he noticed strange lights in the woods. He stopped his car on the side of the road and told the scouts to stay put while he went to check out the lights. Armed with only a machete and flashlight he went into the woods. After a length of time the boys became worried when their scout master failed to return. They walked to a phone booth and called the sheriff's department. A deputy arrived to find the scout master had returned, dazed and scared. He related a bizarre story about coming in contact with a metallic disk-shaped craft ringed with lights hovering over a clearing in the woods. He claimed while watching the thing it shot a stream of hot spray at him which rendered him unconscious. The site of the incident was investigated by Air Force Captain Edward Ruppelt, who at the time was the chief of Project Bluebook. The investigators found the grass and tree tops in the clearing were scorched by high heat. The scout master's hat and arms were also burned. [Source: Project Bluebook files, 1952]

September 16, 1952: At 4:30 a.m., a metallic disk with windows and blinking red and amber lights along the rim and underside was seen over Belle Glade and blamed for scaring cattle.

March 24, 1952: Capt. Donald Holland, a U.S.M.C. pilot, reported encountering a round UFO over Florida. When he attempted to aim his gun cameras at the object it flew off at an extreme rate of speed.

July 1952: A U.S. Air Force colonel piloting a B-29 responded to a McDill AFB radar target and reported seeing a maneuvering egg-shaped glowing object in the vicinity of Tampa Bay. The pilot was on landing approach when the object was visually observed by three crewmen on board. Radar registered the object traveling at 220 knots at altitudes between 20,000 and 40,000 feet.

March 24, 1954: A pilot reported a round UFO seen over Cape Canaveral at 3000 feet. When military jets came near the object it sped away.

June 15, 1955: Witnesses on Daytona Beach reported 3 fireballs moving slowly along the beach before flying straight up and vanishing.

November 2, 1955: Two Williston law enforcement officers felt a stinging heat as they observed 6 oval shaped objects. The UFOs were also witnessed by a dozen citizens.

December 11, 1955: Navy pilots allegedly attempted to night time dogfight over the Atlantic with a round reddish-orange colored UFO that was tracked by radar over Jacksonville. The object was also observed at 9 P.M. by the crews of two airliners. Based on the official report, when two navy pilots tried to engage the target at 30,000 feet, the unidentified object dived and buzzed around their aircraft before zipping off at a high rate of speed. The entire ordeal was confirmed by radar at the Jacksonville Naval Air Station.

November 8, 1956: A UFO, 4 to 5 times larger than a conventional aircraft, was tracked traveling 4000 mph by weather radar in Miami over South Florida. The object seemed to be playing "aerial tag" and was believed to be under intelligent control.

STRANGE FLORIDA II

March 29, 1957: The crew of Pan American flight 206A flying at 16,000 feet observed a brilliant pulsating light off the coast of Jacksonville. The object was on radar for twenty minutes and was the size of a normal aircraft. [Some reports describe this object as a fire ball making a sound like a jet engine].

July 1957: Blue Book records lists an unidentified object over Oldsmar, Florida.

October 6-7, 1957: A white oval object was seen on consecutive nights over Cape Canaveral.

November 29, 1957: A round orange colored object was seen for 2 minutes over Sarasota.

December 18, 1957: People in Sarasota reported television interference as an unexplained white light drifted over the area.

May 17, 1958: Two witnesses reported an orange colored light over Fort Lauderdale. When a spotlight was turned on it, the object grew more intense then sped off.

June 4, 1958: A white oval-shaped UFO played zigzag over Sarasota.

January 14, 1958: A white glowing object was seen at 7:30 p.m. over Sarasota.

April 3, 1959: In Ocoee, two credible witnesses reported seeing a large greenish-yellow light ascending and reflecting against the water of a lake. The object faded out then reappeared, hovered for a minute, then disappeared after speeding off at a high rate of speed.

December 5, 1959: A navy man on leave in Miami, using an Argus C-3 camera, snapped a photo of five white spots in the sky followed by what appeared to be a disk shaped object. The man claimed in a newspaper article that investigators from the Air Force interrogated him and examined his camera. This account is credited to a story that appeared in the Miami Herald dated December 6, 1959.

October 20, 1959: Military personnel reported a slow-moving star-like UFO over Key West that was joined by a second fast moving object before vanishing from sight.

May 4, 1960: An architect in Sarasota observed a long cigar-shaped UFO with four portholes on the side.

May 20, 1960: A UFO hovered, climbed, and dived over Tyndall AFB in Florida's panhandle. The object was seen by several base personnel including Air Police and on base radar.

January 22, 1961: An elliptical metallic object approached Eglin AFB from the Gulf of Mexico, then made an abrupt U-turn and headed back over the Gulf. The object was filmed by a business using an 8 mm home movie camera.

May 18, 1962: At 7 p.m., a housewife saw a hovering cigar-shaped UFO northwest of Pompano Beach. The topside of the object was dark but the underside was brilliantly lighted. The object remained motionless for about 9 minutes, and then slowly moved toward the west before speeding off like a "flash of lightening." The underside dimmed as the object accelerated.

November 11, 1962: A UFO was observed over Lakeland doing loops and leaving "gossamer filaments" in the air. Presumably, this refers to a phenomenon known as "Angel Hair," a fine transparent spider web-like substance frequently associated with UFO sightings. [Source: Lakeland Ledger, 11-12-1962]

STRANGE FLORIDA II

November 19, 1962: Three star-like objects were seen over Tampa and appeared to be under intelligent control. [Source: USAF Project Bluebook 1962 Summary]

August 1963: In Ashton, just a little east of St. Cloud, a UFO made the news when local witnesses observed it sucking up water from a lake. Note: There were six other out of state reports during this same time period about UFOs siphoning water through hoses from ponds].

August 6, 1963: The National Investigations Committee on Aerial Phenomena, NICAP, investigated a sighting over Sanford that was witnessed by 13 people. The UFO approached from the northwest as a red star-like object, pulsating and turning white. It hovered for awhile before moving south over Seminole County where it bobbed up and down, and swayed back and forth, while emitting a flare of greenish-white light.

1965: In Weeki Wachee Springs a man came upon a five foot alien creature wearing a silver suit with a fish bowl helmet. [Yes, I know, this sounds ridiculous, but we could use a laugh at this point]. He said the alien gave him a thin piece of paper containing a cryptic message which the man claimed had been decoded by Air Force investigators, presumably from Project Blue Book. The message allegedly said the alien was from Mars. Great story, but no record of the investigation or incident could be located in available Air Force files.

March 1965: A hunter was deep in the Everglades when he saw a cone-shaped craft land. He began waving his arms in a friendly gesture as he approached within close range but was struck down by an intense beam of light. Allegedly, the hunter was rendered unconscious for 24 hours. He struggled back to civilization and reported his close encounter to the sheriff. He was admitted to the Fort Myers hospital with partial blindness and internal injuries. An investigation revealed scorched vegetation at the location of the sighting. Skeptics charged that it was all a hoax; however, medical records did confirm the man had experienced trauma while in the Everglades.

July 1965: Unidentified craft was seen over the Atlantic Ocean out from Fort Pierce.

March 1966: Strange craft was observed hovering over the Florida Straits off the Keys.

April 1966: Florida Governor Hayden Burns, accompanied by news journalists, observed a disk-shaped craft over Marion County while flying to Tallahassee. When the disk appeared to be pacing the Governor's Convair 340 airplane, he ordered the pilot to turn and give chase after the UFO which suddenly veered off at supersonic speed.

June 1966: UFO seen over the ocean off the coast of Cape Canaveral.

September 1966: The U.S. Navy recovered a strange object, shaped like a rocket, off Miami Beach in forty feet of water. The Navy said it was not a missile but otherwise could not identify the object. This led to speculation by UFO buffs that the Navy had recovered a crashed UFO.

1967: A fisherman from Oak Hill reported a close range sighting of "a glowing flying saucer moving slowly over the water" while fishing in Mosquito Lagoon adjacent to the Space Center.

May 1967: A triangular object with glowing lights on each corner was sighted near Gainesville.

April 1973: An electrical blackout darkened much of South Florida. People reported seeing several strange bluish-green lights hovering over the nuclear power plant at Turkey Point.

STRANGE FLORIDA II

December 3, 1977: A chevron-shaped UFO with running lights was seen over Ft. Lauderdale.

March 25, 1981: Pompano Beach observers reported triangle-shaped craft moving south to north.

August 1987: A witness in Flagler County claimed to see an object shaped like a pair of inverted bowls on top of each other. It was white, metallic-looking with blinking lights around the rim, a red light on top and green light on the bottom.

November 1987: In Gulf Breeze, Florida, Ed Walters, a contractor, spotted a space craft hovering over his house. He took five Polaroid pictures of the Tea Kettle looking contraption before he was struck with a blue beam. Ed saw this thing on several occasions which generated a lot of press coverage. Folks flocked to Gulf Breeze for their own close encounters while Ed wrote a best selling book. Ufologists began shying away from the Gulf Breeze encounters after a UFO model was found in Ed's house and a local kid confessed to having helped Ed create a hoax. Ed, along with his loyal supporters maintained it was a genuine close encounter. UFO buffs looking for extraterrestrial space craft, still visit Gulf Breeze, now dubbed Florida's UFO hotbed.

October 17, 1990: A silent low altitude triangle-shaped object was seen over Flagler Beach.

Fall 1993: A motorist claimed to have been chased by a red UFO while driving through the Merritt Island National Wildlife Refuge on Route 3 near Kennedy Space Center. In the same proximity, a Canadian visitor claimed that while camping on a spoil island in Mosquito Lagoon, he witnessed a triangular-shaped craft and snapped a Polaroid photo of an space alien, which he copyrighted and offered to sell for a fee. Amazingly the alien in the photo appeared to be wearing a hockey mask. This led me to wonder if extraterrestrials played hockey. Investigators concluded that both reports were false. The red UFO that chased the motorist turned out to be a red beacon on top of a microwave tower that was seen in the driver's rear view mirror and as for the alien encountered on the island, it was a hoax.

April 15, 1994: A dark gray, V-shaped craft with red lights was observed near Brooksville.

October 1994: A boomerang-shaped craft with three lights on the underside was seen over the Indian River Lagoon by a NASA worker on his way to work at the Space Center.

February 14, 1997: Several observers [6 or 8 witnesses] in Ormond Beach saw a dark-colored chevron-shaped object seen slowing moving over the Halifax River.

February 2002: A streak of light making right angle turns was seen in Gadsden County. In Pompano Beach an orange-colored, cigar-shaped craft, with yellow tips, was witnessed by several people before it zoomed off at high speed and disappeared from sight.

April 2002: Strange light was observed over Tampa, zig zagging in and out of the clouds.

April 2002: Blue flash of light seen by boy scouts in night sky over Ocala National Forest.

May 2002: Lee County residents observed a large, orange triangular, or chevron-shaped, object over Pine Island.

May 2002: Three large triangular objects were seen over Orlando at 2:30 in the morning. Objects were described as black with a series of lights on the front and flying in an erratic manner unlike conventional aircraft.

STRANGE FLORIDA II

May-June 2002: Unidentified silent triangular object was seen by multiple witnesses over the Spring Hill community in Hernando County. Most observers reported seeing six white lights outlining the edge of the object. One report claims the object appeared to be accompanied by conventional [possibly military] aircraft.

July 2002: Oblong object described as two acres long with flashing red and white lights was seen over Polk County.

November 3, 2005: A huge flying wing or triangular craft was seen flying over Naples at a fast rate of speed. The craft was silent and had no lights.

January 4, 2006: A witness sent a private email to me describing an unexplainable aerial event off Satellite Beach. "We were aboard a deep sea fishing boat about 15 miles out from Satellite Beach, [Brevard County]. It was late afternoon about 4 p.m. when the four of us saw a large round platter-shaped object about 1000 feet altitude above the ocean. This object was motionless and at a distance of mile at best. It appeared to be surrounded in a fog or mist. I estimate the object was 100-200 feet width and 30-40 feet thick. During the observation another identical object emerged or morphed out of the first one. The two objects hung motionless for a minute or two and then tilted up on their ends and dove into the ocean and disappeared. We didn't see a splash or wave where they went into the ocean. I notified the coast guard but no one ever followed-up with me or the other observes even though they have our phone numbers."

July 4, 2006: Black, non-reflective sphere, estimated at cloud level, was video taped east of Osteen by a man watching the space shuttle launch. Author examined the video footage and could not readily identify the object.

THE STRANGE CASE OF UFO Hill
DID FLORIDA WRITER, *WILLIAM MORIATY*, STUMBLE UPON A POSSIBLE GOVERNMENT CONNECTION TO THE UFO PHENOMENON?

In a separate feature, you'll read about Florida author William Moriaty's account concerning a mysterious beam. Moriaty amazes me with how he can root out unpublished Florida secrets that most of us would never hear about; which accounts for his large following of readers. The story is a Moriaty exclusive, totally unpublished, well, except for his article that appeared in *Nolan's Pop Culture Review,* Florida's leading online magazine. Okay, fasten your seatbelt for a trip back to December 1980 to UFO Hill in Gadsden County.

It was through a former colleague that William learned about a bank security guard in Pensacola who had experienced a close encounter of the unexplainable kind. The security guard liked to hunt in Gadsden County, southwest of the small hamlet of Wetumpka in the woods along Sadberry Road. Although the rural location contained an overgrown grid of streets leftover from an abandoned subdivision project, it was a lucrative hunting area with an abundance of wildlife. After a day of hunting in 1977, the security guard said, he headed west down the road, to where it circled a small hill, to check for signs of wildlife.

About 300 yards south of his location, the man was startled by a strange sight, which he described as, "a metallic disc-shaped object hovering over a hill." He said, "it as 25 to 30 feet in length and making no sound." The object hovered over the tree tops for a few moments, then moved slightly higher before shooting straight up and, within seconds, became the size of a small star in the evening sky. It then made a 90-degree turn and, in a split second, zipped across the night sky where it vanished beyond the horizon.

The security guard later related his encounter to a few hunting buddies who, as one might expect, scoffed at his story. A few days later, hoping to find some evidence to support his story,

STRANGE FLORIDA II

the security guard took his buddies out to the hill and, to their surprise, there in front of them was the same metallic disc, or one just like it. To their amazement, the strange object repeated the same performance previously witnessed by the security guard. On following visits to the site, the object was seen on several occasions by the men. The strange craft, or whatever it was, would do a repeat performance at virtually the same exact time of the evening.

The security guard, determined to get a better understanding of what was going on, decided one cold night to camp on top of the hill. At first, nothing happened and there was no sign of the object. Then, in the middle of the night, he awoke to a feeling of terror. He recounted how something seemed to be communicating non-verbally with his mind, ordering him to immediately leave the top of the hill. Looking up at the night sky, he saw a pin point of light that moved across the sky until it was directly overhead. When it appeared to be descending toward him, he quickly rolled up his sleeping bag and made a mad dash to his pickup. He climbed into the safety of his truck and looked back at the hill where the object was now hovering just like the first time he had seen it. While he watched, the object emitted a blinding pinkish light and then grew smaller until it was just a grapefruit-size ball of pink light.

The hunters also noticed something else strange about the area. On each visit, the vegetation seemed altered. Four foot tall saplings would grow to ten feet in a matter of days and 90 foot tall pines would simply disappear, without any sign of removal. The security guard decided to do a little investigating and obtained (from the Gadsden County Property Appraiser's office) aerial photographs of the subject area covering a twenty year period which showed unnatural changes to the vegetation and tree canopy. He then talked with some local backwoods folks, living near the sighting location, who claimed the "weird lights in the sky has been going on for so long that we just ignore them."

When William Moriaty got wind of the story, he decided to investigate it in July 1981 while on a trip to Tallahassee, which is only about twenty miles east of Wetumpka. I seriously doubt there's a square inch of Florida that Moriaty hasn't visited at sometime to check out history or trees...or in this case a UFO claim. It was William Moriaty who dubbed the site "UFO Hill" in his initial report. Using a hand drawn map provided by the security guard, and along with two friends, his party had little difficulty in locating the hill, but was stopped from accessing it by a ten foot electrified fence. The fence, running north to south across the road, had U.S. Government emblems on it and an attached metal sign reading, "Restricted Area." The government's interest in securing the location may never be known, so we are left perplexed about what witnesses claim was an encounter with something from outer space, something that may still be going on.

Just like tourists, the ufonauts keep returning to Florida...

Since starting this book, I have received at least half dozen reports of aerial phenomena from all over the state. Hundreds of others have been logged with the National UFO Reporting Center. These reports have included all shapes and sizes from triangles to rectangles. Maybe the aliens are trying to confuse us with so many shapes. Or perhaps we are being visited by different extraterrestrials, each piloting different vehicle.

Perhaps we are dealing with a combination of phenomena and not just visitors from another planet. Maybe some of these sleek contraptions are time machines from the future taking tourists back for a look at the past, or perhaps they come from another dimension, or from inside the earth as suggested by hollow earth believers. Or perhaps, there's a worldwide mass hallucination that's been going on since biblical times which causes some folks to see strange flying objects. Whoa...that would be more bizarre than the UFO phenomenon! The truth is out there, some place, but we can forget about it if it's stashed away in the government's secret files. UFO researchers are up to their necks in evidence, but the basic question is still begging to be answered, "Is there intelligent life on those other planets?" Personally, I'm still looking for intelligent life on earth.

STRANGE FLORIDA II

[[[[[[Encounter with a Mystery Beam]]]]]]
Did a secret government experiment go wrong?

When I first heard about this bizarre real life incident that happened in Florida's Panhandle, I paid little attention to the fine points since it happened over a half century ago. After researching another subject related to top secret government experiments, I decided to revisit this intriguing story which comes from one of my favorite books, titled *William Moriaty's Florida*. It's one of those rare books that should be on the shelf of every true Floridian as it is an insight to how we natives remember the Sunshine State before developers replaced our orange groves and natural habitat with shopping centers and theme parks. Allow me to digress for a moment about William Moriaty who is popularly known for his internet column *La Floridiana*, a feature of *Nolan's Pop Culture Review* online magazine. Here's another claim to fame about Moriaty, he has planted thousands of trees across the state which makes him a folk hero in the eyes of real Floridians. In 1983 he founded the Tampa Bay Reforestation and Environmental Effort Inc., a non-profit organization aimed at protecting a major part of our environment. Will Moriaty and I are fellow natives and friends. However, we have our differences, such as he wears white suits and I wear black ones, but our love of the Sunshine State is the same, whether it's nature, history, or a bizarre mystery as in the following strange story.

To get to the beginning of this bizarre story we must travel back to the 1949-50 time line. Will's parents left Tampa on a trip to take his half-brother to attend military school in Biloxi, Mississippi. At Perry, they connected with U.S. Highway 98 for a drive along the Gulf of Mexico around the peninsula's big bend into the panhandle and very near several military installations, including the sprawling Eglin Air Force Base. Although Highway 98 still lacks the heavy traffic of other Florida roads, in the late forties it was a desolate stretch of pavement with very few cars, especially at night.

Will's mother was at the wheel while his father dozed in the passenger seat and his half-brother slept in the backseat. As she drove through what was then a remote section of Walton County, adjacent to the huge Eglin Air Force reservation, an uneasy feeling came over her as if she were being held against the seat by a great unseen force. Suddenly, she was hit with a sensation like being electrocuted. The car began to act up, sputtering and jerking, as if in bad need of a tune-up, then the engine just stopped. The headlights and dashboard lights went out as the vehicle continued to roll through the darkness on its own momentum. Fortunately, at that time of night, there were very few cars on the road.

Will's mother was trying to figure out what was going on when, after a few moments, the engine re-started by itself and the lights came on as if nothing had happened. "What in the world is going on," she wondered, checking the gauges and interior lights. Then without warning the same weirdness happened again. The engine cut out and the lights went black, and she experienced the same strange sensation, although to a lesser degree. Then, just like the first time, the engine re-started and the lights came back on.

Having no further bizarre experiences, she continued on through Okaloosa County without relating the incident to Will's father and half-brother who had slept through the whole nightmare. We can imagine that the experience must have played on her mind as she drove through the night toward Pensacola. She knew it could not have been a hallucination because not only had she physically felt the unexplained sensation, it had affected the vehicle's electrical system as well.

After dropping Will's half-brother off at military school in Biloxi, his parents paid a visit to some friends, a colonel and his wife, living at nearby Keesler Air Force Base. It was the first time Will's mother would relate her weird experience. After patiently listening to the details, the colonel, in a rather adamant tone, replied "...In this man's Army Air Corps, there are certain things we must never talk about and what you have told me is never to be mentioned to anyone! Ever!"

Needless to say, she was perplexed by the Colonel's strange, but serious, response. Did he know something about a military secret? Was something sinister at work that night in 1949? Did it have something to do with her experience as she drove through the desolate darkness of Walton County next to the sprawling Eglin military reservation? Was the Colonel trying to keep the security lid on a secret government project? Whatever it was, he had only added more mystery to the mix.

Twenty years went by from that night on Highway 98 and nothing was said about the strange incident. In the meantime, the Colonel retired from the Air Force and settled with his wife in Clearwater. Will found the Colonel interesting and would often tag along when his mother went to visit the couple. Then, on one visit in the spring of 1973, Will's mother asked the Colonel if he remembered her telling him about the strange thing that had happened to her on the drive to Biloxi. When he denied knowing anything about it, she responded, "I can't believe you don't remember it." She then proceeded to recite the full story to him again. It was the first time Will had heard about his mother's bizarre experience. When she was finished, the Colonel shook his head, "I just don't remember you telling me anything like that." Obviously the mystery was still alive and well. It seemed that even in retirement, the Colonel was still holding the lid on an old secret.

With a little gin and tonic a secret is revealed...

As a young teenager, Will would often visit the Colonel to hear his combat tales of World War II and Vietnam. Sometimes, they would sit up into the wee hours of morning with the Colonel sipping gin and tonic and talking about airplanes, world politics, and his exploits during several decades of military service. Will would sit there drinking a coke while taking in the Colonel's intriguing stories. His stories seemed to get better after downing each drink. Then one night, after several gin and tonics, the Colonel opened up, "You remember that story your mother told me a few weeks ago, about the strange electrical incident that happened to her when she was driving up to Biloxi? Well, I lied about that—I know damn well what happened to her that night—and to others, too."

Will hung onto his chair. He was all ears and on the verge of hearing a genuine secret if the Colonel would just keep talking...and sipping his drinks. Will adhered to an old rule of weird research, when secret stuff is being exposed, keep quiet and listen. The Colonel took another sip, then holding his glass between his palms, began to unravel a twenty year old mystery. "We, [referring to the USAF or another government agency] were conducting microwave experiments at the Eglin reservation. That evening we were trying to project a microwave beam thirty miles out into the Gulf when a horrific accident occurred. The trajectory of the beam did not arc properly to reach its target, and instead shot almost straight out from its projector. Two of my technicians were killed and your mother was caught several miles away in the stray beam…"

In 1973, Will, like the rest of us in those days, had little knowledge about microwave technology. As a matter of fact, he saw his first microwave oven in the 1980's when he worked at a Montgomery Ward store. Nevertheless, Will sat straight up soaking in the details as the Colonel poured himself another drink. At this point, Will would have fixed the Colonel's drinks himself just to keep him talking.

The Colonel took another sip and started again, "Immediately upon being informed at Keesler of the incident, I was summoned to fly to Eglin in order to investigate the accident. When I got there, smoke was pouring out of every orifice in the two techs' bodies—eyes, nostrils, ears…they were literally cooked from the inside. I was not aware at that time that your family was caught in that beam. I flew back later that morning for debriefing at Keesler. Once I established from your mother what time she estimated her incident took place, I realized it corresponded with the time of the mishap." The Colonel paused and set his glass aside, then added, "Yeah, I knew all about her story—more than I wish I ever knew."

Will was left stunned by the Colonel's admission. It took him quite awhile before he could find the courage to tell his mother about what the Colonel had confessed. According to the Colonel's account, Will's parents and half-brother had stumbled unwittingly into the beam of a secret government experiment. If true, then they were victims of government secrecy. The mystery now was what kind of physical effects had this encounter had on them? Sadly, Will's half-brother, who had been asleep in the backseat that fateful night, developed melanoma at the young age of twenty-seven. At age thirty-three, after a long battle it claimed his life on September 18, 1973. Indeed, it is possible that exposure to a powerful microwave blast may have contributed to cell mutations leading to his cancer and premature death. This happened about the same time the Colonel became convinced he was being watched by government agents. Had he told a sixteen year old kid too much? Had he spilled the beans of top secrecy?

Upon first hearing William Moriaty's bizarre story, I began researching to see if I could substantiate the Colonel's confession. This is not easy to do when it involves secret government projects, plus there's the usual disinformation that is deliberately planted to steer nosy researchers off course. What I found was that Eglin Air Force base has been the location of untold numbers of secret weapons projects, including many which involved microwave research in the late forties and through the Cold War period of the fifties. The typical household microwave oven generates less than 1,500 watts of power, compared to the some of the government microwave experiments that produce millions of watts. One of the Pentagon's so-called "less lethal" military experiments, the Active Denial System [ADS], is known to have fired a 95-gigahertz microwave beam. Although referred to as "less lethal," the true biological affects of this weapon are still top secret. The Freedom of Information Act is useless in requesting information on secret government projects if they are still classified, which means in many cases a secret can last indefinitely. Even when released, declassified documents often contain up to ninety percent blacked-out parts which only adds frustration for a researcher trying to get to the bottom of something.

In the late forties and early fifties, microwave experiments were more difficult to control and occasionally resulted in horrible tragedies at test facilities. One of the projects during this time at Eglin involved the development of a beam, or ray, to disrupt electrical systems of aircraft. That sounds very much like what happened in Will's story.

Using a 1950 road map and 1954 military topographic map of Eglin AFB and the Walton County area, I was able to roughly estimate the position of Will's mother's car when she encountered the unknown. It most likely occurred on a part of Highway 98, slightly more remote than other sections, on a thin stretch of land separating the Gulf of Mexico from Choctawhatchee Bay and the Eglin military reservation. One 1940's era military topographic map shows a "test range" and "test facility" which would have been in direct alignment with the approximate location of Will's parents' vehicle on Highway 98. Later grid maps circa 1950 do not indicate these facilities; instead the word "abandoned" is used. However, if the government wanted to shoot a powerful microwave beam into the Gulf of Mexico, then this thin piece of land cut by Highway 98 was, at least in 1949, the least populated area between Eglin AFB and the Gulf. If such an experiment really occurred, as the Colonel claimed, then you can bet that somewhere in the Pentagon's deep, dark file cabinets are classified documents explaining what happened that night so long ago.

Another old secret involving Eglin AFB...

In 1962, Eglin AFB was to play a role in a highly classified lunatic scheme to create an excuse for the United States to invade Cuba. The unbelievable plan, hatched at the Pentagon by General Lemnitzer and the Joint Chiefs of Staff, was code named Operation Northwoods. It called for innocent people to be shot on American streets, terrorist acts in Washington, D.C. and Miami, sinking boats filled with Cuban refugees, bombings, and hijacking of passenger planes. As bizarre as it sounds, the United States actually planned to attack itself, or its own taxpaying citizens, and blame it on Fidel Castro so as to gain public and international support for launching an invasion of Cuba.

Part of the insane plan involved Eglin AFB, where a radio controlled drone aircraft would be painted and numbered as an exact duplicate of a civilian passenger plane that was to take off from the Miami area. On board the real passenger plane were to be *selected* passengers with alias names. At a specific time the real passenger plane would rendezvous south of Florida with the duplicate drone aircraft from Eglin AFB. The passenger plane would then turn around and head for an auxiliary landing field at Eglin while the duplicate drone would continue flying a route across Cuba. At Eglin, the passengers were to be evacuated and the real plane returned to its original status. Meanwhile the phony plane was to start transmitting on the international distress frequency a message that it was under attack by Cuban Mig fighters. A radio signal would then trigger explosives on board to destroy the phony aircraft. The intention was for radio stations of the International Civil Aviation Organization to notify the United States about the attack to add realism to the whole scheme. Then, presto, like sleight of hand magic, the United States would have produced a great excuse to go to war along with public support.

The phony aircraft attack plan was only one of several deceptive plots under Operation Northwoods which remained secret for over forty years until declassified documents surfaced in the National Archives, which can now be found on the internet. None of the plans were ever carried out, however, another hyped-up deception known as the Gulf of Tonkin incident, led us into the Vietnam quagmire and claimed the lives of over 58,000 Americans.

I'm reminded of a statement made in June 1997 by Air Force General Kenneth A. Minihan, Director of the National Security Agency. "The public has a duty to watch its government closely and keep it on the right track." I will tag that with my own statement, "We the people do not belong to the government; the government belongs to us." That's true democracy, folks.

Strange confessions from Florida's leading medium
Evil Spirits in a Winter Park Home

According to Susan Thompson, who has communed with the dearly departed since childhood, most spirits are benevolent and should not be feared. As one of Florida's most publicized mediums, she operates the *New Smyrna Beach Historical Ghost Tour* and has been featured in dozens of publications, DVD videos, and on numerous talk radio shows discussing the subject of spiritualism. "While malevolent entities are rare," she explains, "they do exist, and on occasion will reveal their wicked ways through unexpected manifestations. Evil spirits are earthbound souls who exist in that narrow space between the physical and spiritual worlds." She says that earthbounders remain attached to their earthly possessions, in some instances even to a living person, and this keeps them from crossing over to the afterlife. Some are confused and frustrated souls who do not believe they're really dead which, according to some theories, may contribute to poltergeist phenomena.

"Most earthbounders are good. Unfortunately, as in physical life, we also have a few bad ones," remarked Thompson, who has participated in numerous exorcist-style house cleansings to evict evil doers. "Once a medium can get them to go to the light they'll let go of their earthly connections and will shed any wickedness."

Susan Thompson knows from experience that being a medium does not give the living immunity against evil spirits. In 1991 she began her own four-year episode of terror at her Winter Park home. Actually it started with a good spirit and small stuffed animal. "Candice, my youngest daughter, was sixteen at the time," she explained. "She would find the stuffed toy moved to different places in her room, things would disappear...then reappear, and sentences of jumbled letters would mysteriously appear on her computer screen."

Susan, using her strange craft as a medium, soon determined that the entity was a good spirit who meant no harm. "Candice was not frightened at all and even named the entity 'George.' But, I could sense a presence of sadness, like helplessness, and I could tell he was earthbound." George, according to Susan's visions, had been a skinny blonde-haired boy of sixteen who had died in a terrible accident. It seems that just before he died, George had been abducted by thirty-six people wearing strange costumes and held in an abandoned house where he was tortured in some kind of ritual. "The facts surrounding this entity came in bits and pieces over several contacts with him," she said, recalling how deciphering spiritual communication can be a little foggy. In hopes of attracting help, George had set a fire in the abandoned building which got out of control resulting in the deaths of him and his tormentors. "His former captors were now earthbound evil entities who had followed him to our house," she explained, still a little nervous about recalling the terror that followed. "I feel they wanted to settle the score with him for causing their deaths. This is when we began experiencing absolute horror in our house."

"George had hung around our house for some time. He would move objects and we could hear footsteps on the tile floor in the hall, but nothing really scary," said Susan. "The bad stuff started when Candice was a high school senior. She had a mid-term photography project to complete and, early one morning, asked me to go with her to an old abandoned castle on Bear Gully Lake to take some pictures of the sunrise. This place was about ten minutes from our house, down an over-grown dirt road in a wooded area."

Research into the facts behind this story indicate the castle-structure was actually a three-story boat house for a larger, medieval-style mansion built in the early 1970s by a rags-to-riches multi-level marketing guru named Glenn Turner. In 1975, Turner's empire crumbled after he was charged with operating a pyramid marketing scheme. Turner spent years defending his innocence, but eventually served five years in prison for fraud. During his expensive legal ordeal, Turner lost his sixty-acre castle property to creditors. For several years on each Halloween, the local Jaycees used the abandoned castle as a haunted house for their annual fundraiser. A developer bought the property in 1989 and, following several suspicious fires, the unfinished castle was torn down leaving only the medieval-style boat house on the lake.

"We got to the old castle about five-thirty in the morning and while Candice went about her early morning photography, I sat in the car drinking my coffee. The doors and windows of the castle were all boarded-up and, even with the walls defaced with graffiti, it was still an ideal subject for photography. Candice shot several rolls of film and we talked about how the place had a strange feeling, then we drove home. The strangest thing happened when Candice developed her pictures…there was no graffiti on the walls and none of the windows or doors were boarded-up…and in one of the top windows was a shining light…the castle actually looked brand-new! We couldn't understand it."

"We jumped in the car and went back out to the castle and walked through the tall grass to get a close look," said Susan. "It was just as we had left it, still boarded-up with graffiti all over the walls. We looked to see if there was any way for light to be in that window, like in the photograph, but the window was boarded-up too. We pulled back some boards and stuck our heads inside. It was very dark inside. An unearthly feeling of terror swept through us. For a moment we could not move our legs, we were frozen. Once I could move again, I grabbed Candice's arm and we got out of there."

The next week Susan returned to the castle to see if she could pick-up the strange feeling again. "There was evil associated with this abandoned place," she explained. "After that I did not go back there. Then Candice began having recurring nightmares which seemed connected to our visit to the castle. I tried to communicate with George, the friendly earthbound spirit in our house, but each time I would feel negative vibrations, like he was frightened. I finally got through to George and learned how he had been killed in a fire, it had something to do with that castle and he was being followed by evil entities." Susan was soon to find out that his presence had attracted the evil ones to her house. "I first noticed it when I walked down the hall and every door would open and slam shut. Lights would flicker on and off." But that was mild stuff compared to what came next. "I was sitting at the table having coffee with my friend Joline, a medium, and Candice when, all of a sudden, this huge head of a woman came flying towards us from the kitchen. The head was suspended in the air, she had wild, black hair and no eyes, and it just bobbed up and down in front of us. It looked solid, fleshy-like, we all saw it. I demanded that the creature leave and after a few swoops she flew into the wall and vanished."

That night Susan went to bed with the eerie event still playing in her head. "I'm laying there trying to sleep when I heard a whizzing-like noise. I got up and heard Candice running down the hall. As she asked me what the noise was, the front door flew open. I quickly closed the door and locked it. As we turned to walk away, it flew open again with a bang. I knew this was not going to be a good night. I finally got Candice to bed and went into the kitchen to make a cup of tea. The whizzing noise became louder and seemed to pass over me. I could see faint shadows whipping around me. Then, from the corner of the kitchen, the huge head of that woman came rushing at me again. It was just a head dangling in the air, about four feet across, the eyes were just black holes, and when the mouth opened long fangs appeared." She had witnessed similar phenomena during exorcisms, but none as terrifying as what she was experiencing in her own home. Susan rushed to check on her daughter. "Just as I looked into Candice's bedroom, she bolted-up in bed and said, 'Mom, they're here, all of them are here'." She frantically hurried back to the kitchen. "There were thirty-six of them, all evil entities, whizzing like shadows around the kitchen. This went on for hours, I could feel them as one by one all thirty-six passed through me. I felt like throwing up, it was shear horror for nearly a week. I knew something had to be done, so I called my friend, Joline, to meet at my house to see if we could get George, the good entity, to go to the light and cross-over. As we concentrated on George, the evil ones became angry and were circling him and making a blood-stirring, unnatural noise. Never have I heard such painful moaning and screaming as emanated from these things. Finally, George ran for the light and crossed-over and the evil ones ceased to exist, they just went puff…disintegrated, and were never seen again."

Since her frightening ordeal, which has been corroborated by several witnesses, Susan Thompson's house has been peacefully quiet; however, she is still a practicing medium, along with being a lecturer, radio personality, ghost tour guide, and frequently, acting as a one-woman ghost exterminator helping others rid their houses of evil.

… STRANGE FLORIDA II

A STRANGE CASE OF SUICIDE.
Did he know too much about a secret experiment?

In the early morning hours of April 20, 1959, a police patrol stopped to check out a station wagon parked in a Dade County park. The vehicle was rigged with a hose leading from the exhaust pipe into the interior. Slumped over in the driver's seat was a 59 year old male, unconscious from a heavy dose of carbon monoxide poisoning. To the investigators it appeared to be a standard case of suicide, however, others have their doubts and believe Jessup was silenced to prevent public disclosure of details about a 1943 secret project since known as the *Philadelphia Experiment*.

The victim in this curious case was Dr. Morris K. Jessup, an astrophysicist, astronomer, and author of several books. Born in Rockville, Indiana, in 1900, he was named for his philanthropist uncle whose name can be found on any map of Greenland where at the extreme northern tip you will find a place named *Cape Morris K. Jessup*.

Following a stint in the army during World War I, Morris Jessup pursued studies at several universities and gained an extensive background in astrophysics, mathematics and astronomy. During his career, Doctor Jessup was involved in several research projects including work for the Carnegie Institute and U.S. Department of Agriculture. While involved with the Carnegie Institute, he explored the unexplained mysteries of the Mayan and Inca civilizations and was the first to suggest an extraterrestrial connection to these ancient cultures. Jessup ran short of funds before his findings could be published, however, many decades later *Erich Von Daniken* authored a popular series detailing a possible outer space connection to early empires of Central and South America. In the mid-1950s, Doctor Jessup conducted extensive scientific research into aerial phenomena and released an objective book about the enigma, titled *The Case of the UFO*. He embarked on a cross-country lecture tour to promote his book and to appeal for a serious scientific investigation into unidentified flying objects. The U.S. Air Force's *Project Blue Book* at the time was the only official UFO investigative agency. Serious researchers increasingly looked at Project Blue Book as nothing more than a pacifier for public curiosity. Jessup thought that both government and private research was lacking in UFO research, where, he believed, new energy sources might await discovery. In particular, Jessup focused on how UFOs might be the secret to harnessing electro-magnetic and gravitational energy fields. Since such new energy concepts would dip deep into the profits of the petroleum giants, many believed that the oil industry was using political connections to keep the lid on UFO research.

Jessup's book and lectures brought in bundles of mail from readers including several handwritten letters that put him on a head-on collision course with a confounding mystery that still intrigues conspiracy enthusiasts. The first letter arrived in October 1955, postmarked Pennsylvania and signed by a *Carlos Allende*, who changed his signature to *Carl Allen* in later letters. In the letters, which drifted in over a period of a year, Allen described his first hand knowledge of a bizarre Navy experiment secretly carried out in 1943 at the Philadelphia Navy Yard. He said the project was code-named *Operation Rainbow*, since known as the *Philadelphia Experiment*. In this experiment the U.S. Navy attempted to render a ship invisible. The subject ship used in the testing was the U.S.S. Eldridge, a destroyer escort.

STRANGE FLORIDA II

The first test was attempted on July 22, 1943 and was allegedly successful with the vessel being made partially invisible. The navy halted the project after members of the crew complained of serious nausea. The project's objectives were then changed to making a ship invisible to radar. According to Carl Allen, he had witnessed this experiment as a crewman aboard a ship moored near the Eldridge. The next test was conducted on October 28, 1943. This time the ship disappeared in a bright blue flash and in an instance, appeared 375 miles away off the coast of Norfolk Virginia. A few minutes later the Eldridge reappeared at the Philadelphia Navy Yard. We're talking teleportation here that allegedly had a profound physiological effect on the crew. Several crewmen suffered serious mental effects, some vanished forever, and five were actually fused into the metal of the ship. Because of the horrifying results, navy officials immediately halted all future experiments. If we are going to believe any of this, then we might as well stretch this account a little farther. According to the Allende letters some of the crewmen were brainwashed so they would forget about the experiment, some were institutionalized, and others vanished during a brawl in a Philadelphia dockside bar. They probably "vanished" when the shore patrol arrived to haul them off to the brig.

At first Doctor Jessup thought the Allende letters were a hoax, perhaps from a deranged writer, but there were specific details which eventually convinced him to investigate the matter. Supposedly the experiment had involved some brilliant minds, which included Albert Einstein and the whole project was allegedly based on his unified field theory.

The U.S. Navy has consistently denied conducting any such experiment, and most of the information has come from the Allende letters, however, there are a few supporting facts to the Philadelphia Experiment. The letter writer, Carlos Allende, was later identified as Carl M. Allen, and was indeed a registered merchant seaman who had been onboard a ship moored in Philadelphia harbor. There was in fact a U.S.S. Eldridge, [Number DE173] the only problem is that according to its 1943 deck log, [Ref: Microfilm NRS-1978-26] the Eldridge was not in Philadelphia during the alleged tests. Maybe that's because it was teleported 375 miles away or its records were falsified to fit security needs. It is also a fact that Albert Einstein was employed by the Office of Naval Research during the subject time frame and there was an operation code-named Project Rainbow, but it had nothing to do with making things invisible. It is also a fact that the navy was interested in the writings and research of Morris K. Jessup.

The Office of Navy Research contacted Dr. Jessup in 1957 and asked him to examine a copy of his book they had received. Jessup willingly complied and what he was shown by the navy was a copy of his UFO book with annotations handwritten in the margins. The annotations appeared to be by three people using three different colors of ink and referred to UFO technology and the Philadelphia Experiment. The annotations suggested the writers had a superior knowledge of the theories in Dr. Jessup's book. An examination of the handwriting suggested that the three annotators were probably one man, Carl Allen. The return address on the package in which the book was sent, turned out to be an abandoned farm house. For some reason it seems Mr. Allen did not want to be tracked down and apparently he stayed on the move during this time, surfacing at one point in Colorado.

The navy informed Dr. Jessup that they were reproducing 100 copies of the annotated book through the Varo Corporation, a Texas based government research firm. This is rather strange, since if there was nothing to the Philadelphia Experiment, or UFOs, then why would the Office of Naval Research go to the effort to contact Jessup, track down Allen, and reproduce so many copies of the annotated book? The navy claims it was not for official use but for personal use of ONR officers with three copies furnished to Dr. Jessup. Well, that's a convenient answer for public inquiries. I wonder if the taxpayers were bilked for this "personal use" project.

There's no good evidence that the Philadelphia Experiment ever happened, of course if it did happen we can assume that the government would keep the lid on any evidence to keep it from leaking out. Was that why the ONR was interested in talking with Jessup? Did Jessup know something? Was he unknowingly spilling the beans in his book? Did Carl Allen fabricate the whole mess that has become a legend? Have researchers of this mystery been on a wild goose chase? Like with most secrets, you can bet that we will never know the truth.

After his brief contact with the ONR, Morris Jessup may have continued communicating with Carl Allen and probing into the Philadelphia Experiment. Some think he may have discovered the truth about the project. In 1958 his life began a downhill turn when his wife walked out on him after which he moved to Coral Gables. After moving to Florida, several of his manuscripts were rejected by his publisher, a common experience for any author, and he became depressed, but other than an automobile accident, there was nothing to suggest he was suicidal.

According to public records, Dr. Jessup was still breathing when the cops found him slumped over in his carbon-monoxide filled car in that Dade County Park. He either died enroute to, or at, the hospital. While no autopsy was conducted, which is normally standard in suicide cases, tests were done on his blood. His blood alcohol levels were far above the lethal limits and combined with medications in his system it should have been fatal. The question arises about how a person so impaired could have driven himself to a county park and rigged up the hose to his car? So, what caused this once enthusiastic scientist to become so despondent as to commit suicide? Or was there something more sinister at work? The questions are many and we may never know the shadowy details of Jessup's later life. Shortly before his death he announced that he had made an important discovery regarding the UFO phenomenon. Perhaps he got too close to exposing a secret or maybe his death was just another suicide.

STRANGE FLORIDA II

A CURIOUS TALE OF A DEAD MAN'S GREETING
Is it an embellished legend or a missing piece of history?

The following gruesome story was discovered in an 1888 newspaper which reported it as factual history. However, there is a mystery here; is the story a lost piece of Florida history or just another farfetched legend?

There was once an old house in New Smyrna, for which it is said, few know the mournful history. Actually, the story begins in Savannah, Georgia, with the murder of a wealthy planter. Don't ask me for the date, if I knew I would tell you, but the article mentions no date. The victim was 70 years old when he was found with his throat cut and a dagger sticking out of his chest. Robbery was the obvious motive of his murderer or, in this case, murderers, since three of the old man's horses were missing. The trail led to a cabin on a small stream called Mud Branch, belonging to a man and his two sons. Their last name was Gainter and they were notoriously known as a vicious and unsocial lot. On the night of the murder, the Gainters seemed to vanish.

What the Gainters did not know was that the old planter had briefly regained consciousness long enough to dip his forefinger in his own blood and scrawl upon the wall in trembling letters "G-A-I-N" before his life drained away. Immediately, a group of men began tracking the three Gainter men, but they were long gone and, as one person put it, "It was like the earth had opened up and swallowed them out of existence."

After three months of aimless wandering, the Gainters showed up in New Smyrna where they found an abandoned house and moved in. Now, according to the story, the house, which had a large tree growing through it, was made of coquina rock and was built by the Spanish as a place of security. On the outside was a niche where once stood a Crucifix and on the wall was supposedly carved the date 1511. I know, the date is much too early for any Spanish structures, but there was indeed a house similar to this description. It was called the Rock House and it once stood on the north side of present day New Smyrna. Historians have for years debated over whether this house was built by the Spanish or British. Today, only a photograph of the house remains, as it was demolished in the early 1900s and crushed up to be used as ballast on the Florida East Coast Railroad. At the time of the Gainters, the Rock House would have been one of only a few inhabitable structures south of St. Augustine.

The house soon became a rendezvous for all the notorious characters of Florida's east coast, at least if you believe the story. The Gainters became agents for pirates and slavers from Cartagonia on the Spanish Main. A stockade was built in the rear of the house where stolen slaves were kept until they could be resold to the Spanish.

Ten years after taking residence at the house, a hurricane blew a schooner into the coast. The Gainters came upon the stranded vessel and found it deserted by the crew, but in the hold were ten Africans held in chains. Eight were men and the other two were a woman and an infant who were near death. The Gainters marched the men to their stockade but, before leaving the ship, the elder Gainter killed the woman and infant.

The notorious Gainter clan had also salvaged a large quantity of rum from the abandoned vessel, which they stored at their house. About a week later, after feeding the slaves back to health, the Gainters began a drinking spree consuming enough rum that, by 10 o' clock, all three were drunk as skunks. Assuming skunks drink. While they slept, the slaves were busy inside the stockade, hatching a plan for escape. The leader was a big mulatto whose wife and child were the ones killed by the elder Gainter.

The next morning, the three Gainters were awoken from their drunken stupor by eight blacks standing over them. The elder Gainter was the first to meet his fate. Taken to the front door, he was held in an upright spread-eagle position while the slaves nailed his hands and feet to the door frame. His tongue was then cut out and placed in his pocket. The two sons were served in the same manner being nailed to an inner door frame. Before escaping into the forest, the slaves stabbed each one of the Gainters in their hearts.

A couple of days later, Lieutenant Rafael Gomez with a mounted squad of Spanish soldiers emerged from the woods after a long ride from St. Augustine. In the distance he could see the house and the upright figure in the doorway. To Lieutenant Gomez it appeared that the elder Gainter was waving at them. He turned to his sergeant and said "Look, Senor Gainter is welcoming us. He is glad to see us." Apparently, the lieutenant needed to get his eyes checked because, as the Spanish soldiers drew closer, they quickly saw the horrible scene was not one of welcome, but of death.

Lieutenant Gomez ordered his soldiers to take the bodies down and give them a decent burial. Whether or not any of this story is true, we may never know, but it was published in 1888 and allegedly quoted directly from the age-yellowed manuscript of Don Enrique Gonzalez. Don't ask me who he was. Unfortunately for historians, no record of this document has ever been found, nor has anyone by the name of Gainter been found in existing records.

From *History of New Smyrna*, Copyright 1976, 1987, 1990, by Gary Luther.

New Smyrna's mysterious Rock House

This curious house once stood on a high shell mound commanding a view of Ponce Inlet. Could this have been the house mentioned in the Gainter story? In 1901, the Rock House was torn down, crushed up, and hauled away for railroad ballast. No one knows exactly who built the Rock House but according to New Smyrna historian Gary Luther, the earliest record of occupation of the house is an 1803 land grant made to Henry Martin. In 1808, the wooden parts of the house were burned by the Seminoles. In 1821, the house was the last inhabited dwelling south of St. Augustine.

STRANGE FLORIDA II

The Wizard of Central Florida

The Great Harry Wise

Magician, illusionist, mentalist, wizard, and circus ringmaster

America's last real ghostmaster!

Harry Wise is among the greatest entertainers to have ever emerged out of Florida. He spent fifty years in show business and is considered to be America's last ghostmaster. What's a ghostmaster, you ask? Ghostmasters were the hosts and lead acts for live horror shows that once played movie theater stages across the country. Between 1930 until fading out in the late 1960s, these vaudeville-like stage shows were popular in theaters as live midnight horror shows during Halloween. Ghost shows featured a little magic, scary illusions, monsters that would roam into the audience and always, at some point, a total blackout of the theater. Rubber snakes were often thrown into the audience just before the lights went out which created a lot of screams and sometimes near panic. You could say that Harry Wise scared the "yell" out of his audiences and, after everyone was sufficiently terrified, the theater would run a horror movie, as if they needed more scaring. You can't have that kind of fun these days due to insurance coverage, potential law suits, local ordinances, and most of all because most modern movie theaters no longer have stages.

Harry Wise began the ghost show circuit in 1957 playing Frankenstein with the famed Johnny Cates Show based in Texas. By 1963, Wise had his own ghost show on the road, under the banner of *Dr. Jekyl and his Weird Show*, playing up the Pacific west coast, across mid-America, Canada, and down the east coast to almost every theater in Florida. It was the hey-day of ghost shows. But, long after other shows had faded into horror

STRANGE FLORIDA II

New Smyrna Beach making him the last of America's original ghostmasters.

In the early 1960s, in-between his other shows, Harry Wise became Mr. Magic on Central Florida television. For several years, Mr. Magic was a household name known to every kid within broadcast range of Orlando's WDBO television. He remained a television personality until 1965 when he went on the road coast to coast with a big stage show featuring two hours of flashy illusions called the "Symphony of Magic." In addition to playing under names like Mr. Magic, Dr. Jekyl, and Ray Darkvale, Wise also appeared briefly in 1981 as the "Great Hans Voglar" in his own "Miracles of the Mind" mentalist act. Voglar was promoted as an "Internationally acclaimed hypnotist with thirty years experience whose uncanny ability in the World of ESP had amazed audiences around the World." Of course, Voglar was actually Harry Wise and, as a mind reading mentalist, he had never left the states. He was in fact a real hypnotist, although he used pseudo-hypnotism on stage. I know, because my first time in front of an audience was as a stooge for one of his hypnotic acts. I made a fool of myself pretending to be hypnotized. Many years later, in 2004, when I was writing his show business biography, "A Wizard's Tux and Tales," Wise confided that as a magician he had never done a mentalist routine and basically spent two months putting his ESP act together from information gleaned from a couple of books on mentalism. "For the most part, mentalism is psychology," he explained. "You learn to read people, their body language, mannerisms, and you can do a cold reading of some people and they will think you're some kind of miracle worker. In many cases, I just repackaged my magic and called it mentalism."

The most famous of Harry Wise's show posters advertising his live theater thriller the infamous Dr. Jekyl's Weird Show.

When Wise needed a stage name appropriate for a mind reader, he used his mother's maiden name, Voglar. "It was amazing at what I could get away with as a stage mentalist," admitted Wise. "I played shows for colleges where both students and faculty members actually believed I was reading their minds. It was an hour and twenty minutes of good entertainment, but they thought I was some kind of psychic. For me, it was scary shows for colleges where both students and faculty members actually believed I was reading their minds. It was an hour and twenty minutes of good entertainment, but they thought I was some kind of psychic. For me, it was scary knowing these educated people were so gullible. Here I was, a ninth grade drop out, leading around college faculty members by the nose. That's one reason I got out of the mentalist business."

When Wise turned forty-six, he did something that he had wanted to do since he was a kid, he joined the circus. "It was the Franzen Bros. Circus, a European-style circus. I was the ringmaster for the show, billed as Wise the Wizard, Florida Television's Original Mr. Magic. After spending a season under the Franzen big top, Wise went on to serve as the ringmaster for several other circuses. "I got off the road in '86, the last show was the Tommy Tyme Circus. I was getting tired of the road, but I finally got something out of my system that had been there since I had seen the Wallace Bros. Circus when I was ten years old. It just took me forty years to get around to doing it."

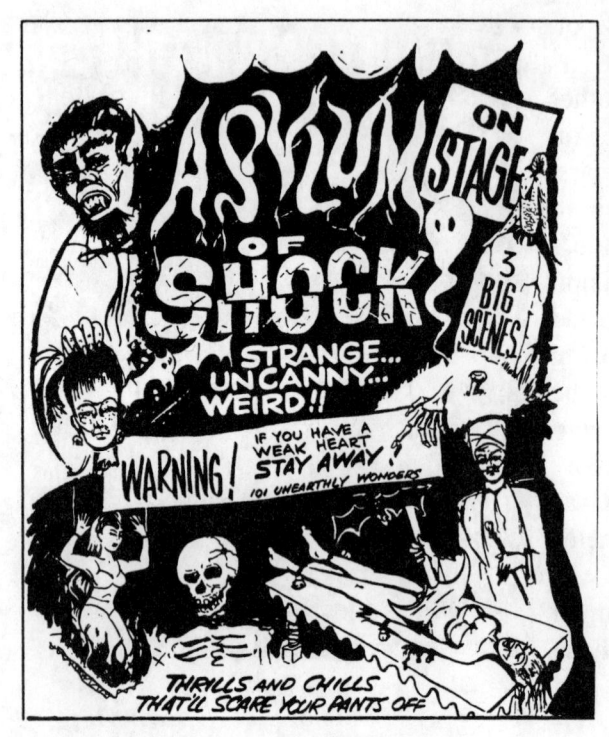

Above: A typical ghost show theater poster from the 1950s.

There is another side to Harry Wise beyond being a magician, ghostmaster, ringmaster, wizard, and showman. It is possibly the most mysterious side of his life, the part that goes beyond the theater stage and circus ring. I discovered two, well-worn, limited edition paperbacks distributed by Collegiate Distributors of Los Angeles. One was titled, *Fragments of Forever,* published in 1983, and the other, *Xanadu and You,* printed in 1984. Both are collections of mystical prose, sonnets, and poetry by an author named "H.W. Wise." In addition, there are four other enchanting works which have been found: *Cicada's Serenade, Goddess Encounter, Secrets of Ravenslair,* and *The Reality of it All,* all written by an H.W.W.

There were a number of clues within these works to cause me to wonder if these publications had been written by Harry Wise the magician. For example, in one there is the mention of the circus. But the big clue was in Fragments of Forever, where I found the name Ray Darkvale, the stage name of Harry Wise. Yet, Wise had never mentioned anything about being a writer. Perhaps I had discovered another dimension to the Wizard. He finally admitted that he had written these publications that were far more mystic than theater magic and ghost shows. Throughout this collection of parables and poems are found esoteric metaphors into which Wise has woven the meanings of life according to his own observations and dreams. Some are clearly cryptic, requiring a little more effort to decipher. Of course, trying to decipher the secrets of a wizard is not an easy task, but supposedly there is a secret embedded in his writings. The following example is the easiest one to figure out, except everyone who reads it draws a different meaning from it.

STRANGE FLORIDA II

Sunday, Nov. 12, 1971, 12:07 a.m.

"The magician Ray Darkvale is dead and buried now. His notes follow as my last legacy to his memory...for I have glimpsed that which he knew! I will follow soon...I MUST...search for and FIND his dream world of Xanadu! I know three things...the beautiful girl exists...The bridge, river, and mill are there at Mansfield, and...I looked across the river and saw the Unicorn too. After I follow on my best friend's DREAM QUEST, the only one left to know any of this...If it matters to anyone at all, will be...Alan Milan! The roaring fire is now merely glowing embers. Sleep is overtaking me...I must rest now."

The clues stick out like a sore thumb if you look for them. On stage, in the 1970s, *Ray Darkvale* was the alter ego of the mysterious Wise. He writes of *Darkvale* being dead and buried. Some have interpreted this to be a mystical suicide message while others believe it is cryptic instructions for an illusion. *Mansfield* refers to Mansfield, Indiana, and its river, covered bridge, and mill where Wise briefly found sanctuary from the public in 1982. The problem is that Wise had never been to Mansfield until '82 and his writings are dated 1971. Either he is a time traveler or clairvoyant or made a big mistake with his dates. He told me that visiting Mansfield was like a déjà vu experience. Did he dream of this place eleven years before visiting it? He also mentions *Alan Milan*, the showman who inspired him to become *Hans Voglar*, the mentalist. *Alan Milan*, however, was actually the stage name of a magician named *Don Davison*. This can get confusing, like shape-shifting, two people using so many names. There are copious references to the mythical unicorns throughout his writings, perhaps cryptic symbols of our cravings for a tiny sparkle of magic in our monotonous nine-to-five world. According to Wise, wizards pursue unicorns in mystical forests while the rest of the human race "seems content with pushing a shopping cart around crowded supermarkets or fussing with their lawn mowers."

Harry Wise admits that his stage acts were illusions, mere tricks for entertainment. However, he adds "there is a lot we don't know about the physics of the universe, and some alchemists and ancient magicians may have known secrets that only a privileged few know about. Some of it is best left alone." What's he talking about? Is he a magician trying to conjure up a little mystery? I learned another fact about Wise; he is a bona fide member of a modern version of a secret society dating back to 1118 A.D., known as the Knights Templar; he wears the ring, too. Could Wise be a real wizard?

In conversation with one of his former stage hands, I learned of a bizarre rumor concerning Wise the Wizard. Supposedly, he has a secret hidden in a safety deposit box of an undisclosed bank. The bank is believed to be in Georgia and, according to the story, there are three safety deposit boxes. The first two boxes each contain a key to a third box. Only two people have keys to the first two boxes. It then takes two keys to open the third box, which is suppose to contain a secret having to do with instructions of some kind. Whatever it is was accidentally discovered by Harry Wise during his days as a magician. Some people think it has to do with levitation. Wise was known for his famous floating lady act and other gravity defying stunts, but those were illusions...or were they?

The World of Harry Wise is a world of fantasy, mystery, and illusions. He has been featured in numerous newspaper articles and in his own biography. In his hometown of Sanford, Florida, his legacy is preserved in a permanent exhibit at the City Museum. As for his mysterious secrets, he leaves us standing between reality and fantasy, wondering if he is really a wizard or just a cleaver magician creating another illusion.

STRANGE FLORIDA II

A folksy place natives call the crossroads of Florida...

YEEHAW JUNCTION

The Historic Desert Inn

If you haven't heard of Yeehaw Junction then you're probably a newcomer or tourist. Yeehaw Junction is a real place in what genuine natives call the *Real Florida*. There's not much to see at Yeehaw Junction, except the historic Desert Inn which sits in the middle of nowhere, at the crossroads of U.S. Highway 441 and State Road 60 in southeast Osceola County.

The Desert Inn offers lodging and has a bar, gas station, and restaurant, where patrons range from local cowboys and passing truckers, to traveling businessmen in suits or an occasional tourist. It's not exactly a first class establishment by any stretch of the mind, but what really counts is it's a piece of Old Florida...and it has some haunted tales. If you are a first time visitor to the restaurant don't be alarmed if a giant spider drops down in front of you while your're waiting on your frog dinner. Yes, they serve real frog dinners, but the spiders are phony. Above each table, there is a spider attached to a string running across the ceiling to the bar. While unwary patrons are waiting for their food, the bar keeper will lower a spider on a web and dangle it in front of them. While I was there a couple of tourists practically turned over their table jumping up when a spider suddenly dropped down in front of them. Two local cowboys sitting at the bar got a good laugh, they had seen it all before. Everybody gets the spider treatment, it's like an initiation, or you might say it's Yeehaw Junction's strange way of saying, "Welcome, ya'll."

The history of Yeehaw Junction reaches back to the 1890s when it was originally called *Jackass Crossing*, a remote hub for cattle drives. In the early 1900s, Henry Flagler ran a railroad through this part of the Florida palmettos and constructed a small depot near Yeehaw Junction. In the 1920s, a small clapboard hotel was built as a way station for weary travelers. According to local folklore, a hobo, named Dan Wilson, was kicked off the train and took up residence near Yeehaw Junction, or *Jackass Crossing* as it was called back then. Wilson must have liked the place because he somehow acquired the small hotel and expanded it using lumber stolen from the railroad. During one period of its existence, the place was notoriously known for booze, rip roaring times, more booze, and even a few shoot outs, oh yes, and a very busy bordello upstairs on the second floor.

In 1946, Fred and Julie Cheverette purchased the Desert Inn and it became a popular U.S. Highway 441 truck stop. After Fred passed away, his wife continued operating the business until her death in 1986. In 1987, Beverly Zicheck, the most recent owner, bought the historic establishment and has passionately tried to preserve its history.

The upstairs rooms, the ones once used as a brothel, are seldom rented anymore but for the weary traveler there's a row of eleven motel rooms out back of the main building. The Desert Inn, which sits only a few miles off the Florida Turnpike, is now officially listed on the National Register of Historic Places.

THINGS THAT GO *BUMP* IN THE MIDDLE OF NOWHERE...

The Desert Inn, once the only lodging for about 65 miles in any direction, has seen its share of weirdness and tragedy. Many lives have ended in screeching car crashes at this crossroads. Beyond the accidents at the intersection, other lives have ended on the grounds and in the rooms of the Desert Inn. It has been said that over the years several fatalities, to include deaths from a gunfight or two, have allegedly occurred at the hotel. In the 1990s, a distraught gentleman hung himself in one of the upstairs rooms. Allegedly, over the years, there have been numerous suicides in the second story rooms.

While I sat at the bar washing down a platter of fried catfish with sweet iced tea, the bar keeper spun out several stories for me about the strange things that go on there. Two employees claim to have seen a ghost of a man walk into the restaurant and disappear. To any respectable ghost hunter stories of such ghastly occurrences would be a good reason to expect the place to be haunted.

Sounds of someone pacing the floor have been heard and objects have been seen to move across rooms in the hotel, objects as large as a desk. People claim doors open and close by unseen hands. Some have seen a wispy apparition while others tell of hearing creaking foot steps on the stairs. Former employees have heard what sounds like a voice whispering and a few recalled "feeling uneasy" about the upstairs area. Some folks like to believe that the ghost of Julie Chevertte is haunting the building. In life, Julie was a person of humor who liked to pull a few pranks. Some believe she invented the spider prank. Maybe she's still joking around, but since witnesses have reported objects mysteriously moving about, perhaps the old hotel may have a bad case of poltergeists.

I can't really say whether or not there are any ghosts at the Desert Inn, but the next time you are in that neck of the woods, stop for lunch, or better yet, spend the night so you can say you've spent the night at Yeehaw Junction.

STRANGE FLORIDA II

A Florida Psychiatrist Communicates with the Famously Dead
Strange Messages from Beyond the Grave

When most spiritualists precede their name with the title "Doctor", it usually means they've completed a course in metaphysics. But in Gary Frick's case, it means a genuine medical doctor or, to be exact, a practicing psychiatrist on the staff of a major Florida hospital. When a psychiatrist talks about exchanging messages with the dead, you either listen to what he has to say or suggest he see a psychiatrist. I've had the pleasure of talking with Doctor Frick and, while his claims sound bizarre, I can say from my observation as a researcher of strange stuff that he is a well-educated, compassionate, and sincere practitioner of his profession. He daringly faces the risk of ridicule in sharing his experiences with others through lectures, talk radio shows, and a book titled "Mother Teresa's Message from Heaven." Don't be misled by the title, Mother Teresa is only one of many legendary spirits who communicate with him from the afterlife. Yes, even Elvis and John Lennon talk with Dr. Frick along with his own maternal grandmother, various U.S. presidents, and Frank Sinatra who, for some strange reason, doesn't quite like the good doctor.

After years of trying to write a book about his strange experiences, which he originally believed to be products of his subconscious mind, Dr. Frick finally concluded he was receiving messages from the afterlife. Spirits were trying to write a book through him. "They've been communicating with me my entire life," the doctor said. "However, I was not consciously aware of my spiritual guides until I was in my early thirties." What makes this spiritually connected psychiatrist different from other mediums is that he has somehow tapped into a network of deceased famous people, like John F. Kennedy, Abe Lincoln, and Albert Einstein. "The only reason they chose me is because they could. Somehow I was receptive to their energy in such a way that they could write a book through me." He said it had nothing to do with him as a person but adds "One thing is for sure, if I didn't have a certain degree of respect for myself or other people, my spiritual guides wouldn't want much to do with me. I don't think they expect any more from me than from the average person."

"A true mystic will tell you that life itself is a spiritual experience. God is always with us," explained Dr. Frick, who says we do not need to communicate directly with spirits in order to have a spiritual experience. "I have always been aware of the fact that there is a God and an afterlife, and that God and his helpers communicate with us through our intuitive minds."

When asked if he has a special spiritual mission, Dr. Frick responded, "That's difficult to answer. Whenever I try to figure out my life's purpose, I almost always find myself being even more confused than if I didn't think about these matters at all. With regards to being an author, my spirit guides inform me that my writing a book is optional. Then they tell me that they certainly wouldn't mind if I communicated a special message for them. What makes it complicated is that spiritual guides are not like people. They love us unconditionally, whether we fulfill a particular mission or not."

There is no complicated message in Dr. Frick's book, or I should say the spirits' book. Certainly, there is a lot of spirit talk, but the message within this talk can be summed up in one simple word, "Peace." Considering the turmoil in today's world, perhaps Dr. Frick is the selected conduit through which spirits are trying to awaken us before it is too late.

STRANGE FLORIDA II

The LEGEND of TOMOKIE
A Timucuan fable or white man's yarn?

The Timucuan village of Nocoroco stood on the western shore of the Tomoko peninsula, a few miles north of present day Ormond Beach. We know this to be a fact because Spanish explorer Alvaro Mexia toured the area in 1605 and said it was there. Since then, archaeological excavations have identified Nocoroco's location. It was a busy population center a thousand years before Ponce de Leon discovered Florida in 1513, which means it existed longer than any modern American city. We must wonder at what Spanish explorers thought they had discovered, since nothing was really lost to the hundred thousands of Timucuan Indians living along Florida's east coast.

Chief Tomokie Statue at Tomoka State Park

At some point, so the story goes, the people living on the Tomoko peninsula were ruled by Chief Tomokie, described as a giant of the warrior class. Being a *giant* matches well with real history. Drawings made by Le Moyne in 1565 and excavated skeletal remains indicate Timucuans were of tall physical stature; some standing seven feet tall.

According to the legend, there was a spring nearby with waters known to possess curative powers. Only certain special folks were allowed to drink this "water of life" using a sacred cup that had never been touched by human hands. Each evening, a messenger from the Great Spirit was sent to drink from the miraculous spring. Was this the mythical fountain of youth?

Chief Tomokie thought this water-of-life stuff was a bunch of nonsense and offended neighboring tribes by drinking from the spring without permission. To make matters worse, he seized the sacred cup and took off with it. Needless to say, this really fired everyone up and a band of warriors were soon on the big chief's trail. The local tribes combined their forces to hunt down and kill the chief. He was soon cornered with arrows flying at him, but emerged unharmed, presumably still holding the sacred cup. Just about the time he thought he was safe, an Indian maiden named Oleeta lunged forward with her bow and sent an arrow straight into the heart of Chief Tomokie. She then ran to snatch the sacred cup from the hand of the dying chief, but was struck with a poison arrow from one of Tomokie's loyal warriors. Her body was buried in ceremony near the spring. According to the legend, the sacred cup was passed down through the centuries and is allegedly in the present possession of Florida Indians. Is the story based on fact? Or was it a fabrication of Mary E.M. Boyd? Her early 1900s manuscript is the main source for the story, although she claimed it came from an earlier reference. Extensive research has turned up no other references to the legend.

STRANGE FLORIDA II

The Horrifying Mystery of Sam McMillan
Don't lose your head over this ghastly but true newspaper story

This is a true tale that will scare the paranormal pants off any non-believer. Christine Kinlaw-Best, a prominent Central Florida historian, said, "It's probably Florida's most horrifying ghost story and it has been lost to history." It begins with Samuel McMillan back in 1872, when he settled in what is now west Seminole county. What Sam did not know in 1872 was that he would end up in this book as a ghost story.

Historian Kinlaw-Best explained that "Sam McMillan never married and was one of the first orange growers west of Sanford. Everybody said he was a miser who kept a lot of money hidden at his place on Twin Lakes."

According to the South Florida Journal, dated October 24, 1882, the ghost stuff got its start on September 30, 1882, when Sam came up missing. A few days later the local Justice of the Peace, Edgar Harrison, found Sam's body in Crystal Lake weighted down with an iron stove pot filled with nails. His killer had not planned on body gasses bloating the corpse up like a balloon. Sam then simply floated to the surface, well most of him, because his head was missing. Buzzards had already been working on the floating corpse when it was discovered by Edgar Harrison.

"It was the most heinous murder of the time," remarked Kinlaw-Best. "They had to bury the poor soul without his head." But four days after burying Sam, his head was found and buried in a separate grave. Okay, body and head in different graves, this is where everybody got into trouble. Neighbors began hearing eerie noises coming out of Sam's house. Then if that was not enough to shake up the neighborhood, a bent-over, headless corpse was seen walking around Sam's homestead. Witnesses reported that "the ghastly form seemed to be searching for something." Apparently they had not read many ghost books or they would have known that headless specters always search for their missing heads. Then to make matters more frightening, people began seeing a ghastly head fly up out of the water and taunt the headless body. Witnesses watched as the headless form chased after its head trying to catch it. People reported hearing spine chilling cries of "Why did they part us? Where's my body?" Hey, I'm not making this stuff up, it comes from an 1890 article that was published in the *Atlanta Constitution*.

Historian Kinlaw-Best says, "It was in several newspapers, and in 1890, five reporters decided to investigate the case for themselves. They hung out at Sam McMillan's house waiting to see if there was any truth to the hauntings." According to what the five reporters wrote, "We waited until midnight and was about to give up when we suddenly heard a loud, unearthly groan that painfully pierced our ears and with our eyes we witnessed a headless form." The apparition was described as having blood running down its headless neck and was walking around in a bent over fashion looking for something. Then it walked down to the lake where to our horror we witnessed a bloody head with hideous wounds and open eyes rise up from the water." Once the head had floated out of the lake the chase was on. The headless form let out an awful moan as it ran for the head but, each time; the head would make a sound between a gurgle and a laugh, and would fly off out of reach. The corpse, with long, outstretched arms, would again race frantically after it. The reporters said "this blood curdling spectacle went on for two hours. Finally, the headless form, unable to capture its head, issued a roar of rage and then faded into the mist of a small family graveyard." The head continued darting wildly along the edge of the lake before vanishing beneath the water. One witness to the paranormal scene, remarked, "It was the most dreadful sight I have ever seen and for days and nights afterward I could not get the bloody visions off my mind." What is really weird about this story, it that it was actually reported in several newspapers as news.

Following the reporters' frightening encounter, three local men decided to dig up Sam's head and rebury it in the grave with his body. The uncanny shenanigans ended, apparently re-uniting the head and body must have satisfied Sam's ghost.

The sheriff makes an arrest in the case...

The sheriff soon arrested Archibald W. Newton for the murder. Newton, [not to be confused with a Fig Newton] was an Englishman, who lived next to McMillan. He was tried and convicted, and sentenced to be hanged. However, historian Kinlaw-Best, discovered through her diligent research, that the case was appealed to the State Supreme Court, where, due to "technical difficulties" in the investigation, Newton was set free.

Today, the area where Sam McMillan lived is covered with residential communities, shopping malls, industrial buildings and roads. Graves in the old Taber family cemetery were relocated in the late 1950's, well, at least the marked ones. Unfortunately, most of the burials, including Sam McMillan's, had wooden markers, which over time had rotted away. In November 2000, during the highway construction of the Central Florida Greenway, human remains were unearthed on the site of the old graveyard. The remains were identified by an inscription inside a wedding band, as belonging to a woman who, in 1912, had been buried in the Tabor cemetery. This was proof that all graves had not been removed. "It is doubtful that McMillan and his head were ever relocated," said Historian Kinlaw-Best, who based her assumption on the fact that historical records do not list Sam McMillan as one of the relocated burials. It's a safe bet, old Sam is resting under the asphalt of modern times, perhaps just waiting to haunt anyone daring to disturb his peace.

STRANGE FLORIDA II

The *Bloodsucking* Critter of South Florida
Does the vicious creature called El Chupacabra really exist?

If skunk apes are not enough, now we have a pesky red-eyed, spike-headed creature with fangs killing our livestock and pets. Translated as 'the goat sucker', El Chupacabra seems to have originated in Canovanas, Puerto Rica, where it is believed to be the result of a secret government experiment or, depending on the source, some kind of high-bred critter connected to space aliens. I think the U.S. Government made this thing by crossing a chicken with a Tasmanian devil, or maybe the infamous Jersey Devil has retired to South Florida.

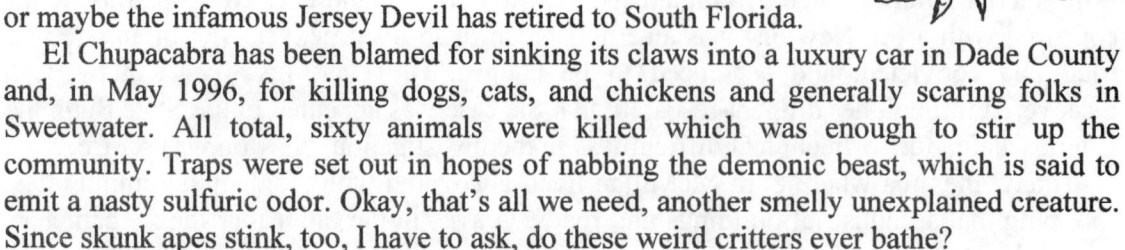

El Chupacabra has been blamed for sinking its claws into a luxury car in Dade County and, in May 1996, for killing dogs, cats, and chickens and generally scaring folks in Sweetwater. All total, sixty animals were killed which was enough to stir up the community. Traps were set out in hopes of nabbing the demonic beast, which is said to emit a nasty sulfuric odor. Okay, that's all we need, another smelly unexplained creature. Since skunk apes stink, too, I have to ask, do these weird critters ever bathe?

Witnesses have described the Chupacabra like a beast right out of science fiction. It can change colors on a whim, usually blue or green, and is shaped like a kangaroo with glowing red eyes. It has sharp teeth, webbed wing-like arms, claws, dorsal fins, and spikes on its head. In 2005, a picture appeared on the internet of a bluish-colored Chupacabra captured in Texas. It looked to me like the poor Chupacabra had the mange. I was almost right, as it turned out to be a coyote with a severe case of sarcoptic mange, which leaves animals emaciated and hairless with bluish gray skin.

When the Chupacabra first surfaced in Puerto Rica, 200 civil defense volunteers went looking for it. It was true that something had been prowling the Canovanas countryside mutilating 200 cows, dogs, chickens, and hogs. The carcasses were shown, through autopsies, to have strange puncture wounds inconsistent with any common predator of the region. However, in spite of twenty eyewitnesses claiming a close encounter with the weird looking creature, a biologist suggested it was nothing more than a deformed animal. One woman claimed to have found a Chupacabra's nest and submitted specimens of dung, hair, and traces of flesh for examination. I don't know why anyone would want to mess with the nest of a ferocious, bloodsucking beast with fangs and claws. Anyway, the specimens collected by the woman were sent for DNA evaluation, but the results were inconclusive. It seems like lab results on weird stuff are always inconclusive.

Ninety-nine percent of all Chupacabra claims in Florida come from Hispanic communities around Tampa, Miami, and Orlando. This brings up the big question, is the devilish beast mere cultural folklore imported from Puerto Rico? If it is just a folk yarn, then what killed all the animals? Unless you have a better explanation, I'll stick with my theory that the *Jersey Devil* has retired to South Florida.

STRANGE FLORIDA II

FLORIDA'S STRANGE FORCES OF NATURE
Don't Mess With Mother Nature, she can be very unpredictable!

When most people think of Florida's weather they think of sunshine and a subtropical climate broken only by seasonal thunderstorms and an occasional hurricane. Well, I have news for you, the truth is Florida can be a rather strange, unpredictable, and even deadly place to live. Not only is the sunshine state one of the world's lightning capitals, it has been ravaged by tornados, giant sinkholes, droughts, floods, freezes, heat waves, tidal waves, earth tremors, water spouts, fierce hurricanes, and yes, even snow!

In 1774, a snow storm blew across North Florida dumping several inches of angel dandruff in what was called "the great white rain." Snow is not all that unusual for Florida, it has been recorded as far south as Fort Myers and Miami. In January 1800, five inches of snow fell along the St. Mary's River and, in 1899, up to four inches of the white stuff landed on parts of Union County. In February 1951, Crescent City and St. Augustine both received about two inches of snow. Tallahassee, Jacksonville, and the Suwannee River region all received from 1.5 to 3 inches of snow during the winter of 1958, which dumped a half inch of snow on Bartow. In February 1973, more than three inches of snow fell on Milton, while Pensacola and Quincy reported up to two inches. Some undocumented accounts mentioned six inches of snow blanketing the small community of Jay. While Northerners may view these snowfalls as trivial and hardly enough for a decent snowman, it is none-the-less a weather oddity for the Sunshine State.

One such temperature oddity occurred in July 1996 when swimmers found the ocean much too cold. Within hours, the water temperature along Florida's east coast had mysteriously dropped from the average of 80 degrees to a rather frigid 68 degrees. Unusual oceanographic conditions had pushed the warmer water out into the Atlantic trapping the colder waters of the Gulf Stream close to Florida's beaches. Of course anyone from Michigan might consider 68 degrees suitable for swimming, but to warm-bloodied Floridians it felt like the ice age had returned. I'm sure some Florida folks were shivering on March 26, 2006, when the temperature in Palm Beach dropped 16 degrees below normal to a record low of 47 F.

The most deadly event of Florida's weather has always been its dreaded hurricane season. Since statistics only date from about 1835, no one really knows for sure the power that was packed into earlier hurricanes. Geological evidence found in Alabama silt may be proof that monster hurricanes, far exceeding category-five strength, may have hit the region in prehistoric times. The frequency and strength of hurricanes has been increasing in recent years. In 2004, Florida saw one of its worst years when four major hurricanes, Ivan, Charley, Jeanne, and Frances, slammed the peninsula. Every part of the state was affected to some degree, with many places totally devastated. Historically, the worst hurricanes on record occurred in the 1920's and 30's. In September 1935, a monster storm wiped out a great portion of Florida's coastline from Cape Canaveral down to Key West. In 1926, a hurricane killed 500 people in only a matter of hours. The deadly hurricane of 1928, which battered all of South Florida and blew water out of Lake Okeechobee, claimed an estimated 2000 lives. If that sounds like an enormous death toll,

STRANGE FLORIDA II

consider the 1900 hurricane that hit Galveston, Texas, claiming 6000 lives, or the 8000 deaths in 1974 when hurricane Fifi struck Honduras. In 2005, Katrina wiped out the central gulf coast leaving thousands homeless in Louisiana and Mississippi. Throughout recorded history, killer storms have killed a quarter of a million people in our part of the world. The infamous Labor Day hurricane of 1935 pushed an 18 foot wall of water over Islamorada Key, washing a train from its tracks and killing 700 workers on board that were trying to reach safety. The storm destroyed the entire Flagler railroad line to Key West. In Tampa, the barometer fell to 26.35 inches, the lowest reading ever recorded in the Western Hemisphere.

When Hurricane Andrew slammed into South Florida on August 24, 1992, it destroyed over 3000 mobile homes, 70,000 acres of mangrove, and 63,000 residential homes, killing 39 people and leaving 250,000 homeless. The huge storm even tossed a 210 ton Freighter ship five hundred feet inland and actually blew the iron rails from a section of railroad track. The Dade Metro Zoo was blown apart and 1.4 million homes were left without power. Hurricane Andrew, a category-four storm, reached winds of 169 mph, at which point the Hurricane Center's wind velocity instrument was literally blown away. Therefore, the exact maximum wind speed is unknown, leaving the speculation open that winds may have reached 200 mph gusts. The damage caused by Andrew was incredible and certainly an awakening for newcomers. Every agency of the government responded to the aftermath, including all military branches. Insurance companies were financially devastated and many now refuse to cover residents along the coastline. The recovery in the wake of Andrew was estimated to have cost every Floridian 1,500 dollars. In spite of its wrath, Andrew still only ranks as the 23rd worst hurricane on record.

Andrew claimed 39 lives, but rumors insist the figure was much higher. Supposedly, one platoon from the U.S. Army's 82nd Airborne Division pulled eighty bodies from a single apartment building. There were other reports about bodies being discreetly transported to a Navy refrigerator ship anchored off shore and later dumped into the Atlantic. According to research, there was indeed a navy refrigerator ship brought into Miami following the storm. However, authorities, when quizzed by an investigative reporter, denied that bodies were being dumped at sea, stating that the refrigerator ship was used for the storage of perishable substances. Yet, one must wonder, what happened to thousands of illegal immigrants who were living in flimsy quarters and labor camps across South Florida? Did they manage to evacuate to safety? Where did they go? Some conspiracy theorists believe the government did not want the public to know how many illegal folks were living in South Florida and, therefore, deliberately fudged the statistics. Perhaps there are some grounds for this suspicion if we consider the 1928 hurricane which claimed 2000 lives from a much smaller population. Yet, we are told that Andrew took only 39 out of a much greater population. The rumors, true or not, persist today that more people were killed by Andrew than was reported to the media.

If fierce hurricanes are not enough for you, try all the sinkholes that, without warning, open up to swallow a house. This has been going on for thousands of years on the sunny peninsula; many of those perfectly circular lakes around which are built lakefront residences are actually ancient sinkholes. The best example of an ancient sinkhole is the Devil's Millhopper, a big old hole in the earth north of Gainesville. Now a state park, this gigantic funnel-like hole is an old sinkhole formed in two stages ten thousand years ago. It is 500 feet across the opening, nearly a half mile around the rim and 120 feet deep.

STRANGE FLORIDA II

Early pioneers thought the hole resembled the funnel, or hopper, on a grist mill. Local folk tales promoted by evangelist preachers told how the hole was *"a gateway to hell through which bodies were fed to the Devil."* With that kind of publicity, it's no wonder the geologic marvel became known as the Devil's Millhopper. But we don't have to look to prehistoric times to find giant sinkholes; they still form today, even in the middle of a city. In 1981, a large sinkhole ate a portion of downtown Winter Park. In less than twenty-four hours, this hole went from a tiny depression to a 100 foot deep hole, 300 feet across, gulping down a house, parking lot, a swimming pool, six luxury cars of a dealership, and part of two city streets. The price tag for the destruction was estimated to be four million dollars. Sinkholes are becoming more frequent with the increasing population as more water is pumped out of the aquifer. In this case, running out of water is only part of Florida's problem; not knowing when or where the next sinkhole will open up is the other.

Okay, if severe storms, tornadoes, lightning, and sinkholes haven't scared you off, then I'll throw in a gator and a tsunami. On September 8, 1844, a hurricane created a tidal wave that buried the upper Gulf coast town of St. Joseph under tons of sand. In more recent times, on the night of July 3, 1992, a gigantic wave slammed into Daytona Beach washing over hundreds of parked cars. At least seventy-five people were injured when the freakish 18 foot wall of water hit the World's Most Famous Beach without warning.

In Washington D.C., U.S. Geologic Survey officials dismissed the idea of a tsunami explaining that a tidal wave would have affected a greater range of the east coast. The wave that hit Daytona was higher in the center and tapered off along about twenty miles of coastline. Okay, it wasn't officially a tidal wave, but when an 18 foot wall of water comes rolling out of the ocean washing over hundreds of cars, I call it a tidal wave.

The weird wave seemed to have no explanation, which left Daytona officials with a mystery on their hands. Scientists from geologists to oceanographers began scrambling to find the cause of the bizarre wave. Some offered the possibility of an off-shore earthquake but admitted it was only a theory since seismic instruments had indicated no geological disturbances. Both the Weather Service and U.S. Coast Guard had reported normal seas off Daytona's coast. Monitoring buoys stationed forty miles out recorded no abnormal conditions before or after the odd wave.

The Army Corps of Engineers Coastal Research Center proposed that the wave had been caused by a squall-line pushing down the coast from Georgia. The theory suggested the system had simply piled up a swell of water which eventually struck the coast at Daytona. This hypothesis was pretty much eliminated when scientists using a laboratory experiment could not duplicate a scale model of the event. University of Florida geologists said an undersea landslide was a more plausible theory. However, other experts were not convinced and pointed out that the continental shelf was too broad and shallow for a landslide to have caused the wave.

Then came the major freak-out theories, which seemed as good as any of the others. Some folks suggested a UFO had crashed into the ocean while conspiracy theorists blamed it on a secret government experiment or military testing. Others accused the Bermuda Triangle or claimed the wave was caused by a surfacing submarine or a huge meteorite that had crashed into the ocean. While the meteorite theory sounded crazy, a few experts found it worthy of consideration. Such an impact would have produced a wave higher in the center with tapering ends and a short coastal range, just like the one that soaked Daytona. The theory gained support when an eyewitness came forward with a meteor sighting. The observation had been made ten miles out by a boat captain who described seeing an aerial object that "was flaming, reddish white with a tail, and making a swooshing noise as it flew overhead." He did not mention an impact but did report being "almost swamped by a twenty foot wave about fifteen minutes after seeing the object." In a press release, scientists from the University of Florida had estimated "a meteorite one meter in diameter could have impacted the ocean about eleven miles northeast of Daytona." This makes a good explanation until you consider that a meteorite would have been visible from the populated east coast, yet only a single boater had reported any such thing. Then it was discovered that the supposed meteorite sighting was on July 4th and not July 3rd, the date of the wave. Assuming no one was sipping from the joy juice jug, this only added more ingredients to the mystery. Did two bizarre events happen on consecutive nights, at the same time and place, with both creating big waves?

One petroleum scientist suggested the ocean had simply "burped." Okay, with all the garbage dumped into the ocean, I can understand it letting out a big belch. The petro-expert explained a known phenomenon called "hydrates" where disturbed pockets of natural gas beneath the ocean release a gigantic bubble. Without listing what could have disturbed one of these hydrate pockets, he explained how a released gas bubble could have created concentric ripples, or waves, on the surface. The burping theory, like the others, was shot down by other scientists who stated the area's geological environment could not produce such phenomena as hydrate pockets. So the mystery of the Daytona wave lingers on.

In 1993, a shrimp boat encountered a "large bubble-like boil in the ocean" a short distance off Florida's east coast. The crew described it as circular bulge of water that came out of the ocean and almost tipped over their shrimp boat. According to the first mate, "We have no idea what caused it. It just bubbled up like an air pocket, maybe it was a whale, but whatever it was we had never seen anything like it."

On April 21, 1996, four years after the mystery wave at Daytona, another strange wave swelled out of calm seas and capsized a fishing boat nine miles out from Cocoa. The renegade wave dumped three people overboard and was described as "like a little tidal wave." The U.S. Coast Guard referred to it as "a freak of nature."

Whether it is a freak of nature or just natural forces at work, it's a fact that Florida's nature can be very unpredictable with often deadly results. Compound these natural events with humans trying to control or change the natural environment and the consequences can be deadly. This is a lesson unlearned by politicians who continue to allow greedy developers to irreversibly alter Florida's natural order. In short, don't mess with Mother Nature and heed her warnings, for even in sunny paradise she can be very unpleasant at times.

STRANGE FLORIDA II

The Sunshine State's *Slithering Secrets...*
Stray gators in our pools may be the least of our worries.

In 2005, there were 15 reports in Central Florida alone of black bears wandering into residential neighborhoods and more than 200 incidents of alligators ending up in people's swimming pools and garages. This does not include hundreds of gators which had to be removed from neighborhood lakes and golf course ponds. Hey, lets face the truth here, this isn't a case of animals invading Florida neighborhoods, but rather the over-population of humans who have invaded wildlife habitat. As greedy developers continue destroying wilderness areas, Floridians can expect more and more critters to be squeezed out into our backyards. But there may be something more dangerous to worry about than indigenous species like gators and bears. Read on and you may never want to venture down a Florida nature path again.

There have been 165 giant pythons captured or killed in Florida since 1995, including 95 captured in the Everglades just in 2005, alone. One was described as being "as big as a telephone pole." Most of these have escaped or have been released by their owners. In Florida's subtropical climate, such species can exist very well, to include reproducing more of their kind. One park ranger jokingly commented that, with so many constrictors captured or killed, we now have a "Florida python."

In 1997, a woman in Pompano Beach woke up in the middle of the night with a 5 ½ foot rainbow boa constrictor across her shoulders and legs. In 1998, Gainesville emergency personnel used several blasts of carbon dioxide to remove a 5 foot python that had wrapped itself around a woman's arms. In the same year, a six foot monitor lizard was shot by police after it terrorized a Deland neighborhood. In 1999, a Port Orange man was killed after a 12 1/2 foot long reticulated python clamped it jaws on the man's head then wrapped itself in a strangulating hold around his body.

In 2001, a Pompano Beach woman was bitten by a five foot long Monaco Cobra. A few months later, a 13 foot King Cobra was found in an Orlando man's garage. After four hours of trying to capture the reptile, the homeowner finally shot it. In Jacksonville, a 10 ½ foot boa constrictor had to be killed to remove it from a man's arm. In 2002, four Burmese pythons were found in someone's closet. The snakes had escaped from their cage in neighbor's house. In Bishop, Florida, an 8 foot python was found in a neighborhood backyard. In 2003, an 80 pound python escaped from its cage and had to be removed from an elderly woman's leg. Workers in Manatee County, in April 2004, found two giant pythons in a roadside ditch.

In Vero Beach, a 16 foot Burmese python was captured on a city street by Animal Control. In Dade County, an African rock python got stuck in a fence after eating a live turkey. Two months later, also in Dade County, a 12 foot python was reported to have eaten someone's 18 pound Siamese cat. In November 2005, a South Florida fisherman caught more than he expected when he reeled in an 11 foot Burmese python.

STRANGE FLORIDA II

Most of these incidents have only been local press reports, so the rest of us never get to see the big picture. However, one astonishing incident made statewide news when a helicopter pilot, flying over the Shark River Slough in the Everglades, discovered the aftermath of a 13 foot python's battle with a 6 foot gator. It appeared that the giant Burmese python had attempted to swallow the big alligator alive. Both animals were dead when found, with half of the gator bursting out of the serpent's middle most likely due to the gator's struggle to free itself. Think about this, either one of these critters would be able to swallow a human with little effort.

These are the reports that have been documented in press releases, we can only guess at how many giant, or poisonous, snakes are out there waiting to catch someone by surprise, perhaps ready to put someone's Jack Russell Terrier on its menu. There are several stories that have missed the news, like the alleged story about two King cobras being killed in Collier County and a fisherman's sighting of an anaconda in Southwest Florida. There have also been unconfirmed stories about people releasing or catching Piranha in Florida waters. Usually these are Pacu, a tropical fish closely resembling the Piranha. I can't imagine why anyone would want to keep fish that can devour a full grown steer in minutes, but possessing Piranha is against the law in Florida and special permits are required to keep poisonous snakes. Of course, everyone does not obey the law so we are left to wonder how many poisonous snakes have been released by their illegal keepers or have escaped captivity to slither into our woods or even into our houses. I am sure that anyone in illegal possession of a deadly King cobra would not voluntarily report its escape to the authorities.

In conclusion, I am reminded of an old urban legend from the sixties about a truck carrying a crate of Egyptian cobras that had a wreck while crossing the Everglades. It's believed that the deadly cargo of toxic serpents escaped into the sawgrass where they have been breeding ever since. Maybe this legend isn't so farfetched after all.

STRANGE FLORIDA II

The Spookhunters
Searching the Paranormal with Florida's own ghost busters

Usually recognized by his trademark, an orange-colored ghostbustin' jumpsuit, Owen Sliter is the lead spook hunter for a band of a dozen paranormal sleuths. He organized this unusual group after watching a reality based TV show called FEAR. "They sent normalpeople into very spooky, supposedly haunted places," he explained. "In one episode, there was this girl who couldn't last five minutes in an old abandoned prison. I said 'Hey I could do that…'and so I talked with a few friends and we started the group."

Ironically, the chief spookhunter does not exactly believe in ghosts. "I have a set core of beliefs," remarked Sliter. "I believe in God and the afterlife. I am not sure if I am a true skeptic, just skeptical of ghosts and hauntings. If a ghost materializes in front of me, or someone captures a spirit in a jar so we can study it, then I might reconsider."

The spookhunters are a collection of both skeptics and staunch believers, which sets them apart from other ghost investigators. It's a good balance of beliefs according to Owen Sliter who puts it this way "It helps keep what we might see or experience grounded for what it is and not something else." In their investigations, they employ the latest scientific devices from electronic voice phenomena [EVP] recorders to electro-magnetic field detectors, digital video equipment, the skills of live mediums, and even Ouija boards. I guess anything will help when searching for unseen entities.

I first met this unusual paranormal investigative group several years ago when they invited me on a ghost hunt at Ashley's Restaurant in Rockledge, Florida. This was about a year after I participated in a video documentary filmed at this famous eatery, which is known for its poltergeist activity. You know the kind of weirdness I'm talking about, where cups and saucers fly off the shelf, lights flicker, and other creepy stuff. The management is not shy about their haunted history which is printed on the back cover of their menu. But I must say the Spookhunters impressed me from the start, probably because Spookhunter Diana paid for my dinner that evening. I'm always impressed anytime I get a free meal. I asked Spookhunter Diana, a realtor, if she believed in ghosts. "Absolutely," she replied, "but it is always God-driven." She went on to explain how her deceased father had frequently intervened to help her through a few tough spots in her life. That night at Ashley's Restaurant, she was touched by the unexplainable. "I felt like something was touching my face, like caressing it," she said. At Ashley's, being touched by unseen hands is a common experience of patrons.

Spookhunter Brooke, a former Disney World cast member, was inspired to join the group after reading my book, *Weird Florida*, for which she gets my blessings. Brooke explained her thoughts this way, "I believe in the possibility that there are several

STRANGE FLORIDA II

Spookhunters using an Ouija board during an investigation. The team experiments with both conventional and non-conventional devices in their hunt for ghosts.

dimensions and they are all separated by a baby's breath of thin layers. One of these could be the spirit world. I feel some people, like psychics, are more in-tuned with their subconscious while the rest of us get lucky and tap into it. We take ghosts seriously, in a funny sort of way."

Based in Central Florida, the Spookhunters are well-known for their ability to legally [at least most of the time] get into just about any haunted place in America. You might say they've gone where no ghost busters have gone before. This includes investigating the abandoned launch complex at Kennedy Space Center where three astronauts died in a tragic fire. In 2004, I accompanied the group to St. Augustine where, by special arrangement with the National Park Service, we spent most of the night in the Castillo de San Marcos. We actually had the whole place to ourselves and it was a true adventure just being in the musty old fort without a bunch of tourists milling about.

Across the country, they have investigated oodles of haunted places in California, Arizona, Florida, Texas, Nebraska, Kentucky, Nevada, Utah, and Georgia. "The best hunt was the Apollo launch pad," opined Owen Sliter, referring to Kennedy Space Center's launch complex 38 where a tragic fire claimed the lives of three astronauts. "We were able to walk in areas where people hadn't been in forty-plus years. Three men sacrificed their lives on that very spot. It was not so much haunted, but powerful nonetheless."

As chief skeptic, Owen admits he has twice experienced possible proof of ghosts. The first was at the abandoned Waverly Hills Sanatorium in Kentucky. "I have four pictures of the same window and in each picture there is a different shape. We were there with the owner and no one was inside, but something showed up in that window. I can't explain that." His next unexplainable incident happened when the Spookhunters were given a private tour of the *New Smyrna Beach Historical Ghost Tour*, guided by real life medium Susan Thompson. "We were at this abandoned building where the medium said a spirit named Albert once lived. I challenged the medium to talk to this spirit and have him do something to make me believe. She was quiet for a moment, then my cheek started to tingle. She looked at me and said he was touching me. I asked her where and she said on my right cheek. I was floored! I didn't know what to think. The tingling sensation worked its way down my cheek into my right arm and leg. I can't say if it was the power of suggestion, wishful thinking, or a real life encounter with a ghost."

It was on this same ghost tour in New Smyrna Beach where Spookhunter Brooke recalls having an eerie experience. "We went inside the Indian house, a haunted house on a hill. I was downstairs with Spookhunter Corey and the sound recorder. Spookhunters Greg and Owen were upstairs with the video camera. We recorded the sound of a man screaming on the video camera and recorder; yet none of us physically heard it except on the recordings. The interesting thing is that the scream is the same volume on both recorders even though we were nowhere near each other."

As Florida's premier paranormal detectives, the Spookhunters have their own website [www.spookhunters.com], an online bookstore, and have ventured into video production. In 2006, they released their first in a series of popular DVDs titled "Hunt for the Devil," a mixture of humor and fright done in unique Spookhunter style. By the way, every personality mentioned in this article is in the cast, including me as *Florida's Master of the Weird*, but don't let that discourage you. In the Fall of 2006, Spookhunter filmmakers cranked out another video in which team members explore the paranormal claims of the ill-fated Titanic. The Spookhunters' claim to fame is in their ability to get into places that most ghost groups will never see.

"The sky is the limit for the Spookhunters," exclaims Owen Sliter, who visualizes an expansion into television and who knows what else. "My main priority is to entertain," and along the way they may even catch a ghost.

Asked what is next on the spooky agenda, Owen said he would like to visit Alcatraz and spend the night in the old prison. "Dudleytown, Connecticut, is another possibility," he said. "The whole town allegedly went mad and died." Sliter is also focusing on New Orleans for a hunt. "If we turn up no ghosts, we could always go down to Bourbon Street and find a few spirits.

STRANGE FLORIDA II

Florida's Slippery Sea Serpents and Water Monsters
What unknown things are lurking beneath our waters?

Do these things really exist? Before you say hogwash, let me bring up the prehistoric Coelacanth fish. According to science, this big, weird-looking fish became extinct sixty million years ago. That's what scientists believed until 1938 when a live one was caught off the African coast. Since then several more have been hauled in by fishermen. The coelacanth is living proof that just because we can't go out on any sunny day and conveniently snap a picture of a sea monster does not mean they don't exist. Are we to deny multiple eyewitness accounts like the 1891 Jacksonville newspaper article reporting that bathers had been chased from the surf by a sea monster? It said that bathers swimming at Jacksonville Beach scrambled frantically to get out of the water when an ugly-looking sea serpent reared its long neck from the surf. It was described as having a long skinny neck and a dog-like head. There are three possibilities for this historic sighting. Either everyone on a populated beach misinterpreted a known marine animal for a sea serpent or it was a severe case of mass hallucination, which would be weirder than encountering a sea monster. The third possibility is that swimmers splashing around in the surf may have attracted an unknown sea creature which surfaced for a quick look. I can imagine the creature returning to the ocean depths and trying to convince his buddies that he had seen weird two-legged creatures on dry land.

The following account, dated February 14, 1904 demonstrates how a known sea creature can be misinterpreted as a sea monster simply by the way it is described by a witness. "I shall never forget the scare I got," said John Mansfield in a newspaper article. "My boat was anchored in the Indian River in Florida. I was [resting] on the stern looking idly into the water and thinking about anything except a sea monster. Suddenly a vast form made me pull my head back instinctively. The thing was so dark that it looked almost black. It was shaped like a huge carrot with a broad tail like a lobster. It looked weird, I couldn't imagine what it was. Suddenly it bent that big lobster tail backwards, doubling it beneath itself. Instantly, its progress stopped as if it had put on brakes. It then stood straight up on end and I saw two bony things like arms shoot out from the upper part of its body. The head was small, about which the most remarkable thing was its cavernous mouth. The bottom jaw was alright but the upper jaw was split like the upper lip of a rabbit only forty times as large. It appeared to be a veritable cross between a cow and a seal, and a fish and a water bug." What Mr. Mansfield was describing in this case, as he later mentioned, was his first sighting of a manatee. This is a good example of how misinterpretations of common animals, or objects, can easily lead to claims of sea monsters sightings. On the other hand, some sightings simply cannot be explained.

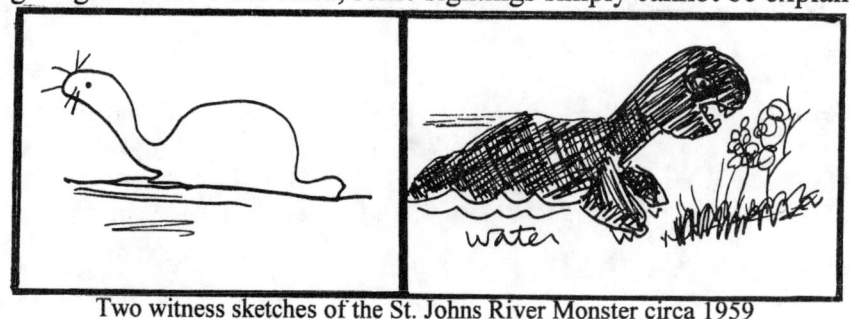

Two witness sketches of the St. Johns River Monster circa 1959

STRANGE FLORIDA II

In the 1950s, several stories appeared in Central Florida newspapers about people seeing a prehistoric water monster in the St. Johns River. Most of these sightings occurred between Lake Monroe and Lake George with a concentration around Blue Springs, a habitat for manatee. I'm quite sure that many sightings of the St. Johns River monster were misinterpretations by people not familiar with manatees which can reach 14 feet in length and weigh 1500 pounds. However, one man claimed to have found "a path made by the monster in the bushes along the river." He said "The grass and everything was mashed down where this thing had been eating." Another witness allegedly observed a "brontosaurus-like creature" out of the water, grazing on grass along the river bank. It should be pointed out that manatee have a grey elephant-like hide and are vegetarians that can consume hundreds of pounds of water plants in a day. They also blow and snort quite loudly which could be startling if one surfaced near a boater unfamiliar with the species, as in the previous mentioned 1904 manatee description by Mr. Mansfield. But manatee cannot explain the 1975 sighting on the St. Johns River near Jacksonville where a group of pleasure boaters had a close encounter with a river creature. The witnesses called it a "dinosaur-looking thing or dragon" which had a "horned head like a snail." Maybe it was of the same species that, in 1891, chased the bathers from the surf at Jacksonville Beach.

Another historical account from 1885 relates how a ship, sitting in New River Inlet, hauled up its anchor to find it had hooked the decaying carcass of a sea serpent. Whatever the creature was, it had two large front flippers and a six foot wide body that was over forty feet long, including a long skinny neck. Now that sounds like Scotland's Loch Ness Monster, but this was in Florida long before anyone had heard about Nessie. The decomposition of the plesiosaur-like creature made it impossible to handle and, unfortunately, the remains were simple disposed of without scientific examination.

The creature-carcass of New River Inlet sounds very much like a 10-30 foot monster sighted in Lake Tarpon, near Tarpon Springs, Florida's sponge capital. This monster even has a name, "Tarpie." Lake Tarpon is a land-locked body of water, but so is Loch Ness and it has its "Nessie." The theory is that the lake is connected to the Gulf of Mexico through the underground aquifer, which allows "Tarpie" to go and come from the sea. If you choose to believe local yarns, "Tarpie" is said to be responsible for the disappearances of a few folks, although no one I talked with can recall any of the creature's victims. Serious researchers believe the Lake Tarpon monster to be a brand new legend based on misinterpretations of alligators, floating plant clusters, or perhaps even giant catfish which are said to inhabit the lake.

In 1943, a couple sailing in the Gulf near Fort Walton Beach encountered a strange marine animal with its long neck sticking four to five feet out of the water. They said the bizarre creature had a large round head with a furry cat-like face. It had two large eyes set directly in front of its head which seemed to study the couple as it made several circles around their boat before vanishing beneath the sea.

The only documented case involving an attack by an unknown sea monster occurred in 1962 about five miles off Pensacola. Five scuba divers were diving from a small boat in the Gulf of Mexico when they saw the dark clouds of a storm on the horizon. As they prepared to head for shore, they noticed a terrific splashing in the water near their boat. Then all of a sudden a long thing that looked like a telephone pole with a head came rushing out of the water toward them. It was some kind of marine animal with a 10 foot rigid neck and a head with tiny eyes and a wide open mouth. In all respects, it looked like the classic sea serpent. The thing began whipping and thrashing about like a serpent and then disappeared beneath their boat. At this point the details are unclear, one account has the creature tipping the boat over and another story says the men jumped overboard when it appeared the creature was going to attack the boat. The five men became separated in the choppy water as the serpent-like thing whirled and splashed among them. According to a news article, there was only one survivor of the frightening ordeal. He managed to evade the attacking creature by swimming to shore. He alleged that whatever it was, it had attacked at least one of his lost companions and assumed the others met the same fate or had drowned trying to save themselves.

In 1873, Charles B. Brainerd wrote about a "devil fish" encounter in the Scientific American. "The strength of these creatures is beyond comprehension," he said, referring to a giant marine creature that seized a deep sea diver working on a sunken wreck off Florida's east coast. The diver, described as weighing a hefty 300 pounds, claimed the creature "landed on his shoulders and pinned his arms tight." He said it felt like he was being "cracked into jelly." The monster refused to let go as the diver was dragged aboard the floating platform from which he had descended. He fainted from the ordeal as men on the platform seized the devil fish by one of its arms. They tried to pull it off the diver but could not break the power of its suckers. It was only removed after "being struck across the sack containing the stomach" and that "the lobster-like eyes gleamed like fire." Can we assume he was describing an attack by a giant ray? His descriptions may be of some other type of sea creature that, for a lack of a name, he called a devil fish.

Then there's the thing that, in November 1896, washed ashore at St. Augustine Beach. It was early evening when two local boys made the unusual discovery while riding their bicycles on the beach. It looked like a half-buried gigantic mound of rotting flesh, a carcass of some kind of marine animal weighing at least five tons. The boys dropped their bikes and approached the pinkish blob for a closer examination. It was easy to tell that it was no whale or anything else they had ever seen. They were baffled by the enormity of the thing; it was 23 feet long, 4 feet high, and 18 feet across. What was this creature, they wondered, was it an unknown sea monster?

Unable to identify the massive blob, they mounted their bikes and rushed off to report their strange discovery to Dr. Dewitt Webb, a local physician who dabbled in science enough to have some expertise on the matter. He quickly proceeded to the beach where he found several local beachcombers trying to dig the thing out of the sand. At first, Webb thought it was the remains of a whale but upon closer examination found it contained no skeletal structure. He knew by observation it was not a fish or any species of squid. He soon concluded, based on the bulbous head, that it was the decaying remains of a gigantic octopus. Webb was a little reluctant to say outright that it was an octopus since the largest on record at the time had only weighed a mere 125 pounds. If it was indeed an octopus, then it far exceeded any size known to science. Although there were no witnesses, one man claimed to have dug out of the sand several tentacles measuring from 23 to 32 feet long.

Dr. Webb took it upon himself to prepare a report of his observations which was sent to leading marine biologists and various scientific institutions. Professor A.E. Verrill of Yale University, an expert in cephalopods, reviewed Webb's report and, at first, concluded the carcass belonged to a giant squid. He then retracted his opinion and proclaimed it to be a previously unknown species of octopus.

THE THING THAT WASHED ASHORE AT ST. AUGUSTINE.

ABOVE OLD PHOTOGRAPH SHOWING THE BLOB ON THE BEACH WITH STEEL CABLES WRAPPED AROUND IT IN AN ATTEMPT TO DRAG THE THING TO HIGHER GROUND. THE MAN IN THE PICTURE IS BELIEVED TO BE DR. DEWITT WEBB.

RIGHT TWO 1896 DRAWINGS, DONE FROM PHOTOGRAPHS, SHOWING DIFFERENT VIEWS OF THE THING THAT WASHED UP AT ST. AUGUSTINE. WHAT LOOKS TO BE REMAINS OF TENTACLES ARE VISIBLE IN THESE TWO PICTURES.

[*PHOTO CREDIT FLORIDA HISTORICAL SOCIETY*]

STRANGE FLORIDA II

Dr. Webb invited Professor Verrill, along with other scientists, to come to St. Augustine and examine the subject which was getting quite ripe. But, for some strange reason, they all declined. Maybe they were afraid of the smell. Webb became the sole investigator of the mystery as the blob slowly rotted away on the beach. Actually the putrid carcass remained on the beach for several months which gives us some idea of its enormous size. Concerned that tides were threatening to wash his slimy subject out to sea, Webb hired a mule team to pull it to higher ground. He found his efforts to be in vain when high tides of a March storm carried the mass, or mess, out to sea. That was the last time the dead thing was ever seen; however, Webb had managed to collect and preserve some tissue samples which were "rubbery and hard to cut." He sent tissue specimens to Professor Verrill and to Dr. William Healy, curator of the National Museum, later renamed the Smithsonian. Once again, Verrill changed his mind and stated the tissue specimens were from a whale. This was in spite of the fact that he had previously said the low fat content was inconsistent with whale blubber. It seems Verrill could not make up his mind. Then the National Museum, without forming an opinion of their own, joined Verrill's conclusion, stating it "was not worth the effort to study."

Dr. Webb was disappointed because he knew the subject had not been a whale and none of the scientists were willing to examine the blob on the beach. He became disgusted by the lack of scientific seriousness and returned to his medical practice.

More than fifty years went by with no mention of the thing that had washed up on the beach. Then, in 1957, a marine biologist came upon a brief story about the monster. The yellowing article referred to it as a giant octopus with a girth of 25 feet and arms reaching out 75 feet. Amazingly, the source of the story was none other than Professor Verrill, the one who had said the blob was a whale. Most likely, the story was published before Verrill had changed his mind again. The marine biologist wondered why he had never heard of Verrill's Giant Octopus or, in scientific lingo, Octopus Giganteus Verrill. No credit was given to Dr.Dewitt Webb who had been the sole researcher of the subject. In fairness, it should have been labeled Octopus Giganteus Webb.

The discovery of Verrill's old article started a quest to find answers to what really landed on St. Augustine's beach in 1896. After locating most of the correspondence, photographs, and drawings Dr. Webb had sent to Professor Verrill, researchers headed to the dusty shelves of the Smithsonian where a specimen jar was found containing the original tissue samples. Using modern technology and the latest knowledge of cellular biology, several researchers analyzed the specimen and a soon reached a new and more precise scientific conclusion. The thing that had washed up on the beach was indeed an enormous octopus. It was estimated, before decomposition, that the huge creature may have measured 150 to 200 feet from the tip of one tentacle to the other. There is no way of knowing the maximum growth size of this species of octopus.

In 2004, two Japanese divers took the first live pictures of giant squid that can grow up to sixty feet long. We can only wonder what other unknown giants live at the bottom of the ocean, waiting to be discovered at some point in the future.

STRANGE FLORIDA II

Man Awakes From Sleep
After 37 Years in a Florida Cave!
Is this Florida's Own Rip Van Winkle Story?

This sounds like one of those sensational stories from a supermarket tabloid or Florida's version of Washington Irving's 1819 tale about Rip van Winkle. Okay, from the *Atlanta Constitution*, dated 1888, I'll present you with the amazing facts. Readers are encouraged to draw their own conclusions, I'll add mine later. Anyway this event allegedly happened two miles from Marianna in Jackson County, which is known for a number of underground caverns.

On April 1, 1874, [just ignore the fact this happened on April Fools Day] a party of explorers, consisting of two men and five ladies, visited a cavern. Following a path, they soon came to an underground spring of crystal clear water flowing from the rocks. In the light of their torches, they traced the stream of water some fifty feet until it disappeared under a mass of limestone. It was at this point that one of the men used his cane to detach a large piece of loosened rock from the wall. Fragments of rock fell from the wall reverberating throughout the cavernous depths. The falling wall fragments had exposed a hole to another chamber. Their torches lit up the chamber, allowing their eyes to meet with an astonishing sight. The report says "For a moment, they were motionless with horror and fright." A few feet away, laying dead-still on the stone floor, was the body of a man clad in the garb of a soldier with his musket beside him.

One of the men of the party entered the chamber and, upon examining the man's cold body, found no outward signs of respiration although the soldier did not appear dead. The men of the party wrapped the body in a waterproof coat and dragged it to the cavern spring where they left it. The ladies were sent to town for help while the men waited at the cave entrance. After awhile, the women returned with two black men and all the men re-entered the cavern but, to their amazement, when they got to the body the man's eyes were open and he was breathing. Upon close examination they found him to have a distinct pulse. The men picked up the cave man and quickly hauled him outside in the fresh air. They poured brandy down his throat to help revive him, then carted him to a nearby cabin. There, they left him and hurried off to town to fetch a doctor. News of the discovery had already reached Marianna and every physician, and fifty curiosity seekers, were on their way to the cabin. Upon reaching the cabin, the doctors administered stimulants to the man and he began moving and talking. The doctors would allow no questions until the man was fully recovered, which happened to be the next day.

Okay, buckaroos, hold on to your hats; here's what Rip Van Winkle of the cave told his rescuers. He said that, in 1837, he was sent from Pensacola to Fort Dade with important military papers. When he was near Marianna [quite a ways off course, if you ask me] he was followed by a band of Choctaws who were on the warpath in sympathy with the Seminoles. Being hard pressed, he abandoned his horse and squeezed into a hole in the ground. Fearing the Indians would discover his trail, he went deeper into a cavern.

Suddenly, inside the cave, he found difficulty with his respiration and a feeling of drowsiness came over him. That was all he could remember.

The newspaper account says the old soldier could not believe that thirty-seven years had passed while he was in his cave coma. He soon grew tired of all the questions and said he didn't want to be the object of curiosity. When his strength fully recovered, he disappeared and has not been heard from since. Some of the good folks of Marianna thought the story was dubious and suspected a hoax, according to a reporter in the Atlanta Constitution. Their skepticism was soon dismissed when one of the women in the group that found the sleeping soldier discovered her pet dog was lost. The dog had been with the group at the cave. Three weeks after the slumbering soldier was found, another party found the dog inside the same cave chamber. The dog appeared dead but, when removed from the cavern to the open air, he came to life and was as frisky as ever. That seemed to satisfy everybody as to the truth of the sleeping soldier story. "The people of Marianna," wrote a reporter, "are very cautious about telling the story to strangers."

Perhaps the minerals in the cave helped preserve the soldier and dog. Maybe the lack of air caused some kind of suspended animation. Maybe I should have found a more believable story, but this one does demonstrate that with all legends and weird tales, there is always some degree of truth. In this case, the truth is the cave exploration part. My guess is that the cave is based on what is today's Florida Caverns State Park near Marianna. Florida may seem like a strange place for a subterranean world; however the Florida Caverns are equal in beauty to the likes of Carlsbad Caverns and the Mammoth Cave, although not as large. Once a hiding place for early Indians, Florida's caverns are 60 feet below the surface with a year round temperature of 65 degrees. This is where the Chipola River flows underground for several hundred feet, forming a land bridge. Like the Mammoth cave, there are dazzling stalagmites, stalactites, flowstones, rimstones and other remarkable geological features, and perhaps even a sleeping caveman.

A Piece of the Gondwanaland Jigsaw Puzzle
Back when geological things were really moving...

Millions of years ago, the Florida peninsula was part of a super-sized continent called Gondwanaland, which sounds like the name of a theme park. This super landmass broke up 300 million years ago into South America and Africa. Florida then became wedged between the pieces of Gondwanaland and North America to form another mega-continent called Pangea, which is easier to pronounce than Gondwanaland.

Florida's Subterranean World Begins Forming...

Throughout geologic history, the Florida peninsula has spent most of its time underwater. Florida's cavernous underground was created during recent Ice Ages when most of the water was trapped in huge glaciers, resulting in lower sea levels. Actually, the sunny peninsula was up to a hundred miles wider back then. With our increasing population we could sure use the extra land today. Gradually, freshwater drained downward through Florida's limestone base and created caves and caverns. As the glaciers melted, the sea levels rose to near present levels, a situation which threatens to reverse itself over the next century if global warming goes unchecked.

STRANGE FLORIDA II

That "*sinking*" Florida feeling...
Now I know why I didn't buy that condo on the beach.

It's just common sense that you can only get so many people in a boat before it goes down. However, it's not Florida's over-population that's worrying scientists; it's the thawing out of glaciers. The same thing happened about 10,000 years ago at the end of the Ice Age when glaciers melted causing sea levels to rise to present day levels.

We've heard the warnings about global warming and how it will affect the major ice sheets of our planet. Now new studies, released in March 2006, indicate that a long-term meltdown of massive ice reservoirs has already begun. Temperatures are already close to that of 130,000 years ago which began the last big thaw suggesting we may be on the threshold of the same thing happening again. If that ain't bad enough, one paleo-climatologist has added more gloom, "We are 100 years ahead of schedule!"

If the data is correct, by year 2100, sea levels may be up as much as 20 feet along the east coast, or enough to sink barrier islands and the Florida Keys. If you're planning a trip to Key West, I suggest you take it now before the place sinks. One study added that projected sea level rise may even be "understated." Well that's just dandy; no good news here, folks. According to researchers at the National Center for Atmospheric Research, changes in the Earth's tilt and orbit are causing intensified sunlight to reach the Arctic. Combine this with global warming effects and we are facing a major melt of the Arctic's ice sheets. To make matters worse, some climatologists believe that, in addition to warmer conditions in the Arctic, certain factors are at work which will cause thawing in Antarctica to be worse than the last big meltdown of prehistoric times. In other words, Florida is in for a double warming whammy.

What does all this mean for Florida? Well, here's a clue. Instead of reading this book, perhaps you should be gathering lumber to build an ark. If we choose to believe the scientific projections instead of listening to skeptics, our sunny peninsula is going to sink, or at least a major part of it. Laboratory models show much of Florida's eastern seaboard being under water. Future Spring Breakers take note; Daytona Beach will cease to exist. That's right; according to one model, all coastal islands and the Keys will be submerged. Yes Miami, too, as a matter of fact. Judging by the scenario presented in some climate models, all of South Florida, southward from Lake Okeechobee, will disappear under water. Standby with life preservers, it sounds like we're going down!

When will this happen? Nobody knows for sure because scientists are still in the process of collecting data to support their predictions, however, it could come much sooner than expected if we don't change our ways. Carbon Dioxide emissions in our atmosphere, caused by greenhouse gasses, will triple by 2100 raising temperatures by 8 degrees warmer than today. Let's put it this way, it's expected that we will see the beginnings of this meltdown during our life times. Can it be stopped? Maybe, but the window of opportunity is short and narrow. Certainly, we may have a chance to halt the process, or at least slow it down, by reducing greenhouse gasses. Of course, it will take a worldwide effort of adopting low-emission technologies to clean up the atmosphere. I'm afraid that by the time this gets done, I'll be floating around on my ark.

CASSELBERRY'S MYSTERY FROM THE SKY
Local witnesses believe it came from outer space!

On the evening of July 4, 2004, thunderstorms rolled across Seminole County, delaying fireworks displays in several communities north of Orlando. Local historian Christine Kinlaw-Best described the stormy weather as unusually bad. "I remember that storm, it started about 6 p.m. and lasted to around 9 p.m., it was horrific. It was a downpour with the worst lightning I have ever seen, and I've lived in Florida all my life."

The skies over Central Florida began clearing about 9 p.m. as the thunderstorms pushed out of the area toward the east coast. With a break in the weather, people began gathering in surrounding communities to watch annual fireworks displays. Although Casselberry did not have its own festivities planned, many of its residents claim there were a series of sonic booms louder than any skyrocket could ever make and a brilliant flash that covered the entire sky above their town.

"We were inside, sitting at the kitchen table," recalled Randy Avery. "All of a sudden, there were several booms, like the sonic booms the space shuttle makes when it returns, except there were four or five big booms in a row. The whole house shook. A picture fell from the wall and it rattled the windows. Me and my wife ran outside to see what had happened and the whole sky was lit up, it was a strange orange color. The neighbors were out in the street wondering what in the world had exploded. It wasn't thunder, it was much too loud. It definitely was not fireworks; it sounded like the mother of all bombs."

Another resident recalled "The sky was a bright golden color, as bright as lightning but a strange color. It was hard to believe how loud the booms were and how bright the sky was. People were outside trying to figure out what was going on."

As Casselberry residents were trying to figure out what had shaken their homes, calls were flooding local radio talk shows talking about how something had crashed or exploded northwest of the center of Casselberry near Highway 17-92 and Dog Track Road. Strangely enough, other than a couple of radio shows, the major news media did not mention the incident until July 16th when WESH Television reported that people were wondering what had crashed or exploded on the Fourth of July.

Casselberry police went on record stating that nothing had been found to indicate a crash or explosion. Contrary to the police statements, many residents claimed that a construction site off Dog Track Road had been sealed off by authorities and that they had observed a team from NASA searching the area. It should be noted that Casselberry is only an hour's distance from Kennedy Space Center. Although a few reports had the subject site on the opposite side of town near Red Bug Lake Road and Highway 436, the majority of witnesses pointed to the area off Dog Track Road.

Several witnesses claimed that the FBI was involved with security of the suspected impact area while others reported seeing government investigators in black Humvees combing the site. When local residents began calling an Orlando radio station and claiming that a UFO or meteorite had crashed, the station dispatched a reporter to the scene where he was approached by a man carrying a red suit case. According to accounts from listeners, the reporter was talking to the station on his cell phone when the man ordered him to cease broadcasting. Listeners who were tuned in to the station say the reporter's phone immediately went dead. "All I know," said J.W. Bowen, a Longwood resident, "something was going on just off Dog Track Road and the government was interested in it. I know it was the government because I saw GSA license plates on several unmarked cars in the area not long after that big boom was heard. If you want my opinion, I think somebody was trying to hide something from the public."

In other reports following the incident, residents in the vicinity of the alleged crash site began complaining of nausea, respiratory problems, and cases of hair and weight loss. Although the allegations of sickness could not be confirmed by medical reports, such symptoms would suggest radiation exposure. This leads some to believe that space junk may have crashed in Casselberry, which may account for witness reports that a NASA team was seen at the site. A few UFO buffs suspect the government of covering up the crash of an alien space vehicle that blew up, possible struck by lightning during the thunderstorm. The most common belief, among local witnesses, is that it was a meteor or a piece of space junk.

Supporting meteorological data and worldwide media sources indicate numerous sightings of meteors from June through July 2004. In Egypt, numerous meteorites rained down from the sky on July 15th, setting fire to hundreds of homes and injuring several people. In the Palencia region of Spain, meteoroids were blamed for aerial explosions, earth tremors, and smoke seen on a nearby mountain. In the United States, a large meteor shower was observed over Texas, Arkansas, Louisiana, Oklahoma and Tennessee. The National Weather Service recorded numerous reports of fireballs in the sky at 9:30, the same time as the Casselberry incident. In some of these cases, the Federal Emergency Management Agency became involved in safety discussions with meteorologists. In Washington State, a fireball causing several loud booms was seen cutting a brilliant 60 mile wide swath in the sky that extended 260 miles from Puget Sound to Whidbey Island. In another report, dated July 4, 2004, several witnesses in Chatsworth, Georgia, reported seeing a fireball with a streaming tail traveling through the sky toward Florida only minutes before Casselberry's booms. Fireballs are produced by large meteoroids that may range in size from a soccer ball to that of a small automobile. When fireballs explode in the atmosphere, they are called bolides. The largest recorded meteorite to crash into Central Florida impacted Lake County in 1918.

No cosmic debris or space junk was ever found in Casselberry, according to authorities who hold to the explanation that the whole incident was caused by lightning. Residents are still convinced that the booms and strange intense flash were caused by something that came from space, either a bolide or space junk. A few still cling to the belief that the government is covering up the crash of an alien spaceship. It is more likely that it was a cosmic object, possibly a bolide or even space junk, which would explain NASA being on the scene. "I know one thing," remarked Michael Osborne, a former Casselberry resident. "It was not lightning, and anyone who says it was did not hear it or feel the ground shake."

Whatever caused the series of sonic booms and the almost blinding sheet of light in the sky on July 4, 2004, may never be explained. But, whatever it was, it has left Casselberry with a lingering mystery.

STRANGE FLORIDA II

THE ELUSIVE WAMPUS CAT

The strange critter that prowls the backwoods of Southern folklore

In the pioneer folklore of Northern Florida, especially in the lower Okefenokee region, we find tales of a hideous creature called the Wampus Cat. Now, if you're not from the South, you might ask "What in tarnation is a Wampus Cat?" Well, Southerners ain't so sure what one is either, but the creature has certainly found its way into Southern folklore, song, poems, books, and even as mascots for high school football teams. Then there are those folks claiming to have had face-to-face encounters with the Wampus Cat or, as some call it, *Whumpus Cat*. Alleged sightings have occurred throughout Dixie, concentrated mainly in Tennessee, western North Carolina, West Virginia, southern Kentucky, and down through Georgia and, yes, even into northern parts of Florida.

The Wampus Cat is said to be a bipedal black panther or a bear-like cat that walks on its hind legs. It has also been described as having a man's head and the body of a wildcat. Other stories refer to a shape-shifting entity that can transform from a human into a cat-like creature. Okay, that's enough for me to avoid this critter should I see one.

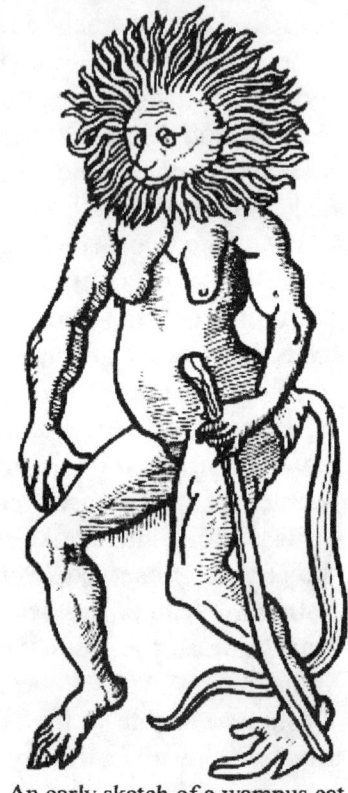

An early sketch of a wampus cat

The Wampus Cat may have its roots in a Cherokee legend about a young Indian woman who did not trust her husband. According to the tale, she dressed in a panther skin one night and followed her husband's hunting party into the woods to spy on him. As the hunters gathered around a campfire, she crawled up to get a closer look, but was caught instead. Since women of the tribe were forbidden to leave the village or to participate in hunts, she was punished by being transformed into a Wampus Cat. As the legend goes, the Wampus Cat was half-woman half-panther and, on moonlight nights, her ghost still roams the hills, howling to be changed back into her human form.

Another tale claims the Wampus Cat is really a witch that kept putting a hex on people's cattle. She was blamed for stealing cows, goats, and other farm animals. People soon figured out how she was carrying-out her deeds; she would cast a spell on herself and change into a panther. Hey, this sounds like old fashioned shape-shifting and if werewolves can do it, why can't witches transform into wampus cats? Folks finally got fed up with her brand of witchcraft and cornered her in a barn while she was still in the form of a panther. According to witch lore, witches can only remain in a "transformed state" for a short time; otherwise they can never change back to human form again. In the case of this witch, she could not get out of the barn in time to reverse the spell on herself and therefore was compelled to exist forever as the infamous Wampus Cat.

In many Wampus sightings, witnesses have said the Wampus critter has glowing yellow eyes, saliva dripping from its fangs, and smells like a polecat. There are numerous accounts of farm animals and hunting dogs being killed by a Wampus Cat. No doubt a few were killed by a genuine panther or bear. It is rather curious that witnesses have said the creature has a skunk-like odor, shaggy hair, and walks upright. That sounds like a Florida Skunk Ape or some other Bigfoot-type creature. Could it be that some Wampus Cat sightings have really been of a so-called "Bigfoot?"

Wampus Cat sightings have also occurred in urban areas, including Nashville and Knoxville. In most urban cases, the animal has been reported to be smaller than a panther. Two of these cases referred to "a large tomcat with glowing eyes that walked upright." There is even one story about the Wampus Cat living in the sewers of urban areas. Maybe as more people move from rural areas to the city, so follows their folklore which becomes twisted into an urban legend.

The Southern slang "catawampus," meaning unruly, misaligned, crooked, or lopsided, is probably related to the Wampus Cat. Or maybe Wampus Cat is derived from "catawampus." And what about "caterwauling?" Does that refer to the eerie howling of the Wampus Cat? Then there is the word "Bearcat" that may be just another name for the Wampus Cat. In Florida, paleontologists recently discovered the prehistoric remains of a previously unknown animal that is described as "a saber-tooth cat with a bear-like body." Could that be the ancestor to the Bearcat, or Wampus Cat?

The Wampus Cat is probably a myth that started with a scary yarn about a panther. There was a time when panthers roamed throughout the South and rural southerners who have heard a panther's cry swear it sounds just like a woman screaming. Such a sound must have sent shivers up a few spines and may have been the basis for stories about a woman being transformed into the Wampus Cat. It seems with each retelling, a storyteller added a new version. Through a little reading, I have found five different so-called Indian legends about the Wampus Cat, none of which can be verified as genuine Native American folklore. It's more likely the Wampus Cat has its roots in Appalachian folklore. But does this mean that folks haven't seen a Wampus Cat? Nope, but it seems more likely 'Wampus Cat' is a general term that has been applied to any unusual animal, or noise, which cannot otherwise be readily explained. So, if one night you encounter a strange shadowy figure, or hear a spine chilling howl, or smell a polecat…just try to keep in mind the Wampus Cat is most likely just a myth—*or is it?*

STRANGE FLORIDA II

Shake, rattle, and roll...
THE NIGHT FLORIDA "TREMBLED!!!"
The midnight terror that shook folks from their sleep!

The evening of January 13, 1879 began like any other winter night in Florida except, as one old Cracker put it, "there was strangeness in the animals, they acted restless and spooked." He noticed that his dog refused to come out from under the porch. Seeing no reason for the odd behavior, the old timer went to bed secure beneath the warmth of an extra quilt. The scene was much the same across the state as folks extinguished their kerosene lamps and settled in for a peaceful night of rest. However, this would be no ordinary night in Florida.

Clocks had hardly reached midnight, eleven forty-five to be exact, when all hell seemed to break loose. Windows began vibrating, awakening citizens to a nightmarish shaking across 25,000 square miles of Florida. Farm animals went wild, kitchen tables danced on floors, cabinet doors flew open, and plaster fell from ceilings. People ran outside wondering what on earth was happening. It seemed that the earth was trying to open up beneath their feet. Some dropped to their knees, thinking it was the end of the world. Others blamed the commotion on the date; after all it was the 13th. Then, as quick as it all began, the terrifying rumbling stopped.

Sleepy-eyed Floridians, most standing outside in their nightshirts, only had about fifteen minutes of calm before the devilish trembling began again. This time it was more violent, sending household items crashing to floors. Frightened families huddled together while chickens squawked and dogs barked. The Chicago Daily Tribune reported, "Mothers clutched their little ones and prepared to save their lives or die themselves." In cities, hotel guests rushed wildly into the dimly lit streets as if something unknown was after them.

The great vibrations were felt from Tallahassee to St. Augustine and down the east coast to Daytona. A few reports claimed the shaking was felt as far south as Punta Rassa on the Gulf coast. The unearthly night left a considerable amount of minor damage, especially to household items, but fortunately no injuries to people.

Very few earthquakes can be found in Florida's past, as a matter of fact, only three are worthy of mention. One can only imagine being a Floridian back in those days, unaccustomed to a phenomenon like an earthquake. It had to be a frightening event, especially without radio or television news to explain the terror.

According to the University of Florida's Department of Geology, the 1879 earthquake was assigned a modified Mercalli intensity rating of six. This was before the use of the Richter scale, but would compare to a 4.0 to 4.4 earthquake. The exact epicenter of the great Florida quake is unknown, however the U.S. Geological Society placed it roughly between St. Augustine, in St. Johns county, and Starke, in Clay county. The most recent earthquake to affect Florida occurred on September 10, 2006 and registered 6.0 on the Richter scale. The epicenter was 250 miles southwest of Tampa in the Gulf of Mexico but it damaged water pipes in Orlando and tremors were felt across Florida and Georgia.

STRANGE FLORIDA II

LOST CONFEDERATE TREASURE
Dixie Gold in Florida awaits treasure hunters...if you can find it.

Florida is known for its buried pirate treasure and sunken Spanish galleons laden with gold and silver, but this story has to do with Confederate treasure that may have been hidden somewhere in Florida at the end of the Civil War.

One account, supported by fairly good history, states that near the end of the Civil War a million dollar Confederate payroll was buried in the Everglades. To keep the money from falling into the hands of pursuing Union soldiers, a Confederate pay officer buried the payroll, including $200,000 in gold coins, in the glades "where the land rises like a camel's back" in the "west hump" near the intersection of two creeks. The location is somewhere between the Tamiami Trail and Alligator Alley, but be warned treasure hunters, this needle-in-the-haystack is on a Seminole Indian Reservation. However, don't let your metal detector be dismayed, there are other Confederate treasure caches waiting to be discovered.

Cedar Key was an active Confederate port until the Federals captured it in 1862. The assault began with a Union vessel sailing into Cedar Key and sinking seven Confederate ships and a ferryboat. The wrecks of these vessels are still on the bottom somewhere and in their wreckage is said to be strongboxes containing silver and gold.

During the Civil War, a Federal warship chased a Confederate blockade runner into Dead Man's Bay, in Taylor County. Onboard the Confederate ship was 500,000 dollars in silver bars. The Rebel sailors scuttled their vessel near where the Steinhatchee River empties into the bay. The silver bars are believed to be buried near the mouth of the river. There is a rumor of another Dixie treasure buried on the banks of the Steinhatchee River, said to have been 140,000 dollars in gold coins. The crew buried it to keep it out of Federal hands. After the war, crew members returned to dig up the money but, due to a flood changing landmarks, they were unable to locate it. Up the Gulf coast at Apalachicola Bay, a Southern blockade runner carrying 500,000 dollars in silver is said to have sunk in the bay just north of St. George Island.

In March 1865, at the conclusion of the Civil War, Confederate Captain John Riley was in charge of shipping Confederate gold out of the country to Cuba. When he became alert to Federal troops on his trail, Riley headed for the Everglades where he hid 500,000 dollars in gold coins. The treasure has never been recovered and is supposedly located somewhere in west central Broward County. As fast as developers are pouring concrete on South Florida, you'll probably need a jack hammer to get to this loot.

Did gold from the Confederate Treasury end up in Florida?

There's no shortage of stories about what happened to the money and gold in the Confederate treasury at the end of the Civil War. Most historians agree that Confederate president, Jefferson Davis, and other high ranking officials hoped for a resurgence of the Confederacy and planned to finance the come-back using treasury funds. We're not talking about worthless Confederate currency; the treasury had millions in gold and silver. Records indicate the treasury's contents were hauled out by wagons as Union forces began their assault on Dixie's capital at Richmond. Historians and treasure hunters have spent decades researching documents and deciphering clues in their search for the lost Confederate treasure. With good supporting evidence, treasure hunters believe it's hidden in the backwoods of Arkansas...or Texas, or Georgia, or Missouri, or Alabama and maybe even Canada. Okay, it appears that it was split up rather than to risk capture of the entire lot. It was most likely hauled out of Richmond in several wagon convoys headed in various directions and buried in several different states across the South. It was a clandestine operation under the directions of a secret society called the Knights of the Golden Circle. The outlaw, Jesse James, is believed to have been a KGC agent. James supposedly led a convoy carrying 80,000 dollars in Confederate gold to New Mexico.

Originally, the secret treasure sites were guarded by a network of KGC agents, who passed the honored duty from one generation to the next. Today, there are few good old boys, professing inside information, who claim the treasure hoards are still guarded by a new generation of KGC sentinels.

According to official records, and Tench Tilghman's journal, one of the wagon trains carrying Confederate gold ended up in Florida. On Monday, May 15, 1865, after dodging Federal troops and traveling nearly three weeks from North Carolina, the small convoy of wagons crossed into Florida. In charge of escorting these wagons were Tilghman and an entourage of select officers, which included Captain Clark, serving as acting treasurer of the Confederate government. The wagons carried trunks filled with official government papers, baggage and papers of Jefferson Davis, and the last remains of the Confederate treasury. The objective was to eventually rendezvous with Jefferson Davis in Cuba or the Bahamas. However, plans became futile after Federal troops captured Davis in Georgia.

On May 22nd, the wagons passed to the right of Gainesville and stopped at Cotton Wood Plantation, on the Fernandina and Cedar Key railroad. This was the estate of David L. Yulee, former senator and railroad magnate who had contributed much to the Southern cause. This was also the end of the line for the wagon train of Confederate treasure. According to Captain Clark's report and letters, prior to disbanding the group, $6,790 in gold was set aside for the benefit of Mrs. Davis, $1,940 in gold sovereigns was distributed to each officer in the convoy escort, and $975 each was given to their scout and five black servants for wages. A "valuable" trunk belonging to Jefferson Davis, and two other chests containing secret papers of the Confederate government, were buried by Lieutenant John D. Purvis in a Yulee horse stable. No one knows what became of the remaining treasure; however Tilghman, in later years, told friends that he had buried his share on the Yulee plantation and implied there was even more gold there. Old rumors have persisted for years about Confederate gold buried somewhere on the northeast side of Archer, Florida.

Aside from the subject of hidden rebel treasure, this wagon train was the real end of the Confederacy. In that respect, we can say the Confederate States of America took its very last breath in Levy County, Florida.

STRANGE FLORIDA II

PIT *of* HORRORS in the OKEFENOKEE
WARNING: Not a story for the squeamish, but it's true!

Called the "Land of the Trembling Earth," the mysterious Okefenokee swamp covers a large portion of southeast Georgia and overlaps a small part of north Florida. It is more impassable than the Everglades and much of it is truly a no-man's land. It is known for treacherous quicksand, often twenty to thirty feet deep, that can swallow both man and beast in a very short time.

In 1887, a fellow by the name of Mr. Crompton recalled for a newspaper reporter his terrifying experience in the swamp. "Talk of strange things," he began, with a nervous twitch in his eye, "the most horrible sight I ever beheld was on an alligator hunt back in the 1850s." Mr. Crompton served as a guide for a party that ventured into the swamp to hunt alligators in the Spring of 1853. Crompton said the group consisted of an Englishman named Dutton and his friend and an old black man to row the boat and carry things. Dutton was known for being a splendid shot with a rifle and, on hunting expeditions, never missed his target. "Picking our way through some tight places and the marshy lowlands, we went as far as we could by boat. We landed and went on foot with Dutton some distance in front. We had gone about two miles when the swamp became dense and, as it was getting late in the evening, we called a halt and decided to return to our boat before night caught us in the swamp.

Before turning around, we waited for Dutton who had gone some distance ahead and was not in sight." Crompton, standing with the other Englishman, was about to send the black fellow to find Dutton when he heard a call for help. "The blood in my veins was chilled by an awful shriek for help," exclaimed Crompton. "If I live for a hundred years I shall never forget that cry." The call came from their right, a direction that was off the route on their map. It seemed that Dutton had ventured from the planned route and was now in trouble. As Crompton started toward the fading cries for help, the black man cautioned him "It's no use to go after him, masser, it be dangerous, you don't wanna go there!"

Crompton ignored the man's warning and, with the other Englishman, quickly headed toward the screams. "We had hardly gone more than a hundred yards when a sight met my eyes, the likes of which I would rather meet my own death than to ever encounter again." In an open space in front of Crompton was what looked like a marshy stretch of ten square yards. It presented the illusion of being solid ground but was actually a bog of quicksand. "In the middle of this was Dutton, struggling as if with some invisible power that was drawing him downward into this hole of slime and filth. Around his body, coiled in sickening masses, were Okefenokee reptiles of every evil description. To reach him with the assistance of a pole was impossible. It was growing dark and he was being drawn down into the bottomless pit. I called to him and implored him to make a desperate effort to come nearer to the edge so I could reach him. He had sunk up to his shoulders by this time. A large snake had coiled itself around his shoulders and neck and had drawn tighter until Dutton's face was turning black. It was apparent he could no longer speak. In an instant he went down, taking the mass of squirming reptiles with him, leaving nothing but a bubble on the surface. I turned to Dutton's friend, who had not said a word, and motioned him to lead the way back to the boat.

When Crompton and the Englishman, exhausted by the horrifying ordeal, returned to the boat, the old black fellow asked "Did they choke him to death?" Crompton nodded in the affirmative as they prepared to load into the boat. A few days later, the surviving Englishman left for England carrying with him the story of his friend's demise.

Crompton was puzzled how his black man, who was not at the terrifying scene, seemed to know that Dutton had been choked to death. When asked, the black man replied, "Masser, it's been twenty years this spring since I said I would never go into that swamp again. I was hunting gators with my only boy, he was seventeen, and I heard that same cry. I rushed to where he was to find myself unable to do anything for him. I had to stand there and watch the snakes pin his arms and strangle him to death and pull him from my sight, down into that awful hole. When I heard that cry from Masser Dutton I know'd what it was, although I hadn't heard it for twenty years."

"Since that time," said Mr. Crompton, "I have lived within two hours ride of the Okefenokee and have never been back there. The very thought sickens me and causes a shudder to pass over me."

A LITTLE MORE OKEFENOKEE WEIRDNESS...

Florida and Georgia share the Okefenokee in which there are probably a few remote spots which have never seen a human. Over centuries, many people have vanished in this swamp, presumably victims of quicksand, snake bite, or they ended as dinner for an alligator. It's a mysterious tangled mess of swamp that holds many dark secrets, spewing forth on occasions. Some of its stories are mere folk yarns but others real enough to inspire the *Okefenokee X-Files* website. There are personal stories about both tall and short Bigfoot creatures seen in and around the edge of the swamp, at least two sightings in 1955 involved an investigation by the Calhoun County, Georgia, Sheriff's department. Another odd sighting, in 1972, was of a chimpanzee-looking creature in the Stephen Foster State Park. In 1952, there were two separate sightings of UFOs hovering near the swamp. One was shaped like a pulsating, wide-brimmed Mexican hat with a light shining down from its bottom. Earl Howard told me how, as a kid growing up in Blackshear in the early 1900s, he was chased across a field by a big ball of light that came out of the swamp. My fellow weird author, Jim Miles, writes in his big *Weird Georgia* book [highly recommended by me] about a big tiger attacking several pioneer folks near the Okefenokee before being hunted down and killed. We're talking about a *real tiger* here, not a misinterpretation of a bobcat or panther.

There are numerous stories dating back to Spanish times about a band of super warriors or giants living in the Okefenokee and phantom pirate ships with skeleton crews seen on the St. Mary's River, which divides Florida and Georgia. Prior to 1845, one of my ancestors, Colonel William Williams, assisted Captain Billy Cone in surveying a portion of Florida's original territorial border. If I'm to believe my hand-me-down family history, the two surveyors accomplished their task by using a wild grapevine. Imagine that, the Florida-Georgia border measured with a grapevine, now that's a little weird too!

STRANGE FLORIDA II

The MYSTERIOUS CALUSA
Florida's Lost Civilization...

The Calusa Indians, one of the least known aboriginal people, inhabited Florida's Gulf Coast from Tampa down through the Ten Thousand Islands. Based on radiocarbon dating of charcoal and pottery fragments, their culture dates back to approximately 2100 B.C. and peaked about 800 A.D. which coincides with the Mayan classic period in Central America. Some believe there was a cultural connection between Florida's Calusa and the Mayan empire of the Yucatan. The ancient Calusa Empire began its decline with the arrival of the Spanish and, by the mid-1700s, had totally disappeared. A few remnants may have survived to 1800 and it is possible that some were absorbed into other native tribes.

MANY CALUSA DESIGNS RESEMBLE ART FROM THE MAYAN CIVILIZATION. COULD THERE BE AN ANCIENT CONNECTION?

The origin of the Calusa, as well as exactly why they vanished, has been the subject of conjecture, but the truth is nobody really knows why this empire disappeared. There's speculation in some circles that the Calusa were descendants of refugees from Atlantis, which excites those who believe in the lost continent beneath the sea. Others imagine the Calusa as descendants of shipwrecked Phoenicians or Egyptians. But the most popular theory seems to be the possible connection with the Mayan Empire.

Anthropologists tell us how the Calusa were a well-organized society of big-boned people, fierce warrior types, who built ceremonial complexes and, like the Maya, practiced human sacrifice. These ancient people built terraced earthworks, dug canal systems, and established villages all up and down the lower Gulf coast of Florida. One site on Chokoloskee Island covered 150 acres, with two graded causeways, man-made canals, and several prominent mounds, one standing 27 feet high. Another site was discovered on Turner's River which consisted of 30 large mounds in a row. Their earthen works were of various shapes, circular, oval, many pyramid-shaped, and some with steps or spiraling walkways to the tops. The volume of material used in building one mound in Collier County has been estimated to equal the mass of three Egyptian pyramids. On top of tall temple mounds, the Calusa built large houses for their ruling leaders. Pedro Menedez, in 1566, described a Calusa lodge that could hold 2000 people. I guess when they talked about being sent to the big house, they really meant it.

Two pyramids were discovered in the late 1960s deep in the Big Cypress swamp, according to the Peninsula Archaeological Society in a 1971 article. Amateur archaeologists said they had found two structures shaped like pyramids made of stone blocks fitted so precisely that a pocket knife could not be inserted between the blocks. They also reported faint designs on the stones resembling Egyptian hieroglyphics. One structure was 12 feet tall and the other 14 feet. Five miles northeast of the location they found a mysterious seven mile long wall of stacked stone blocks ranging between 6 and 8 feet in height. Exactly what these structures are has never been determined, but some think they were built by the Calusa or, if you want to go out on a limb, by refugees from Atlantis when it sank.

Building an empire isn't easy work and would have required skillful engineering, time, and an organized labor force just like that used by the Egyptians and Mayans. The Calusa's hand-dug canal systems were an amazing feat with some extending two miles. The big difference between Egypt and the Yucatan empires is that Florida offered practically no building material except for dirt, wood, and shells which leads us to wonder what would have been accomplished if stone had been available.

The Calusa, like their distant Yucatan neighbors across the Gulf of Mexico, practiced elaborate religious ceremonies, often resulting in someone losing their heart or head.
The ruling class adorned themselves with colorful headdresses, beads, pendants, and other spangles and dangles. One curious feature was the large ear buttons worn by the Calusa which were identical to ones seen on carved stone figures of the Maya. Many of the known religious customs of these early Floridians parallel those of the Mayan and Egyptian societies. For example, the chief was required to marry his sister, a common tradition found in the ancient Inca culture and during certain Egyptian periods. Like the Maya and Aztec, the Calusa practiced human sacrifice and, whenever a ruling leader died, his close relatives, servants, and animals were killed and buried with him along with his possessions. This was a practice similar to customs dating back to 2000 B.C. in Mesopotamia. One Calusa burial mound on Horr's Island is 3400 years old and is believed to be one of the oldest earthen works in the United States.

Calusa effigy resembles Egyptian art.

The artwork of the Calusa may be another clue to their origin; it has an uncanny resemblance to that of the Mayan and Egyptian civilizations. A Calusa cat effigy of a panther god looks more like an artifact from an Egyptian tomb than something from Southwest Florida. In many cases, Calusa designs are almost indistinguishable from that of the Mayan and Aztecs. There are also linguistic similarities found in the journals of explorer Hernando de Sota who mentions the names of four Calusa chiefs, Carlos, Mocozo, Hirrihigua, and Urribarracuxi. The last three undoubtedly sound like Mayan words, which most of us have trouble pronouncing.

Unlike other ancient aborigines, the Calusa did not use a bow and arrow, choosing instead spears and war clubs lined with shark teeth resembling those discovered in the Yucatan. They also used a variety of throwing sticks called "atlatls" by archaeologists. Throwing sticks added leverage to the spear thrower's arm, kind of like a spear launcher. These same devices were common throughout Central America during the same time period. A curious feature of the word "atlatl" is that "atl" comes from the ancient Nahuatl language of Mexico, supposedly meaning "water." When doubled, as in "atlatl" it's supposed to mean "spear thrower." The first four letters are the same as found in the words "Atlantis" and "Atlantic." Mayan tradition held that their ancestors came from the east, across the great sea, from the land of "Atlan." This sure stirs up a bunch of questions for inquiring minds. Could Atlan have been Atlantis? Could the Mayans and Calusa have been descendants of Atlanteans? Was there really a cultural connection between the Maya and Calusa? No one really knows, but keep reading.

The Calusa were a seafaring people, they did little hunting and practiced little agriculture, relying instead on provisions from the sea. They built a variety of boats, some lashed together in catamaran style, which were propelled by large sails. Anthropology accepts the fact that the Calusa sailed across the Florida Straits to Cuba, a mere 90 miles from Key West. Heck, I could swim that distance; well, at least the first few yards. The big question is could they have also reached across the Gulf of Mexico to the Yucatan? Columbus reported on his fourth voyage of having seen a large Mayan canoe, eight feet wide, with a canopy and sails, carrying 25 men, women, and children. Columbus may have sighted the first commercial cruise line in history or migrating Mayans. It's a fact that Caribbean Indians made regular sea voyages from the islands to the tip of Florida. The Calusa could have easily crossed the 90 miles to Cuba, then hugged the Island's coast westward and made the short hop to the Yucatan. Hey, check your map; we're only talking a couple hundred miles of open sea. The return trip to Florida would have been made easy by picking up the Gulf Stream and riding it back to Southwest Florida. The surface speed of the Gulf Stream averages about 5 knots. Navigators of modern shipping have long known the advantages of riding the stream as a sort of power booster.

In 1928, an anthropologist from the Smithsonian, Henry B. Collins Jr., hacked his way through mangrove swamps to excavate a Calusa burial mound on Captiva Island. He unearthed 100 skeletons of mostly adults in an apparent mass burial. He noted there were no signs of disease, old age, or wounds from Spanish bullets and no weapons or possessions were buried with the bodies as was customary. The skeletons were packed close with their faces covered by a sheath of clay pottery. According to Collins, it looked like *"they had marched to the mound and stretched themselves out for a living burial rather than to submit in defeat to the white invaders."* Had Henry Collins discovered evidence of the final fate of the Calusa?

We may never know for sure if the Calusa ever had connections with other ancient civilizations, although we have compelling reason to believe that was the case. We may never know their origin, or what exactly caused their downfall as an empire. Today, little evidence remains of these vanished people. Over-development has destroyed their village sites and most of their great ceremonial mounds have been hauled away for road building material. Nothing is sacred to the bulldozer. Fortunately, a few of their mounds have been preserved as historical reminders so we will not forget Florida's vanished civilization.

STRANGE FLORIDA II

Florida's
SCARIEST THREAT
is not Supernatural!!
It's very real and it affects all Floridians!!

There exists an out-of-control wickedness in the Sunshine State with the destructive power of a skunk ape that is far more frightening than any apparition you'll ever meet. Unlike the mysterious blood sucking chupacabra, you can see this evil every day. It's all around us and it's more threatening to Floridians than any space alien or demon. Like the coils of a sea monster, it is strangling the life out of the Florida peninsula. This is a genuine man-made monster that politicians are reluctant to put a bridle on, even though grassroots groups are organizing to stop it. This monster feeds on greed and we read about its destructive nature every day in the media. But you don't need the news to prove its existence; just take a short drive anywhere in Florida and you will see it rearing its ugly head. It's known as irresponsible growth and development and it's virtually killing Florida's fragile environment.

Florida's Point of No Return.....

Each day an astonishing 1000-plus new people squeeze into Florida and another developer applies for rubber-stamped permission to build another 1000 houses, condominiums, or a shopping center. While we fuss about the loss of the world's rain forests, here in Florida another thousand trees are scraped away by a developer's bulldozer. Believe it or not, the daily loss rate in 2005 of mature trees in Florida actually exceeded the estimated loss of rainforest trees for a single day. It does not take a genius to know that trees are natural air filtration systems and serve a life-giving purpose for those of us who like to breathe oxygen. Government officials at all levels have been guilty of rubber-stamping permits for destruction by developers, whose environmental consciousness has been clouded by greed. Money, in this respect, is truly the root of all evil because it is throwing our nature out of balance. If you trace your finger around the globe you'll see that Florida lines up with some of the world's great barren deserts. Will the Florida peninsula be transformed into something like the Sahara desert which, by the way, was a wet and lush place in prehistoric times. Florida's human saturation point was reached a couple of decades ago and several respected environmental scientists have suggested that we have already gone beyond the point of no return.

No mysteries here...

. The great citrus groves of Central Florida are now theme parks and residential developments. The state's once fertile farmlands are now covered with asphalt parking lots and cement shopping malls. When rain falls on a hot parking lot, it either evaporates...or it drains off, along with oily toxic crap, into our ground water. Now, instead of using our fertile areas to grow food, we are warehousing people in apartment complexes and residential developments. A prime example of this negative transformation is Seminole County, which was once *America's Celery Capital*. In the 1930s, this area shipped an annual average of 7000 train car loads of vegetables. As a matter of fact, in the 1920s, Seminole County produced so much produce that the second largest ice plant in the world was built there for icing-down vegetables being shipped to northern markets. Today, Seminole County is a mass of concrete development and you'll be lucky to find a postage stamp size garden. It's no mystery why so much of our produce now comes from foreign markets; we have traded our fertile farm and grove lands for concrete developments.

Who says Florida doesn't have mountains??

The highest point in Florida used to be a spot 345 feet above sea level in Lakewood, near the Alabama state line, but that claim is now being challenged by the heights of huge man-made mountains of garbage. These waste-mountains are springing up all over the state and are the only way to dispose of all the garbage being generated by overpopulation. One of the most prominent of Florida's trash mountains, referred to locally as "Mount Trashmore," rises above the flat terrain of Key West. On the bright side, I suppose we could create a new tourist attraction by carving the faces of our state legislators on one of these trash mountains.

Florida is now on the verge of running out of places to legally dispose of its growing volumes of garbage, sewage, and industrial wastes. It's a documented fact that most landfills and sewers have dangerous levels of toxic waste which, along with pesticide run-offs from lawns, result in contaminating our ground and surface waters. High levels of toxic metals, dioxin, and acid pollutants can be found to some degree in almost all of Florida's streams, lakes, bays, and ecosystems. In some bodies of water, scientists have even discovered dangerous levels of radioactive elements like radium. Water is also being contaminated by pollutants in the air and, according to one report, Florida has one of the highest toxic emission rates in the country. Why worry about second-hand smoke when millions of vehicles on the state's congested highways are belching out carcinogenic toxins. It all adds up to a serious environmental degradation of our dwindling water supply and certainly leads to adverse health effects. It's no wonder health notices have been issued for over half of Florida's rivers and lakes, warning of dangerous mercury or other toxin levels in fish and shellfish. Hey, we eat, drink, and breathe this stuff; it's enough to turn us all into glow-in-the-dark mutants.

Running on empty...

Numerous environmental reports indicate that Florida has lost a million acres of wetlands to growth and development. This means we have lost many of our recharge areas that replenish our aquifers. Lakes throughout central and north Florida are drying up while saltwater intrudes our drinking water in coastal aquifers due to pumping out too much fresh. Folks, this may come as a surprise, but Florida is running out of water. By some official estimates, and hydrology studies, half the fresh water sucked out of Florida aquifers is lost by the filling of swimming pools and through lawn sprinklers. The only reason people have swimming pools is because our springs and beaches have become too over-crowded to enjoy. To make matters worse, much of this water which drains off lawns contains pesticides and fertilizers that end up in our streams and lakes, triggering algae blooms and fishkills. It is a crisis situation that's approaching sci-fi movie realism, except this is reality and we all are a part of it.

STRANGE FLORIDA II

Is the Sunny Peninsula Doomed Yet?

Is Florida doomed? We can start by asking the wildlife that's been squeezed out of millions of acres of habitat by development and growth. Newcomers are startled whenever an alligator slips into their swimming pool, or when a black bear wanders into their backyard. But who is really the invader here? It's the human who continues to destroy natural habitats to build communities of cookie-cutter homes. It's shameful how species like possums and raccoons are being forced into an urban existence of scavenging from garbage cans. It is even more appalling how man's mismanagement of our natural resources has pushed more species closer to endangerment. In many cases, the government has helped destroy our flora and fauna, as with the gopher tortoise. With a so-called "Take Permit" issued for a fee by the Florida Fish and Wildlife Commission, a developer can entomb the gopher tortoise alive. The tortoise is symbolic of what is happening throughout Florida, we're being entombed by greed. The truth be known, growth does not pay for itself; it only chips away at our quality of life until it destroys it and in the meantime taxes continue to climb, placing an extra financial burden on both residents and visitors. That's right, with extra taxes created by out of control growth; even tourists and other non-residents have a stake in this mess.

The Florida Watch Institute, which documents the impact of growth in Florida, said in one report that the increase in wastes, pollutants, and toxins has already surpassed the regional carrying capacity in large areas of the state. Yet, in these same areas, development continues at a brisk pace, more often with the blessings of public officials. Such projects will only result in more garbage, more congestion, more vehicles, more emissions, more lawns with insecticides, more energy consumption, and a thousand more swimming pools to fill up. When I grew up in Florida we didn't need swimming pools; we had crystal clear swimming holes. As you might guess, these old swimming holes are now lakefront property or have totally dried up due to our shrinking water table.

By the year 2020, it is estimated that Florida's fresh water demand will jump to 9.1 billion gallons per day. We're not making any more water, so where will it come from? What will we do with all the sewage and garbage? In the future, will we have to go to a museum to see a tree? Will the ocean be too filthy to swim in? These are frightening problems Floridians are facing. Already we are looking at all the concrete, congestion, asphalt, and loss of natural habitat, and asking, "What the heck happened to paradise?

If you've experienced weird stuff, then you're not alone. Read a few personal encounters the author has received from his readers.

WEIRD MAIL BAG

Was it geese or a squadron of Unidentified Flying Objects?

I got back from hunting one night with my father and brother and as we got out of the truck, we looked up a saw a huge metal triangle-like thing fly over our house. It went over real quietly. Then we saw another one going in another direction and then a third one following the first. My brother and I were freaking out but my daddy just said it was a flock of geese and walked into the house. It wasn't no flock of geese because we could see it was solid metal things. They might have been UFOs or one of those military stealth planes because we lived near Eglin AFB. I don't know but it was the darndest things I ever seen since then.

--- Andy M.

I think I saw a real ghost

When I was a young girl in Palatka, probably about 13 years old at the time. I had gone down the road to watch my baby cousins one night. I returned home very late that night, nine o'clock was considered late for a young lady back in the 40's. After I had been in bed a few minutes, a vision appeared at the foot of my bed of a woman draped in a green net. She told me she thought I'd never come home again...then she disappeared. I never seen her before and never saw her again. I think I saw a real ghost that night.

--- Ida A.

A lurking lake critter

My father used to go fishing in Lake George and my older sister and I would go too. My sister, Linda, knew I liked reading about prehistoric animals and would always tease me and say there was a plesiosaurus living in the lake and he'd eat me. One day, she and I had just got done swimming and when we got out of the water and turned around, we saw a strange shape floating right where we had been. It looked very large and dark colored and was causing ripples on the water. It looked like it had a long neck. Then it went below the surface. I don't think it was an alligator either, but we never went swimming in that lake again.

--- Tammy H.

Little green man

My uncle swears to this day that he saw an actual space alien while camping in the Blackwater State Forest near the Florida state line. He insists that a little green guy was watching him while he watched him and then just run away. I don't know if he really saw anything or if he'd drunk too much, but it sure gives us something to talk and laugh about when our family gets together.

--- Lee N.

Haunted house

There's a house in my neighborhood...I won't say where...And everybody says it's haunted...sometimes you can hear people talking inside it at night even though nobody lives there anymore...and some people have seen faces in the windows...my dog won't let me walk him past it. LOL.

--- Shane T.

Strange road kill

My grandfather whom we call Poppy, told me a story once about a time just before my dad was born. He lived in the country in Hillsborough county. It was late at night or early in the morning, and Poppy had been woken up by men's voices and lights outside. He walked out to the edge of his farm and there was the sheriff's men surrounding a large, hairy animal that was dead in the middle of the road. It was too big for our Florida bears. He said if he'd not known better, he'd thought it was a buffalo. He couldn't get too close and they told him to go back to his house. He watched them out the window load it up into a big truck and cover it up and drive away. It was never reported to the papers. The officials had told Poppy it was a bear but they were making too much of a fuss for a bear and it was just too big anyway. He said it smelled like it had been dead for days, but he knew it wasn't there early that day.

--- Dan D. Jr.

Was it a skunk ape?

I was dirt biking with two other dudes on private land near Inverness and saw a large, upright, thing that looked like Big Foot cross the trail ahead of us about 50 yards. It had brown matted fur and went very fast in a loping motion. We smelled a stinking smell like you read about the skunk ape leaving. We found several human looking footprints at least 14 to 15 inches long. Do you think we saw a skunk ape?

--- Jason

STRANGE FLORIDA II

What was outside the cabin?

When I was about 16 we had a cabin near the springs in the Ocala forest. This was in the early 1960's and we would spend a week or two there in the summer. I think this happened in July 1962. One night our dog started raising hell, barking and all that. He was inside but was at the window barking. We figured that it was a bear outside because we had seen bear before but this was not a bear. My dad took his powerful flashlight and shined it out the window and what we saw was something running into the trees on two legs that looked in all respects like a big gorilla but much taller. In later years, when I read about Florida's bigfoot being in the Ocala area and in thinking back to that night, I think we may have seen one.

--- Raymond

Blue fireball over the atlantic

[October 2005] While on the beach just before midnight at New Smyrna following a brief thunderstorm that had moved off shore, we saw a very large bluish fireball traveling from the north to the south horizontal to the ocean. The ball was the size of a quarter held at arm's length and appeared to be about 1000 feet above the Atlantic. It had a long tail behind it. It was a very clear sighting that lasted several seconds. I don't think it was a UFO but maybe a comet of some type, although it traveled in a straight line unlike any comet or meteor that I've ever seen.

--- Anonymous

Ghost light

There's a two rut dirt road with a dead end in Columbia County near Olustee and if you go down to the end at night you can see this eerie ghost light rise up from this low swampy area. You can see it better during the warmer months. I have seen this strange light many times and it has been known to chase people. People say it is nothing but swamp gas or ball lightening, but it really does seem to follow behind a car down the road for several yards before it vanishes. I don't know what causes it to follow cars.

--- Randy S.

Hanging phantom

There's a very old oak tree near Brooksville near the Withlachoochee swamp that's called the hanging tree and on moonlight nights they say you can plainly see a form of a man hanging there. I know people who have seen this, but I haven't seen it.

--- Rebel Boy

What's cutting parts from cows?

I read in your Weird Florida book about mysterious cattle mutilations in Central Florida. I can tell you that this has also occurred on ranches farther south near Lake Okeechobee. In 1998 or 1999 there were several dead cattle found with their ears, tails, tongues and sexual parts surgically removed. During this same time there were two or three black helicopters seen in the same area and one was seen landing and taking off where a cow was found dead later. I do not think this is the work of extraterrestrials as some people think, I think it is the work of our own government doing some kind of secret experiment. The mystery was investigated but to this day remains unexplained.

--- Big Buck

What's adding parts to cows?

A guy that lives near me in Manatee County has a cow that was born with five legs. The extra leg is smaller but it has a hoof and just sort of hangs from the rear hip and is not used by the animal. It seems to get around with no trouble but it sure looks very odd. If you want to see it let me know.

--- Jimmy S.

Horse Spooked by Big Hairy Thing

I was told this story by a friend of mine about this girl who was riding her horse on Arial road near Oak Hill about 1989, I think. On either side of this road is a heavy thicket. She got a whiff of a foul odor like a skunk and went to turn her horse around when about forty yards in front of her something large and hairy crossed the road and disappeared into the woods. It was at this time the horse panicked and threw her off. The horse went for home and she did too as fast as she could. She related her story to everyone and they of coursed teased her about being thrown. According to her story, the thing she saw was about 7-8 feet tall with shaggy long hair and stood upright like a human and it stunk to the high heavens.

--- Sandy

Spanish soldier ghost

I know this sounds a little weird but we were exploring an island near Matanzas Inlet and saw a man in a Spanish soldier's uniform with a sword. He was just standing in a clearing. He went behind some palmetto bushes and when we went to check he was gone. The island is small and there were no other boat on the shore. I think we saw a ghost of a Spanish soldier.

--- Rob

Strange people in a cemetery

I used to walk by a city cemetery on my way home from work when I lived in Jacksonville. One evening, I think it was August 2003, I was walking by there and spied a group of people inside the cemetery with black robes on and carrying candles. They looked like they were going in and out of a large stone mausoleum. I stopped to watch and when I did, they stopped and looked back at me. I couldn't see any faces but I could tell I wasn't welcome. I hurried home and as I was walking up to the front door I saw a satanic symbol spray painted on the sidewalk. I think I saw satan worshippers in the cemetery but I don't know how they got a head of me so fast or how they knew where I lived. I felt the symbol was a warning. I moved about three weeks after that.

--- Anonymous

Girl in the glass coffin

There's a house on the road next to the river in either Cocoa or Rockledge that has a dead girl in a glass coffin. The glass coffin was sitting on the porch for many years, now I heard it's in a building in back of the house. I don't know if it's true but there's story that the dead girl's parents put her in the glass coffin when she died and propped her up on the porch so she would have a view of the river. I first thought it was just a legend before I found out that it's a true.

--- Sandy T.

Thrill Hill Road

In Lake County north of Mt. Dora there's a really steep, scary hill called Thrill Hill. This place is really awesome when you drive down the road you come to the top and it looks like you are going to fly off a cliff because the hill is so high and steep, all four wheels will leave the ground if you go too fast over the top, it's like the road falls out from under you. It's the scariest hill in Florida and it's off State Road 44 and 44A.

--- B.C.

The Devil's Den

If you go to Williston you can find the Devil's Den. We used to go there years ago when I was a kid. It is the strangest geological formation in Florida. It is an underground spring in a dry cavern with a beautiful clear water pool. Above the pool is a hole in the ceiling that lets sunlight in to light the inside. Divers have found many prehistoric animal bones in this spring.

--- Bob Barbour

Ghostly experience at St. Pete's Don Cesar Resort

In 1972 we were remodeling the Don Cesar Hotel. We were there for several years. During the night hours much of our work and equipment was being tampered with. We suspected juvenile delinquents. My boss suggested I earn some extra money by spending a couple of nights there in hopes of catching them, as it was getting expensive. I spent part of one night!! Sometime after midnight I began hearing noises, I didn't see anything but the sounds increased to the point that I was scared and called the police. Myself and two officers checked out the first three floors via the stairwell (the cops wanted to sneak up on them) Halfway up the cops had there firearms drawn. The sounds were everywhere, the floors, the stairwell, everywhere, banging, voices etc. it sounded like a large, rowdy party, was taking place. By the time we got to the third floor (terrified) the cops had enough and we retreated. Downstairs they expressed their sorrow at not being able to help me or explain what was going on. I remember them questioning each other (and me) as to what to put in there report. I think they agreed on unidentified noises, no details. Their report can probably be documented, although it won't say what really happened. Needless to say, the three of us left the scene. I would not return at night and my boss chose not to send in another, we opted to string lights through the entire building. The activity eventually stopped, at least for us.

--- D.G.

Strange light falls from sky

This morning [October 27, 2005] at approximately 4:15 am we observed a bright white light that suddenly streaked from high up down towards the river out by INT Golf Village in St Augustine. It was moving very fast but not in a trajectory as a plane or jet. The light hovered and then fell fast then went out but we could still see an object after the lights went out. It then disappeared. It was not a flare. When we got to work a guy that had been behind me about 10 minutes asked if anyone had seen that odd light that fell out of the sky and should we report it. I am scouring the news online to see if anyone else spotted it or if it was an explained phenomenon. I know it was not a meteor as I've seen enough of those besides seeing the darkened object after the light disappeared. We could hear no sound. Skies were clear and full of stars.

--- Ana

Author's note: The above sighting was reported to the National UFO Reporting Center.

He saw a gargoyle-like creature

Some years ago, I think it was 1974; my brother and I were hunting in a preserve in east Orange County. I can't recall the name of the area but it was just southeast of Bithlo. We were hunting turkey so we were on the lookout for anything that my resemble one. It was about sundown and had not bagged a bird so we decided to leave. On our way down this trail to the truck we saw something sitting in a large dead tree. At first we thought it was a large eagle but when we got right beneath it, the thing spread it wings a flew off. It looked like a monkey with wings, or one of those mythical creatures called a gargoyle. It was really weird and quite frightening simply because you never expect to see something that strange.

--- *JamesG.*

Don't go outside after dark

My grandparents lived in a very rural part of Marion County not far from the Big Scrub. [Ocala National Forest]. When I was very little I remember me and my cousins would stay with them. Each night gramps would bring in his dogs to stay with us in the house. He would put a big wooden bar across the door on the inside and told us never to go out side after dark. He always loaded his shot gun and propped it beside the door. I remember bears walking across the property in the daylight but what gramps was afraid of was these things that roamed around the outside of the house at night. They were not bears. They had killed two of his hounds which is why he kept the dogs inside at night.

I only remember seeing these things one time when we were allowed to look out the window. I was about five or six then, I am 59 years old now, so my memory may not be exact, but what I recall seeing was several large black shadowy things milling about outside in the moon light. There must have been at least five or six of these things and they looked like very large humans, but more broad and maybe seven or eight feet tall with very long arms. I do not recall any detailed features other than the general shape and size. Many years later I read about the people who have seen Big Foot and wonder if that was what was roaming around my grandparents place.

After reading your book I thought you would be interested in my memory which I have never told many people. The area is all built up now but back then in the early 1950s it was a very remote wilderness. I have also read how these half human things have been seen around the Ocala Forest.

--- *Mrs. M.E. Crosby*

Leon County's old haunted Jail

I used to live and work in Tallahassee, Florida. Back in the mid-'70's I worked in the Old Leon County Jail just down from the Capitol Building. It is located at 409 E. Gaines Street. I worked for the Division of Archives, History and Records Management and we were officed in the Old Leon County Jail while we were waiting for the completion of the State Museum. I had heard many, many stories about the old jail being haunted. I just did not believe in the afterlife at that time. Windows and doors would open and close, the copy machine would turn on by itself when no one was even near it, footsteps were heard, but no one was in sight, one man (very believable and creditable) told me he was knocked down by an unseen force on the stairwell landing, things would move with no one in sight and strange noises were often heard down in the basement when no one was in the basement. The old cells were still there and some of the workers that worked back in the cells would feel someone tap them on the shoulder, and when they turned around to see whom had tapped them, well. . . no one was in sight. Well, it did not take long for me to become a believer.

--- *Anonymous*

Strange ball of light

I saw this bright orange ball of light hovering about 500 feet above the tree line 3 times during a two week period in the month of January 1993. The first time I saw it I was driving home from work around 6:30 pm EST. I was traveling north on 441 about 7 miles north of Gainesville on my way home. I then noticed this orange ball of light hovering above the tree line. It just sat there. It glowed but didn't move. At first I thought maybe it was a helicopter, but the more I looked at it, I realized it couldn't be a helicopter because the light wasn't a searchlight. It didn't reflect a beam of light: it just glowed. It couldn't have been a plane or helicopter because there were no other lights on it and no strobes. I didn't stop to watch further because I had to get home. It was still in the same place as I watched from my rear view mirror until I was too far away from it to see it anymore. The second time I saw it was in almost the same spot, but it was further north along the road. I saw it again about a week after that. This time I stopped my car on the edge of the road to check it out. Unfortunately the height of the trees next to the road, it blocked my view. I thought surely I would hear an engine of some kind, but I didn't. I have driven this stretch of everyday for the last 13 years and I have seen nothing like that before or since.

--- *A.H.*

Holy chupacabras, what's this?

I live in Tampa. My room mate claims that they have seen a Anteater-looking animal that can jump up onto 5 foot Trash dumpsters. I didn't see it but we're looking more. I guess its brown and black with a medium coat of hair. Long nose about 6 inch or a foot long like an anteater.

— Ryan

Author's note: Several stories have been received from the Tampa area relating to sightings of an anteater-like creature. Chupacabra? Who Knows? My advice, is don't feed 'em and they'll go away.

Okay, folks, it ain't swamp gas

I heard 3 different stories about experiences from the same person. They were sitting under the bridge about this time 2 years ago and over from the top of the bridge you could see the silhouette of someone looking down and over. Two of the people ran to the top of the bridge on different ends and there was nothing there. It happened again a little while later. Another time a bunch of them were sitting on the bridge waiting and waiting and finally just gave up. They parked the vehicles and 2 of them walked off about 20 yards. They heard a faint scream, and running. The scream got louder and closer. They ran over to the rest of the group and everyone quieted down and now the sound of a woman screaming and running footsteps were really close. They jumped in the cars and left. one time when out there they actually saw the lights pull right up and behind them. So stories of it being swamp gas I believe are false.

— Anonymous

Author's note: This person is talking about the Oviedo Light which you'll find more information about in the section titled Florida's Weird Files plus my own encounter with this phenomenon.

A house possessed?

In 1987, my mother and I had a house built 5 miles shy of Lakeland, Fl. in a small town called Highland City. Right after we moved in, I would see a white mist like come down the hallway almost every night. Things would appear and disappear all the time. One afternoon, my mother and I had flipped a coin to decide what we were going to eat for dinner that night, and when we flipped the coin we allowed it to land on the carpet, as soon as it hit the carpet the coin vanished. We searched for it for about 30 minutes but could not find the coin. About 2 days later after vacuuming I put the vacuum up in the hall closet and went to sit down in the recliner where we had lost the coin and looked down and there it was! My mother would hear voices and music every night that she went to sleep in the master bedroom. Several years later after she moved out and I got married and moved back in. I would lay down to take a nap and I would hear music in the master bedroom and have demonic dreams. If I slept in any other room of the house I had good dreams, but that master bedroom made me feel sick to my stomach all the time and the dreams and music got louder and louder, needless to say I no longer live in that house.

— Angela

Strange shenanigans

I wanted to quickly tell a story that currently has no ending. I just moved into an apartment in Saint Petersburg in the old northeast section of town. It is a loft apartment in a 1920's era rooming house. It is very large and has several rooms and very large walk in attic spaces. I have lived here for a little over a month and in the last 2 weeks strange rapping and thumps have been coming from the attic spaces at night.

I have called the landlord fearing possums or raccoons might have taken up house but after an extensive search nothing was found. The rapping continues every night and are more frequent during full moons. They start on one end of the apartment and go all the way to the other end. A few days ago I was awakened by the sound of a pot being beaten on the kitchen counter. I got very frightened and carefully peeked out of my bedroom thinking it might be an intruder. There was nothing, except the boiling pot sitting on the counter next to the sink. Another incident happened last week where I was in a rush to get out the door to work and I could not find my keys. I searched for 30 minutes and was quite frustrated because I always hang them on a hook by the door. I found them underneath the sofa in the living room. It was one of the first places I checked and they were not there that time, only after looking the second time did they appear. It was then I called my landlord and she told me the house, in particular, my apartment was haunted and offered to let me break my lease. Now I know that who ever is haunting this place just wants to let me know it's here. Last night I saw a white little globe of light out of the corner of my eye float past a candle holder near the front window of the apartment. I know I actually saw it because I looked over at it and it vanished quickly.

I am not really scared, just curious about it. My landlord came over and told it not to disturb me and it seemed to work.

— D.B.

STRANGE FLORIDA II

A paranormal double whammy

I have two curious tales to tell. First, I saw one of those floating balls of light early morning at the end of the Interstate4 bridge over the river where the I-4 Dead Zone is, right where the construction was going on, but this was at three o'clock in the morning and construction didn't have anything to do with it. Two cars even pulled over to the side of the road to look at it and it just faded out. Do you think it was one of those spirit lights? The next story I have is not new, it happened about 20 years ago when I was fishing at night with my Uncle Paul in what is called the Mosquito Lagoon over next to the Kennedy Space Port. we saw a round flat object that was glowing under the water. It moved right under our boat and down the intercoastal waterway until we couldn't see it any longer. I don't know what it was but if it had been in the air I would have said it was a ufo but it was under the water. Many people tell me that they see a lot of strange lights in that area. I was wondering if anybody else has seen anything like this?

--- Roger M.

Author's note: There have been two other sightings in Mosquito Lagoon since 1970 involving an alleged USO, [unidentified submerged object]. It should be mentioned that this large body of saline water has certain luminous marine life. Of course this would not account for a fisherman's 1969 report of flying glowing disk seen hovering over the lagoon.

Mystery moray caught

We was fishing In Lake George for specks and something got my line, when I pulled it in there was a five foot eel on the line. WE took the thing to the Fish & Wildlife people and they said it was some kind of moray eel and don't know how it got into the lake. The St Johns River flows thru Lake George, maybe it came in from the ocean. It had a mouth full of ugly teeth too.

--- Alan

Now you see her. Now you don't!

Something I have thought about for years occurred around 1987 on route 27. My brother and I were going to Fisheating Creek when I seen a Lady in a long flowing gown walking toward us on the side of the road. It was mid-day and I said to my brother "Look at that", I then glanced at my brother and looked back to the lady and she had vanished. My brother never seen her and I think she was only showing herself to me.

--- Scotty

Pictures from Heaven

One day in 2000 I was walking to work down Himes Ave. in Tampa when suddenly I witnessed a large framed picture crash to the sidewalk in front of me. As I looked up to see where it came from, I witnessed another like it, and finally a third slightly larger. There was nothing they could have fallen from and as it was 6 am there were no people up tossing framed pictures outside their homes. Not to mention they fell straight down and not at any angles. There were no parabolic trajectories here. I still do not know where they came from. The two smaller ones were blue paintings of clouds and ocean waves. The larger, was orange and had a scene of ducks flying off of a lake like you would imagine right after a hunter's gunshot. The funny thing was that all of them were in frames behind glass, but the largest one was odd since the glass was obviously in tact, before it landed on the concrete, but the painting itself was riddled w bullet holes. the glass had no evidence of having been shot through. They just all fell from directly above the spot they landed on. Also, they all landed in the same spot.

--- Bill

Ghost dog or deer or whatever

One night as I was driving home from my friend's house in Lutz, Florida I was going down a long stretch of non-lit road called DeBuel Road. All of a sudden before me I caught site of something that seemed to be between the size of large dog and a small deer. I'm not sure which it resembled more although it looked a little like a greyhound. We do have greyhounds here in Tampa too. Anyway, it was running across the road, and it disappeared into the woods on the north side of the road. The strange thing about this sighting was that the ghost dog/deer, or whatever it was appeared to be iridescent blue and I could see the lines on the road right through its body.

--- Scotty

Uncanny hotel experience

I have a story to tell you about the old hotel in Cassadaga that was experienced by me and my friend. The room was very quaint and like being back in the past and somehow felt different. After we returned from dinner, about 9 pm we sat in the room and tried doing a séance just for fun. We used a folding card table and put our hands on it to see if anything would happen. Now I must tell you that neither one of us are mediums or possess any kind of psychic ability, but after about an hour of fooling with the table it began to quiver. What I mean is that it became shaky. We removed our hands because we thought we might be causing it but the table continued to shake for about five minutes. I can't say we were frightened but it was very curious because there was no reason for the table to shake like that. We sat and talked about it for a while then turned off the light and went to bed at about midnight. I think it was about 1 o'clock in the morning when something just told me to wake up. I looked at the foot of the bed and saw a whitish transparent woman standing there looking at us. I rubbed my eyes and looked again, she was still there just looking. I nudged my friend to wake up and my friend saw the woman too. I know for a fact that we saw a ghost because two of us saw the same thing. This ghost was there for at least fifteen minutes and then she just slowly fading away. It was a little creepy but really not scary. I think we were too busy trying to figure out what we were looking at. Have you ever heard of a spirit being seen in that hotel ?

--- Shana

Author's note: For those who are unaware, Cassadaga is a unique Florida community where all the residents are mediums. There are several tales about spirits being seen in the Cassadaga Hotel. As for the shaking table, that's nothing new, I have witnessed Cassadaga's spiritualists levitate tables. Some things are really stranger than you think!.

Invisible forces at work

My husband has a true story of a house he rented and lived in on Las Olas Blvd. in Fort Lauderdale. It had spirits that he, his former girlfriend, her daughter, and a babysitter all witnessed. One incident of the daughter and sitter being pushed and held down on a bed by an invisible force was so frightening to them that he and his girlfriend were called to suddenly cut short their vacation in Spain and come home. They even had water dripping continually from an unknown source in the living room ceiling. It was investigated by professional plumbers and roofers and no source for the water was ever found. There were sounds of conversations going on in apparently empty rooms from time to time too. Needless to say, they didn't stay long in that house.

--- Lisa

The meat loaf from Hell

I don't know if this is strange, but it's a little weird. Don't get me wrong, I'm a good cook but for some reason my meat loaf isn't fit for human consumption. I make the worst meat loaf, even the dog won't eat it. My kids would find an excuse to eat elsewhere whenever I made meat loaf. On more than one occasion, it disintegrated; I had to scrape it out of the pan. Another time I had to throw the pay away. I doubt that Big Foot would eat my meat loaf, it would kill him. I don't know what I'm doing wrong, I have used all kinds of recipes, tried various seasonings, and it still tastes like the meat loaf from Hell. The strange part is that I still feel driven by unknown meat loaf forces to keep trying to cook a good meat loaf.

---Susan

Black Ball in the Sky or a UFO?

I always try to watch all of the rockets, especially the space shuttles launch from Cape Canaveral. On July 4, 2006, the space shuttle Discovery took off at 2:37 PM. I wasn't in a good spot to see the launch (trees in the way), so about ten minutes before the shuttle took off, I started driving looking for a unobstructed view of the east. I didn't make it far, and at 2:37 I pulled over into a church parking lot in Osteen that had an open field behind it. By the time I got my camera out, the shuttle was probably about 30 seconds into its launch. I started taping and once the shuttle was no longer visible, I noticed something else in the sky. It was round black object up in the sky off in the distance in the same direction that the shuttle took off from. Judging from the clouds that the shuttle passed behind, and what the object was in front of, the black object was closer than the shuttle, but it was hard for me to estimate a size. After watching the object a bit, I realized it wasn't moving correctly to be a balloon. For example, it would be at one spot in the sky, and then would move back and forth horizontally. Another time it started getting low in the sky rather quickly compared to the speed that it was drifting at at other times. It also appeared to be just barely entering clouds at times. It would fade behind a cloud, but never actually disappear totally.

Looking back at the video later on, it appears that the object was in the area the whole time the launch was going up, but nobody spotted it because everyone was so focused on the shuttle.

---Anonymous

Author's note: Thanks to this witness, I was able to view footage of the object which appeared to be a dark sphere or globe suspended about cloud level. The size was difficult to determine; however, considering the distance and altitude, it could have been the size of a small car. Discounting all possibilities, like conventional aircraft, balloons, birds, etc., and considering the high security of the air space around Kennedy Space Center during a launch, no one could identify the strange object.

Transylvania Transplant?

In Altamonte Springs near my apartment there is a guy everybody says is a vampire. He dresses in black and only comes out at night and usually wears a top hat. Many people have seen him and he has almost become a legend. Some say he carries a cane with a metal wolf's head on top of it. Other people say he was wearing a cape when they saw him. I did not believe the stories until one morning about one o'clock I saw him near the funeral home near the intersection of 436 and 427. He crossed in front of my car and I got a good look at him and he looked like somebody from out of the past. I don't know if he is a real vampire or not but he is creepy looking.

---Lynne

Author's note: I don't know if he is a real vampire or not, but judging by the half-dozen emails I have received about him, he has really stirred people up with his eerie appearances.

A Man-Fish Tale

I remembered this from a young age when lived in Panama City and, after questioning my mother about my memory, she confirmed what she could of it. Somewhere between 1970 and 1973 she believes was when the incident took place. It was ALL over the local news and everyone spoke about it, but strangely, the very next day, all news reports were hushed. A group of teachers responded to children's screams on the shore near Hathaway Bridge. Witnesses described a man with the tail of a fish emerging from the water near the group of children. I remember several adults talking about it. I had almost forgotten until we were having one of our family gab sessions.

-Anonymous

Silver Ball Seen By Fisherman

I was at the beach just south of Jacksonville and was surf fishing late one afternoon and saw a round silver looking ball about five miles out. I don't know what it was but it was no balloon and appeared very large considering I could see it at such a distance.

-Bill Berringer

Flesh Eating Pink Cloud

Have you ever heard the old story about a pink cloud that eats the flesh off people. It is an old legend and is supposed to be around the Tomoka River. I grew up there and heard many stories about it. I have seen swamp gas in that area but it wasn't pink.

-Shannon W.

FLORIDA'S WEIRD FILES PAST AND PRESENT

Boy Survived After Being Swallowed Alive by a Gator

In 1895, a newspaper reported that Edward Rowland was just a boy when he was swallowed whole by a giant alligator.

One day the Rowland family went fishing on Dunn's Creek, young Edward wandered off and found a spot to sit down. Suddenly a huge alligator emerged from the water and started toward the boy. As the child tried to run, he slipped, falling into the water right in front of the reptile. The big gator, measuring nearly 15 feet in length, snapped the boy up and swallowed him whole. Upon hearing his screams, Edward's parents frantically ran to the scene as their son disappeared down the reptile's throat. Edward's father had a gun and immediately shot the gator through the brain. Figuring his son was probably dead, the father immediately pulled out a knife and began cutting open the big gator's belly to retrieve the child's body so it could be taken to the local undertaker for burial. However, upon removing the boy's body from the saurian's slimy cavity, the boy began to show signs of life. The father began to resuscitate his son; amazingly the boy had survived being swallowed alive! The gator's teeth had crushed the boy's ankles and for the rest of his life he had to wear steel ankle braces. Edward Rowland still holds the distinction of being the only known person to have survived being swallowed alive down the throat of a Florida alligator.

Phantom Buffalo Seen In Downtown Orlando

"Yes, I've seen it," said Tricia Earhardt, "It was like smoke in the form of a bison, right there on the corner of Church Street." Others claim to have heard the buffalo's hooves on the downtown streets. So, what's a ghost buffalo doing in downtown Orlando?

On October, 22, 1912, the famous Buffalo Bill's Wild West Show pulled into town for a grand performance that attracted hundreds from surrounding communities. When the show was over and the animals were being loaded onto the show's train, one buffalo, Barney, went berserk. The big bison went on a rampage through the streets of downtown Orlando. Fearing for peoples' safety and damage to store fronts, wranglers quickly put the creature down. It was said that Barney was suffering from "Texas Fever" which affected his wild behavior. Whatever the case, Barney's life ended in downtown Orlando. His carcass was sent to a Jacksonville rendering plant but his spirit must have remained in Orlando if we are to believe the sighting claims of those who have seen the phantom bison.

The Mystery of Florida's Crazy Old State Seal

Officially, since becoming a state in 1845, Florida has had four state seals. the State of Florida has had four state seals. The longest used seal was adopted in 1868; however, it contained numerous inaccuracies. It showed mountains, two of which were snow capped, one that some say is really an Egyptian pyramid, then there was an Indian woman wearing the feathered headdress of a chief, moreover, the headdress was the type worn by Western Plains Indians. If that was not enough flaws, add to it a side-wheel steamboat which appeared to be sinking, a bag of coffee and a cocoa palm, which is not a tree indigenous to Florida.

The artist of the mixed-up seal is unknown, but one account claims the design was actually intended for one of the western states. When the design was rejected, the artist simply sold the design to Florida at a discount. Whether the story is true or not, the state did not correct its weird seal until May 1985 when a new state seal was designed.

Florida's Crazy Old State Seal

Lion Terrorizes a City Hall

October 18, 1946 a 200 pound mountain lion, named Sid, escaped from the Sanford Municipal Zoo, then located across the street from the city hall, and began roaming the center of city government. Sid first strolled over to the city jail and after scaring the heck out of everyone, including the desk sergeant, he headed for city hall. The big lion then leaped against the window of the city manager's office and sent city employees fleeing down the halls. Sid was finally rounded and returned to the zoo.

Schoolhouse Disappears

Following the Civil War there was a one room schoolhouse south of Archer, near where highway 27-41 passes Blue Peter Lake. One day after class when the teacher and students were on their way home, a loud rumbling noise was heard. They looked back and to their amazement the sounds seemed to be coming from beneath the school. All of a sudden water began gurgling up from the ground forming a pool around the school. They watched as the school listed to one side and then sank out of sight into newly formed pond. Today there is a small lake at the location and fishermen say if you row out to the middle, and look down on a clear day, you can still see the sunken schoolhouse.

The Enchanted Halloween Village

Art and Treena Kaye Litka have a secluded place in the woods outside of Sanford, Florida. As you drive the road to their house, you'll be greeted with humorous epitaphs on tombstones along the way. If that sounds strange, well, lets just say this is where it's Halloween all year.

Art, a college professor, and his wife, Treena Kaye, are notorious collectors of Halloween props and memorabilia, usually acquired when retailers sell off leftover merchandise after each Halloween.

Inside the Litka home you'll find a life size talking Frankenstein, skeletons and skulls, and animated props like a realistic mechanical bat that flaps around in an overhead circle. The favorite with guests, is the complete model railroad layout with its ghoulish-themed buildings and creatures, and yes, even Beetlejuice feels at home here.

Phantom Farmer Seen Plowing a Field in Fernandina

In September 1892, the *Boston Globe* ran a news article concerning a ghost seen plowing a field in Fernandina, Florida. The apparition was reported by a man named Peterson, who claimed that a ghost was plowing his cornfield in the moonlight. The apparition appeared at midnight with a team of oxen, but when Peterson sent his oldest son to investigate the phenomenon, the boy walked right through the ghost, plow and oxen. The specter was described by Peterson, as dressed in laborer clothing with a wide brimmed hat concealing his features. Peterson's neighbors came to witness the strange sight, which, according to newspaper reports, was seen on several occasions. Local folks with knowledge of the phantom claimed it was the ghost of the former owner of the farm who had committed suicide in his field one morning.

Mystery Hole Near Brooksville

In May 1894, a mysterious hole was reported in the *Chicago Tribune* that was located near Brooksville. Local folks said it was a haunted hole and referred to it as the "Brooksville Pool." However, in 1894, people described the hole as "like a sink in which water swirls around and drags down floating logs out of sight into its murky darkness."

They also claimed that many people had "mysteriously disappeared into the hole never to be heard from again." If that was indeed true, then their bones probably ended up in the aquifer...the underground source of Florida's drinking water.

It was alleged in early newspaper accounts, and local gossip, that a secret society, under the cover of darkness, once gagged and bound their adversaries and threw them into the mystery hole.

Present historians believe the Mystery Hole story is based on a local water-filled, sinkhole that had a whirlpool in the bottom.

A Living Ball of Snakes

On January 20, 1888, a train on the South Florida Railroad was forty miles south of Kissimmee when it encountered an unusual track obstruction. The engineer was running at full steam on the line that ran through a swamp, when he noticed a large ball about 100 yards ahead of the engine. Before the engineer could apply the brakes, he hit the ball. To his astonishment, it was a big living ball of entwined snakes, with their wiggling heads sticking out in all directions. The ball of serpents was the size of a bushel basket and when the engine hit it, the ball exploded with wiggling snakes flying into the air, some landing on the cab and cow catcher.

With snakes squirming on the engine, the train continued on down the line about five miles to the next station. A newspaper account said, "People standing on the platform gave a wide berth" as the serpent draped engine rolled to a hissing stop. The station estimated there were 150 snakes of various colors on the engine, with black ones being the most predominant.

Did a UFO Crash in Brevard County??

On the night of July 21, 1979, a strange glowing object was observed hovering over Indialantic. People jammed the phones at the Sheriff's Department with frantic reports of a UFO casting an amber light in the night sky. One report claimed the object was circling a house. Authorities contacted Patrick Air Force Base for assistance and called out the Fire Department. The strange object was reported over the Banana River and moving west at 400 mph toward the city of Melbourne. It seemed to elude local law enforcement before it crashed in the river. A sheriff's patrol boat quickly responded to the crash site. Among the tiny amount of debris, the authorities recovered parts of a kite that had been carrying a pen light. This is proof that every light you see in the sky isn't a spaceship, although in this case, the object was truly an *unidentified flying object*...at least, until it was identified.

Submerged City Found North of St. Augustine

This remarkable story appeared in several newspapers, including the *St. Augustine Press*, in April 1872. Following the heavy gales of a hurricane, the remains of an ancient city was discovered seven miles north of St. Augustine on the west shore of the North River.

Reports came from local people who said the city was beneath the water and consisted of coquina walls, wells, and foundations of houses. Nearby they also found a previously unknown coquina quarry. Coquina is the rock made of compressed shells which were used to construct early Spanish buildings in St. Augustine. The discovery was made after five days of heavy winds drove the water out of the river to an extent not experienced before. The quarry showed extensive use, most likely for material in building the mysterious city. The site was about four miles north of where Ponce de Leon landed in Florida.

Recent research into this 1872 story has found no additional follow-up articles to the report, nor do historians know of any submerged city. However, this story may actually refer to an early discovery of the remains of an African-American settlement called Fort Mose. Located north of St. Augustine, and established in 1738, this settlement was also known as Gracia Real de Santa Teresa de Mose. It was inhabited by about 100 escaped slaves from the British colonies to the north. The settlement consisted of a church, a dwelling for the priest, wells, a lookout tower and twenty-two houses. Fort Mose, now under the jurisdiction of the National Park Service, is considered the first free black community in what is now the United States.

Bone Yard Tale Was Really True

A certain downtown section of Daytona was once called the "bone yard" by local kids. Builders brushed the tales of human bones off as mere lore. For century, commercial buildings occupied the site and stories of bones faded into history. Then, in November 2005, a construction crew unearthed a skull and other bones beneath a city sidewalk at the corner of Bay and Beach streets, evidence that the lore of the bone yard was indeed true. At first, the human remains were a mystery until archaeologists identified them as belonging to an early indigenous tribe known as the Timucuans. These early people died out over 200 years ago, but at the arrival of the Spanish, their population was 200,000. Only bones belonging to a single individual were found, leaving us to wonder if we are walking on the dead beneath the sidewalks of Daytona. More historic burials in Florida have been destroyed by construction and development than by vandals in Florida. Early roads were often paved with shell from burial mounds containing human remains, and many present day residential developments and commercial centers now sit on top of sacred burial mounds and old family cemeteries

Ancient Spanish Ship discovered buried on a Florida Navy Base

In 2004, in the wake of Hurricane Ivan, a contractor rebuilding a swimming pool on Pensacola's Naval Air Station unearthed a Spanish Ship four centuries old. Unlike other Spanish shipwrecks, this one is on land under 75 feet of sand. The Navy base is built on what was once the 1698 Spanish settlement, Presidio Santa Maria de Galve.

Secret Government Experiments Exposed

In 1956 and 1957, Floridians were, unknowingly, guinea pigs for a secret government experiment. Scientists from the U.S. Army's Biological Warfare Center secretly released swarms of mosquitoes infected with yellow fever and dengue fever in Avon Park. Hundreds of residents fell ill with respiratory problems, swollen glands, fevers, encephalitis, which resulted in several deaths. Army researchers came to town disguised as health care workers to photograph and test the victims.

The Avon Park case was not the only time Floridians have suffered from a secret government experiment. In 1955, in a still classified project, Tampa Bay citizens suffered from a whooping cough epidemic after the CIA released bacteria from the Army's Chemical and Biological Warfare Center. During the mid-1960s, in yet another still classified scheme, a government agency conducted secret LSD tests on college campuses in Florida.

Strange Coincidence

In 1926, 64 year old Sexton Johnson, former superintendent of schools in Orlando, ran his car over an embankment in Tampa and drowned in two feet of water. On the same day, his brother drowned after falling from a ship in Jacksonville.

A Gravity Defying Hill
Where up is really down...

This is another classic subject of the weird that must be included in any book about Florida's strangeness. In Lake Wales, about fifty miles south of Orlando, there is a hill which seems to defy the law of gravity. You can stop your car at the bottom of the hill, shift into neutral, and your car will roll up hill. The mysterious hill has become so popular that, on weekends, there are thirty cars lined up to defy the laws of gravity.

Pioneers knew about this strange hill when their horses seemed to exert more labor going down the hill than going up it. They found that an orange placed on the road would roll uphill.

Legends have evolved about the area being a sacred Indian burial ground and that spirits are fooling around with the laws of nature. The strange spot became known as Spook Hill. By the time motorcars came into popular use, Spook Hill was already a Central Florida tourist attraction. It still attracts tourists, perhaps because the most unusual thing about Spook Hill is that, unlike other Florida attractions, it's still free!

But has gravity gone haywire here or is there some other explanation? There's no doubt that cars, skateboards, balls, or most any round object, all seem to roll about 100 feet up the incline of the hill. Some say that they can sense that the gravitational pull is working in reverse at Spook Hill. Someone has even promoted the idea that wrist watches run backwards at the mystery hill.

There are crazy hills all over the South. In San Antonio, Texas, tourists are pulled toward "Gravity Hill," a shallow incline that crests at a railroad crossing. "Booger Hill" near Cummings, Georgia, is probably the anti-gravity hill with the most traffic. In Helena, Arkansas, at the intersection of Sulphur Springs Road and Highway 49, you'll find "Gravity Hill." In North Carolina, there's "Mystery Hill" and Princeton, Kentucky's "Gravity Hill" is supposedly haunted by a man and his daughters who were run over by an ice truck. Another spook hill is in Burkittsville, Maryland, the town of *Blair Witch* movie fame, while others can be found in Nashville, Tennessee and near Bonaire, Georgia, where, according to legend, a witch collected tolls in the 1850s. Like Florida's "Spook Hill," there are paranormal explanations attached to all of these strange hills.

For a scientific angle on Spook Hill the author contacted the Department of Geology at the University of Florida. "It's impossible," replied a state geologist. "There are no unexplained gravitational anomalies at work at Spook Hill. You can verify this with a simple carpenter's level." Leave it to a scientist to spoil the fun.

Indeed, a carpenter's level will quickly explain the phenomenon, as the author found out. Cars do not roll up hill, they actually roll down it. Spook Hill is an optical illusion caused by the local topography. If an observer looks in one direction, the hill appears to be an incline, but a glance in the opposite direction exposes the optical trickery of this strange hill.

The City of Lake Wales has placed small directional signs around town so tourists can find the famous hill. However, the real mystery may be in trying to locate Spook Hill. Pranksters occasionally turn the signs, sending hill seekers off in the opposite direction, which the author can verify from experience.

Where is Fort Bragdon?

A historical marker with a green metal plaque marks the spot on a rise in Orlando's historic Greenwood Cemetery. It states that the location was designated as Fort Bragdon in the honor of Major George Bragdon for his service with the Seminole Chapter of the National SOJ Inc. and Col. Geo. F. Unmacht Camp of Heroes of '76.

Although the marker might confuse any historian, this is not a site of a real fort, it's actually the grave of Major George D. Bragdon, who, at the ripe old age of 90, died on November 11, 1968. It seems Major George had always wanted a military fort named for him, so following his passing, his old buddies carried out his wishes by designating the plot as Fort Bragdon.

A Big Fish that Didn't Get Away

From November 1913, comes a newspaper story of a monster fish caught off the coast of Florida by Captain Charles H. Thompson of Miami. Okay, hold on for some amazing figures. It weighed 15 tons and was 45 feet long. Its circumference measured 23 feet and 9 inches. The monster's mouth had several thousand teeth and was more than 3 feet wide when open. The gills were 4 feet long. The tongue was 40 inches long. The pectoral fin was 5 feet and 3 feet wide. Its dorsal fin was 3 feet long and the tail was 10 feet wide. It's skin was 3 inches thick and without scales. It was alleged to have been an unknown fish and not a whale or porpoise, as we might suspect. According to the news report, scientists believed it was an inhabitant of the far-down ocean depths, at least 1500 feet below the surface, and that it was *"thrown up by some subterranean volcanic disturbance which injured its diving apparatus."*

The monster was harpooned off Knight's Key by a crew headed by Captain Thompson. In the struggle the subdue the big creature, four harpoons were shot into it as well as 150 bullets. The skin was so thick that the bullets caused little damage. The fight between man and beast lasted non-stop for two days and a night before the big fish gave up. Using an anchor chain, it was lashed still fighting to the side of Thompson's 30 ton boat. Its tail slammed a powerful blow into the boat destroying the rudder and propeller. Two tugboats were called to help bring the Thompson and his catch to Miami. Upon arrival it appeared dead, but suddenly it came to life again, this time smashing a portion of a dock, destroying a dock house and breaking a man's leg. The huge fish was rolled upon the beach where it became a curiosity until the City of Miami ordered it be removed before it got too smelly. The Smithsonian Institution sent J.S. Warmbeth, a taxidermist, down to Miami to prepare the carcass for preservation and study.

The creature was embalmed using 15 barrels of formaldehyde. The thickness of the hide made the work exceedingly difficult. The skin was mounted on steel ribs to restore the original form and then the whole thing was put on a flat car and hauled to Atlantic City, where thousands of curiosity seekers viewed it. A millionaire, who had seen the fish, had it transported to Indianapolis so he could prove to his friends that it wasn't just another big fish story.

Tampa's Devil Zone

Beginning at Egmont Key and extending just beyond the Skyline Bridge there is an area of Tampa Bay in which strange things occur. The zone roughly covers about twelve square miles and is known by some fishermen and boaters as the Devil's Zone. It's sort of a mini-Bermuda Triangle infamous for a high number of boat engine failures, drownings, suicides, homicides, weird creatures, maritime accidents, failure of navigation devices, sightings of phantoms, and unidentified flying objects. Although skeptics scoff at the claims, Tampa's Devil Zone has been the subject of talk radio shows and is mentioned in many books.

The Legend of Flight 401

On December 29, 1972, an passenger jetliner, flight 401, enroute to Miami crashed into the murky darkness of the Everglades. The tragic accident claimed 101 lives, including the captain and flight engineer. Parts of the plane were later salvaged and used on other passenger planes. Passengers and crew flying on later aircraft having recycled parts from flight 401, have reported encountering the ghosts of 401's captain and flight engineer. Most of the stories come from credible witnesses, including pilots, crew members and maintenance personnel. A retired stewardess told me about seeing the ghosts on a crew member on one of her flights in a lavatory with a sink that belonged to flight 401. The high flying spirits seem to make only brief appearances, but some passengers claim to have actually spoken to them. As we might expect, the airlines companies involved will not comment on the alleged experiences.

Lost Tribe

Prior to 1935, there were several reports, many from Seminole Indians, about an unknown tribe living in the Everglades. They were said to use flint tipped spears, dress in primitive garb made of skins, and spoke an unknown language. Some believed they were remnants of the prehistoric Calusa.

Killer Bees

Forget the dangers of hurricanes and wild gator's, the Sunshine State is being invaded by killer bees. Known as Africanized honeybees, these super angry bees have a real attitude problem and it doesn't take much to provoke them to attack. Since escaping from Brazilian lab in 1972, they have killed 1000 people in the Americas, including 14 in the United States. In Florida, swarms of killer bees have attacked and killed dogs in Miami and Sarasota. In LaBelle, a full grown horse was stung to death by the winged killers. It was estimated the horse had been stung 2000 times on the face and neck.

Apiary experts say the bees normally go after a person's nostrils and mouth inflicting as many as 400 horrible stings. In 2005, utility workers in St. Lucie County were attacked by a swarm. In Lantana, several sheriff's deputies ended up in the hospital after being attacked while chasing burglary suspects in the woods.

So far no humans in Florida have been killed, however, the killer bee situation is becoming a serious problem in some areas. Informational literature about killer bees with bee-proofing suggestions is available from the Florida Department of Agriculture.

The Big One That Was Caught

This will give you a "Jaws" story to think about when swimming in the Gulf of Mexico. In May 2006, Captain Andy Whitbread of Fort Myers caught a 13 foot 4 inch long, 750 pound hammerhead shark off Florida's southwest Gulf coast. The largest hammerhead on record prior to Whitbread's catch was caught in Freeport, Texas in 1976. It weighed 620 pounds.

Voodoo Skull in Luggage

In February 2006, a woman arriving Haiti at the Fort Lauderdale International airport was arrested when airport security screeners discovered a human skull in her luggage.

The grisly skull still contained flesh, teeth and hair, with organic material inside the cranial cavity. The 30-year old woman, a Haitian-born U.S. citizen, explained that the skull was to be used in voodoo rituals in belief that it would ward off evil spirits. She explained that the skull had been purchased from a man in Haiti.

One person suggested, since voodoo is considered a religious practice, she ought be granted Constitutional rights protecting her freedom of religion. Whatever the case, customs agents charged her with failing to declare a human head and transporting hazardous material on an air carrier.

Voodoo is secretly practiced in Florida's Haitian communities.

The Wonder House

After being told by his doctor he only had a short time to live, Conrad Schuck moved from Pittsburgh to Bartow, Florida. In 1925, he defied his doctor's prediction and began building a strange house at 1075 Mann Road which is known as the Wonder House. It was strange enough to be featured in *Ripley's Believe It or Not*.

Schuck continued to add on to his unusual house through the 1940's. He installed an air conditioning system which used rainwater in cooling, a large cement pool in front of the house and several outdoor bathtubs on secluded porches. The most curious feature is the many mirrors he installed which allow you to view the front door from almost any place on the property.

Flying Saucer House

Just up from Gulf Breeze, Florida's so-called UFO hotbed, it appears the aliens have built a house in the shape of a UFO. Known as the Flying Saucer House, this strange circular structure sits on Pensacola Beach. Actually it was built to withstand hurricanes that have an annual habit of slamming into the panhandle.

The white metal house sits twelve feet above the ground, built to lift up and float if the area is ever flooded. That's a good idea considering the aftermath of Katrina.

Although it has no extraterrestrial connections, it does look exactly like a flying saucer which inspired one of its several owners to put pictures of Aliens in the windows.

The Aliens have since been removed from the windows, but if you want to see the Flying Saucer House it's off highway 98 across the Three Mile Bridge, east of Pensacola, on Santa Rosa Island.

STRANGE FLORIDA II

Florida's Weirdest Bicycle Tour

In March 2006, a dozen BMX freestyle bike riders from several states and England struck out on what can only be described as the Sunshine State's strangest bike trip. With a route based on *Charlie Carlson's* popular book *Weird Florida* the riders went on a quest for Florida's weirdest places and roadside oddities. Matt Coplon of Profiler Racing put together the tour that began in Tampa and stretched from Tallahassee down through Key West to Dry Tortugas Island.

This Place Was Once the Coldest Spot in Central Florida

Located between Lake Monroe and Sanford next to an abandoned railroad yard, are the ruins of a strange structure which has quite a claim in Florida's industrial history. This is all that remains of the huge Mountain Ice Company's ice plant built in 1922 to provide ice for railroad freight cars. At one time this was the largest building in volume size in Central Florida, and no doubt the coldest too since it was also the second largest producing ice plant in the world. The colossal, double insulated walls surrounded a football field-size storage area that held a daily average of 700 tons of block ice.

So why was so much ice needed? Well, prior to 1940, this area of Florida was a major agricultural center that shipped an annual average of 8000 boxcar loads of produce. That's a lot of vegetables. This was in the days before train cars had mechanical refrigeration and the only cooling system was big blocks of ice stored in bunkers at each end of a boxcar. Adjacent to the ice plant was Rand's Yards, one of the Southeast's busiest switching yards where long freight trains loaded with fresh produce were put together for northern markets.

The huge ice plant employed 200 workers and was so large that trucks could be driven around inside. The mammoth bunker-like building was also used during hurricanes as a shelter for black farm workers that lived in shacks on surrounding farms. Local African-American historian, Charlie Morgan, recalled, *"I remember when I was a kid how we would all go up to the ice plant when a hurricane was coming. They'd let us stay in the ice plant because nothing was going to blow it down."*

Owned by the Mountain Ice Company of Chicago, the plant operated around the clock, seven days a week, until it closed down in the early fifties. With the invention of mechanical refrigeration for train cars, and with agriculture moving to the larger muck farms of South Florida, the market for ice simply ended. The rail yards are now vacant with only a few remaining side tracks, but cutting through the middle of this place is the shiny CSX mainline used by the Auto-Train which has its southern terminal just three miles down the tracks. Tourists arriving on the Auto-Train must wonder about the weird white walls standing beside the tracks. Little do they realize this was once the coldest place in Central Florida.

It's Not Really a Rock, So what is it?

In the Canaveral National Seashore North District, mid-way down Florida's Atlantic coast, there is something hidden in the sand dunes that is a little known relic of World War II. It is not easily accessible, first you have to drive six miles to the end of the pavement of A1A and that is as far as you're going to go without a special permit from the National Park Service. With a special backcountry permit and a gallon of mosquito repellent, you can hike a winding sand road about two miles farther south to what is called Target Rock.

At first this big rock looks just like a coquina rock, but upon closer examination you'll see that it is really weathered cement with lots of metal protruding out of it. If you stand back and use your imagination this rock seems to have a slight airplane shape. Looking around the dunes you'll find an abundance of lead, the kind that comes from a 50 caliber machine gun. But think about it for a moment and the puzzle starts falling into place, machine gun bullets and a rock with a slight shape of an airplane. That's right, it was a target for fighter aircraft during World War II.

In the 1940s this narrow strip of land between the Atlantic Ocean and Mosquito Lagoon made a good spot for target practice. There were several military air bases in this part of Florida, all needing a place to exercise their aerial attack skills. The Navy hauled a small airplane to the site and filled it with cement and for three years it was used as a target for fighter planes.

STRANGE FLORIDA II

Sarcophagus In the Middle of a Street

In New Smyrna Beach you'll find a tomb in the middle of Canova Drive. The street is named for actress Judy Canova who had planned at one time to put a trailer park in the area, but the grave, a premier attraction on the New Smyrna Historical Ghost Tour belongs to Charles Dummett.

His father, Douglas Dummett, came to New Smyrna prior to 1844 and built a house on Mount Pleasant, an Indian mound overlooking the river. Douglas Dummett was a sugar merchant, the Justice of the Peace and the orange grower who gets credit for starting Florida's famous Indian River citrus. He married a black slave girl and had three daughters and a mullato son, Charles, who was born in 1844. Charles Dummett attended boarding school in the North and in April 1860 while home on school break, he was killed while hunting when his gun accidentally discharged. He was buried by his father on the spot where he died. This could be the first "Spring Break" casualty in history. For the past century this area has evolved into a residential neighborhood, but Charles Dummett's tomb still sits on a little island in the middle of Canova Drive, named for movie actress Judy Canova.

Mystery S.O.S. Calls from the Atlantic

Over several weeks during March 2006 the U.S. Coast Guard on eight separate occasions received almost identical distress calls from a vessel somewhere between New Smyrna Beach and St. Augustine. Each time rescuers immediately searched the Atlantic but found no ships in distress. The calls always came at night over a non-existent radio frequency saying "Mayday, Mayday. Standby for longitude and latitude. We are going down." Was it a hoax or, as one paranormalist suggested, an S.O.S. from out of the past? On March 22, a slightly different but strange call came in urgently requesting help. Once again the Coast Guard responded but this time they actually found the boat. Although the vessel did have engine problems no one on board had sent a distress call and did not need help because the radio did no work. Okay, while the officials claim it was a hoax, let's stir the pot of mystery here, maybe the calls were coming from the Bermuda Triangle.

The Haunted Herlong Mansion

The historic town of Micanopy sits in North Central Florida just south of Gainesville. It is one of the oldest towns in Florida, a place with ancient live oaks, old wooden buildings, and plenty of antique shops. Located near the center of town on Cholokka Boulevard is the Herlong Mansion built in 1845, the year Florida gained its statehood.

Sometime around 1900, the 8000 square foot mansion was left to the six Herlong children by their mother with one stipulation; their father could live there until his death. By the time he died ten years later the mansion was in poor condition. The six Herlong children each wanted the house but the only one who could afford it was Inez Herlong-Miller, a former school teacher. She began a long fight with her siblings over ownership of the family home.

Inez eventually gained ownership and began restoring the mansion. In 1963, before she completed the restoration, Inez went upstairs to her childhood bedroom and several hours later was found unconscious from a diabetic coma. She never recovered and died a month later.

The place was later sold and converted into a Bed and Breakfast but it appears that Inez still haunts the place. Doors are reported to open and close by themselves and guests have told of being awakened in the middle of the night by the voice of a woman and feeling a misty spray on their face. Some have claimed to see an apparition darting across the room. Most of the ghostly activity occurs in a room called Mae's room. The room is named for Mae Herlong but was originally the bedroom of her sister Inez. The owner opened another room and called it Inez' room, but Inez still seems to prefer Mae's room.

The historic Herlong Mansion is one of the most talked about Bed and Breakfasts in Florida and its haunted story is a main attraction for many guests. But if you want to stay in Mae's room you'll need to make a reservation as it is the most popular room because of the resident ghost.

Record Rainfall

In October 1924, a small rainstorm dumped 23 inches of rain on New Smyrna. It was estimated that 4000 tons of water fell.

STRANGE FLORIDA II

World's Largest Confederate Flag

Greeting motorists coming into Florida on I-75 at White Springs is the largest flying Confederate flag in the World. The flag measures 20 by 38 feet and flies from the top of a 100 foot pole. It was hoisted in a dedication on February 15, 2002 attended by over 500 black and white descendants of Confederate veterans.

At the base of the flag pole is a granite wall etched with over 250 names from each of the 13 Confederate states and Indian nations. No public funds were used to build the 40,000 dollar memorial and flag pole which sits on property owned by the Sons of Confederate Veterans, a national historical society of 32,000 members. Florida SCV has future plans to construct such monuments at other entrances into Florida.

Highest Point in Key West

Dubbed Mount Trashmore this former garbage pile in Key West at 91 feet above sea level is the highest point in the Florida Keys. It was closed in 1994 and covered with plastic sheeting and a layer of top soil to seal in any toxic crap. It is now covered with grass but is still monitored for any emissions of methane gas and toxic wastes. On a few occasions methane gasses coming through vent pipes have burst into flames.

Now there's an effort to turn the mountain into a refuge for feral chickens. For years Key West has had a problem with wild chickens running loose in the city, many are descendants of when cock fighting was a popular sport on the island. Mount Trashmore may be the solution to the island's rogue rooster problem. Of course if that stuff sealed inside Mount Trashmore gets to percolating and blows its top, then Key West could end up with a volcano.

The Veterans' Train

You may see this unusual vehicle anywhere along Florida's east coast. It is the Veteran's Train built by Boyd "Buddy" Richardson of New Smyrna Beach. Buddy is an oddity himself, as a combat veteran he has the distinction of serving in the Navy, Army and the Marine Corps. After retiring from the military he has spent his life devoted to honoring veterans. His Veteran Train is made from an old truck converted into a locomotive and a 31 foot travel trailer transformed into a red caboose. It's a walk-thru military museum filled with hundreds of donated artifacts and photographs. Richardson exhibits his train and a massive collection of over 600 flags from every country and state at veteran events. On one occasion he drove his train all the way to Washington D. C. to be in the National Veterans' Day parade.

Elementary School is built on a Cemetery

Most folks knew there was a grave yard there before Palm View Elementary School was built in Manatee County. The problem is that many of the graves were unmarked resulting in the facility being constructed on top of the dead. In 2006, sonar equipment detected thirty graves three feet beneath school property. A Baptist minister spoke against school activities going on above the dead, saying, "It's important to respect the burial places of the dead." There are few official records for the graves since the cemetery dates back to the 1800s.

What's the Citrus Tower without Citrus?

The Citrus Tower in Clermont was built in 1956 on one of the highest hills in Florida. It was originally planned to be only 75 feet tall, but ended up being 226 feet high, or 496 if you count the antennae on top. It contains 5 million pounds of concrete and can stand winds up to 190 miles per hour. From its observation deck tourists could look out over 35 miles and see millions of orange trees. The Citrus Tower is a standing memorial to Florida's changing times. You can still look out over 35 miles of rolling hills, but nowadays you'll be looking at the roof tops residential developments that have replaced the once thriving citrus groves.

White Rattlesnakes

There is an area west of Gainesville which is known for its pure white rattlesnakes. About one albino rattler is found in each ten year period. In July 2001, herpetologist Mike Routh found one that was measured five feet. I guess the benefit to hikers is that white rattlers are easier to see, but regardless of color they are still poisonous.

STRANGE FLORIDA II

World's Most Unusual Monument

This is the first Florida oddity I can remember seeing as a kid when our fourth grade class went there on a field trip. It's in Kissimmee on the lakefront and is promoted as the "World's Most Unusual Monument" and you don't have to pay to see it.

It's a 50 foot tall, irregular quadrilateral pyramid...whatever that is. Officially, it's the "Monument of the States" with 21 tiers containing 1500 stones, rocks, and weird things from every state and 22 countries...and a meteorite from outer space.

The tall monument topped off by its 562 pound concrete eagle, was a project of the All-States Tourist Club of Kissimmee and was dedicated by the governor on March 28, 1943. The estimated weight of the monument is 60,000 pounds, much of it in cement donated by local citizens. But wait, there are more than rocks stuck in this weird structure, look close and you'll see a cannon ball from Michigan, buffalo horns from Montana, petrified wood from Arizona, a rock from the Sahara desert, a human skull, glacier eggs, a petrified apple from Wisconsin, a map of Holland, and some other weird things waiting to be found. This is another one of those rare free tourist attractions.

The Monument of the States, also known as the World's Strangest Monument in Kissimmee.

Mysterious Creepers

In August 1884, an Arkansas man traveling through Florida reported in the New York Times of encountering an army of crawling bugs near Palma Sola. He wrote, "I was startled by a rustling sound in the creeping plants through which I was walking. The noise came closer to me and I ran out to a strip of sand between the bushes and mangroves. I was not there long before the cause of the racket arrived. It was an army of big black bugs, each an inch to two inches long. They were so thick that the ground was black with them. There were millions and millions of them covering an acre and they moved as fast as a man can run. I was barefooted and they were crawling on my feet. I could feel my feet crushing them as I literally walked over them and wasted no time getting off the beach.

Did Extraterrestrials Hitch a Ride on a Meteorite That Fell in Middleburg?

According to old newspaper accounts, in early 1888 a colorful green meteorite crashed to earth in cultivated field south of Middleburg, Florida. Several witnesses to the amazing event approached the still smoking crater and found "a 200-pound block of limestone." Wait a minute, this sounds suspicious. I don't know about you, but I've never heard of a "limestone" meteorite. Okay, skip my skeptical remark and keep reading. A few months later, the mystery meteorite was exhibited at the Sub-Tropical Exposition after which it was put on display in Jacksonville. The stone was examined by a Dr. Hahn, who claimed to have discovered "miniature fossils" of corals, crinoids and shells" in the rock. Hey, this sounds like coquina rock that you can pick up at the beach. Anyway, Dr. Hahn photographed these micro-fossils of extraterrestrial life and published an article in Popular Science. News of extraterrestrial life landing on a limestone meteorite in Middleburg attracted the attention of the scientific community which "condemned Dr. Hahn for heresy." Dr. Lawrence Smith wrote, "Dr. Hahn is a kind of half-insane man, whose imagination has run away with him." Dr. Smith, had never examined the actual meteorite, but in his opinion the fossils were actually "crystals of enstatite."

STRANGE FLORIDA II

Dr. Hahn and his meteorite were saved from oblivion by Charles Fort, who wrote about the event in his 1919 work *"Book of the Damned."* Mr. Fort was a collector of weird news articles and it is from his name we get the term *Fortean* science. Whether or not a big green meteorite ever crashed in Middleburg, Florida, is anybody's guess.

7000 Year Old Brain Found in Titusville

In 1982, a construction project at Windover Farms in Titusville uncovered 155 ancient skeletons in a peat bog. Work was halted until anthropologists could examine the discovery. Through radiocarbon dating, they discovered the bones to be 7320 years old. The most incredible aspect of the find happened when a CT scan showed a brain preserved inside one of the skulls. The Windover brain yielded one of the world's first oldest samples of human DNA.

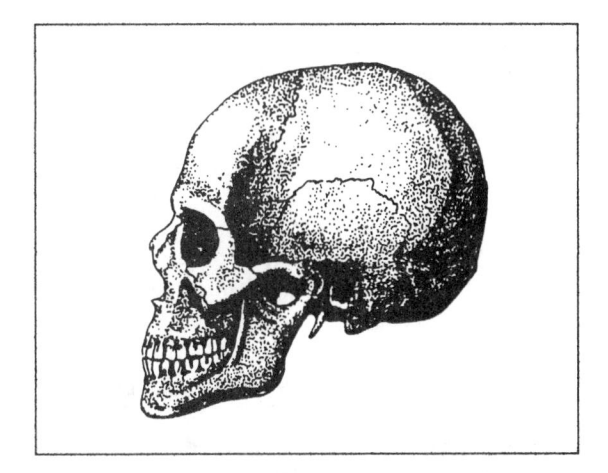

Cat Curiosities

In Key West, at the historic home of Earnest Hemingway, you'll find an unusual family of cats. Generations these cats have all had six toes on each foot.

A Devine Presence

Strange things often happen at strange times like during the Challenger space shuttle disaster in January 1986 that claimed the lives of seven astronauts. Many witnesses to this event claim they saw the image of Christ in the smoke cloud cause by the explosion. The unusual image can be seen in most video tapes and photographs of the tragedy.

Dolphin Dialogue

This strange incident occurred at the Miami Seaquarium. Trainers had placed a group of new, untrained dolphins in a holding pool next to a tank containing trained dolphins. The new dolphins were to begin their schooling the next day, however, trainers found the new students did not need training. They performed like professionals on the first try. The only answer to this mystery is that they had been taught tricks of the trade through communication with the trained dophins in the adjacent tank. Amazingly, it appeared the lessons had been learned overnight.

Author's note: Dolphin intelligence is pretty close to that of humans, however, the two cannot be fairly compared since brain functions of dolphins differ greatly from humans. For example, we humans lack the sophisticated sonar and echolocation ability of dolphins. Considering such abilities, maybe dolphins are really more intelligence than humans.

World's Largest Bird Nest

Talk about a high rise condo, check out this eagle's nest. When it was measured in 1963, this huge bald eagle's nest near St. Petersburg, measured 9 feet 6 inches wide and 19 feet 8 inches deep. It was estimated to weigh about 2 tons. It was probably built over a long period by a succession of feathered occupants. At the time, it was the largest bird nest on record and even claimed it's place in the Guinness World Records.

The Lost English Settlement?

In 1999 a fragment of a pre-1790's English pipe and pieces of plaster were found near Jupiter. The plaster was determined to be the same kind used on houses by the British during the Colonial period. So what were these artifacts doing in Jupiter, Florida? The British period in Florida lasted a mere twenty years from 1763 to 1783, but there are no records of an English settlement in this part of the state.

Historians speculate the artifacts may have come from the lost Greenville Plantation as briefly mentioned in old English historical records.

Florida's Mr. Greene in the Limelight

Tommy Greene should go down in history as one of Florida's most colorful folk heroes. He is as colorful as his name, because since 1964 every thing about him has been Green, his house, inside and out, his clothes, his car, and over the years he has named his dogs Shamrock, Olive, Gangrene, and Lime.

Folks in Madison, Florida, know Mr. Greene as the charismatic publisher of the *Madison County Carrier* who has spent a great deal of his life promoting the power of positive thinking. In front of his publishing company there are three tombstones inscribed with R.I.P. where Mr. Greene has buried the words "Impossible", "Can't", and "If." In Greene philosophy, "there's nothing you can't do if you put your mind to it." He has more than lived up to his way of thinking. He is a successful businessman who has served as a leader of several civic organizations and as president of the Florida Press Association. He once served green grits to members of the association. Madison is the place to go on St. Patrick's Day if you want to see green, you'll most likely find Mr. Greene serving up green pancakes or cooking up green rice and chicken for a fund raiser. He even dyed his hair green at one of these events. Oh yeah, did I mention that he writes with green ink?

A 1905 Tale of Teleportation

In 1905, at a meeting with Presbyterian ministers in New York, Dr. Isaac K. Funk discussed a teleportation account involving a physician who, at the time, was editor of a medical journal. In a presentation on psychic phenomena, Dr. Funk explained that the subject, suffering from a mortal illness, was transported in spirit from Florida to a home of a friend living 1000 miles away. There he conversed with his friend and was then spiritually transported back to Florida. "The startling feature to this experience," said Dr. Funk, "was that both men had immediately written the other describing how they had seen and talked with each other in a kind of apparition form. The letters crossed in the mail."

Dr. Funk concluded that nine-tenths of psychic phenomena is fraudulent, and that the other tenth could be explained by telepathy and clairvoyance.

Prowling Wild Man Creates a Scare

An April 29, 1888, newspaper report tells of a crazy Wild Man prowling and threatening Concord citizens, in Gadsden County, Florida. Described as tall, muscular, with long flowing, pure white hair and beard, the mysterious wild man wore clothing made of skins and bark. He carried a flint lock rifle and an ax handle with spikes on the end. A search party was mounted after the man threatened several people.

Alien Bodies Stored In Florida?

This story has floated around UFO groups for years. It goes like this; one night back in 1973, the great honeymooner himself, Jackie Gleason, claimed to have been taken by his friend President Richard Nixon to a secret facility on Homestead Air Force Base. Gleason was shown the preserved remains of Alien bodies recovered in 1953 from a crashed flying saucer. Hurricane Andrew wiped out Homestead AFB resulting in its closure. I guess we can assume the alien bodies were transferred to another location. In a freedom of information request submitted by me in 1996, the government denied the story, which was their way of saying *"go away and don't bother us, if we did have space aliens we wouldn't tell you because it's a secret."*

Spontaneous Human Combustion

Florida has one of the best documented cases of Spontaneous Human Combustion. No, this is not caused by consuming too many lima beans, although gaseous foods may contribute to it. SHC is defined as the human body bursting into flames. It is a very real, but puzzling phenomenon that first appeared in 17th century medical journals. On the morning of July 2, 1951, Mrs. Resser, 67, of St. Petersburg became a victim of SHC. When the landlady went to the 67 year old woman's apartment to deliver a telegram, she found the door knob too hot to touch. Fearing the place was on fire, she summoned two painters working nearby to open the door. They found little smoke inside and nothing seemed burned except for a pile of ashes, which turned out to be Mrs. Resser's incinerated body. She had been reduced to ashes, except for her skull and one foot still in a slipper. The case was investigated by Assistant Fire Chief S.O. Griffith who found no other fire damage except a greasy spot of soot on the ceiling above the victim. Nearby newspapers, linens and other flammable items were untouched by the heat. The bizarre case was examined by the FBI, county coroner, police, an arson specialist, pathologist, and fire marshall, but no one could begin to offer an explanation. It appeared that Mrs. Resser had simply exploded into flames and was incinerated while sitting in her chair.

Strange Deaths of Orlando Police Horses

On March 2, 1997, while on routine mounted patrol in downtown Orlando a police horse named Partner's Pride, suddenly dropped dead for no apparent reason. Exactly one week later another Orlando police horse dropped dead at the same exact spot at the same exact time. Foul play was ruled out and so was anything else that might have caused the deaths of the otherwise healthy steeds. The mounted policemen reported sensing nothing that would have caused their horses to drop dead. The answer to the mystery was finally found by engineers from Orlando Utility Commission. Beneath the ground electricity was leaking from a defective cable that supplied power to a street light. A timer turned on the light at a certain time in the evening.

The combination of wet grass and metal shoes on the horses' front hooves had sent a 277 volt, electrical charge through the animals' chests. This instantly stopped their hearts. The riders were unaffected because of being insulated by the saddles.

Look East, It's the Bermuda Triangle

Florida is the only state that touches the mysterious Bermuda Triangle, the infamous triangular section of the Atlantic Ocean known for its disappearances of thousands of ships and aircrafts. Some researchers of the weird believe the triangle of extends to some interior parts of the peninsula. The most documented disappearance was that of Flight 19, which you read about in this book. There is a whole menu of theories about the Bermuda Triangle which blame everything from portals into other dimensions to space aliens to the sunken continent of Atlantis.

The area has some of the highest traffic of surface and air craft which means that a certain number will ultimately meet with problems. It is also an area where several weather systems merge to create problems for ships and planes. There are geologic anomalies which may account for some disappearances, but others cannot be explained and that's what makes the Bermuda Triangle a weird spot in the ocean.

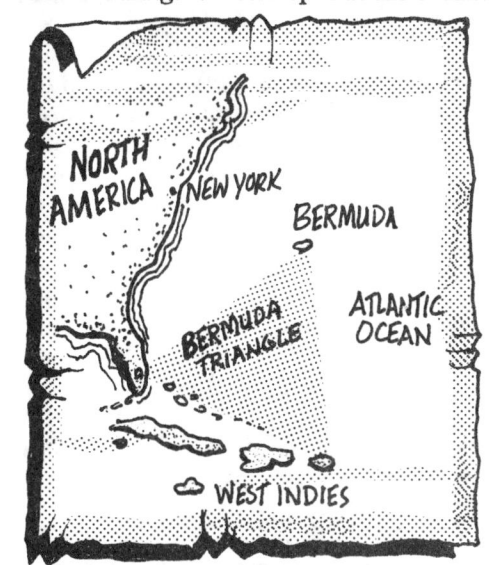

Florida's Lost Volcano

Florida's lost volcano is an old mystery that is still mystifies folks, although many have never heard of it. For more than 100 years a mysterious chimney of smoke was observed rising from a vast swamp 25 miles southeast of Tallahassee. People believed that the smoke was from a small volcano or fissure somewhere in Wakulla or Jefferson counties. On some nights a glow could be seen in the swamp from the top of the old state capitol. The mysterious smoke even made its way into Maurice Thompson's 1881 novel called *"Tallahassee Girl."*

On August 31, 1886, the smoke ceased forever when the Great Charleston earthquake sent tremors across North Florida. Did the earthquake seal-up a volcanic fissure? Although, geologists dispute the idea of volcanic activity in the region.

In 1870, an expedition with a New York journalist, tried unsuccessfully to locate the site of the so-called "Wakulla Volcano." The journalist died of "swamp fever" while in the swamp and a guide was injured when he fell from a tree. In later years others reported finding a blackened, dishpan size hole atop a rocky knoll in the swamp. Prior to 1960, Clarence Simpkins of the Florida Geological Survey made several trips into the swamp and reported finding boulders as "if they had been thrown out of the earth," but no signs of a volcanic crater. The source of the smoke still remains another Florida mystery

Nazis Invaded Florida

During World War II, in the pre-dawn hours of June 17, 1942, a German U-boat surfaced off the coast of Ponte Vedra, south of Jacksonville and unloaded a squad of Nazi marines in a rubber raft. The Nazi infiltrators paddled ashore with a crate of explosives and four suitcases of civilian clothing. They buried their uniforms in the sand dunes and changed into civilian clothes. This was part of Hitler's secret Operation Pastorius. Another group had landed on Long Island, New York. Their objective was to infiltrate the United States and conduct sabotage acts against the defense industry. By the end of July 1942, the FBI had captured all of the infiltrators.

Six of the Nazis were tried and executed in August 1942 and two were sentenced to life in prison, but later deported at the end of the war. The bold act marked the first time since 1812 of a foreign enemy landing on the shores of the continental United States.

The Torreya Tree

On the banks of the Apalachicola River grows a rare botanical species called the Florida Torreya, also known as the Gopherwood or Stinking Cedar. This particular Tree reaches 50 feet and resembles a yew tree, but is found in no other place on earth. The belief that Noah built the Ark from the Torreya, or Gopherwood, has led to speculation that the Garden of Eden was located in Florida.

Florida's Oldest Living Thing

Near Longwood, Florida is the *Senator*, a 3500 year old living Cypress tree. With a majestic girth of 47 feet and standing 126 feet tall, it claims fame as the World's largest cypress. Hey, it's another rare free tourist attraction, too.

The NASA Moon Tree

At the Kennedy Space Center between two exhibit buildings grows a leafy green tree. This is NASA's Moon Tree, grown from a seed taken into space aboard Apollo 14 on a half million mile round trip to the moon.

The Chuluota Ghost Light

I have witnessed this phenomenon on several occasions as did many teenagers growing up in Seminole County. The Chuluota Light, also called the Oviedo Light, is seen where the bridge crosses the Little Econ River on State Road 13 near the communities of Chuluota and Oviedo. This was a favorite Friday night spot for high school boys to take their dates for a good scare. As I recall, the eerie, faint greenish-colored light rises up from a nearby marshy area and floats to about tree top level before vanishes. It appears more like a mist than a solid light. Some claim the light has chased behind their cars and others have reported hearing a hissing sound. The explanation is that the light is caused by methane gas produced by decaying bio-mass. In other words, regular old fashioned *Swamp Gas*.

The Demon of Round Cypress

Down the St. Johns River, west of Sanford, there is a stand of cypress which was once said to harbor a shape shifting witch who often made appearances as a panther. This round forest of trees was also a moonshiners' hideaway during Prohibition and some believe the demon tales got started as a way to scare off nosy people. Remnants of old whiskey stills can still be found in this swamp. Most likely the only real demon was the potent brew made by the bootleggers.

The Devil's Circle

In the Black Water Swamp in Lake County there is a perfectly round circle where nothing will grow. It is a small barren sandy circle in the middle of a swamp where the soil seems to have an unusually high level of sodium, but why is that? Legends have it that Satan danced in a circle at this spot. The stories parallel North Carolina's Devil's Stomping Ground.

The Amazing Maggie Bell

Maggie Bell was a renowned medium from 1919 to 1924 in the rural community of Lake Monroe, in Seminole County. She conducted nightly séances in her parlor and could levitate tables. She vowed to return after death to prove to her friends that life goes on in spirit form. After she died several folks experienced Maggie's presence in the form of her ghost or the sweet aroma from a pipe that she smoked.

I now possess Maggie Bell's spirit table in my collection of weird artifacts. I hope she doesn't mind. In June 1996, using three researchers and two mediums, I conducted a controlled experiment with the table in the spiritualist town of Cassadaga, Florida.

The objective was to see if the table had any special spiritual qualities. During the two hour session, the table levitated off the floor in a wavering motion before settling down on the floor. The wood legs and top of the table seemed to have a liquid-feeling during the event and then became rigid again once the table was on the floor. What we witnessed cannot be explained in conventional science terms. I must conclude that it was old Maggie Bell sending us a little proof of the afterlife. One thing we know for sure, we did nothing to cause the table to float and the experiment was under controlled conditions.

THE MAGGIE BELL SPIRIT TABLE

Three Women Killed By Big Gators

It has happened before and will happen again, someone eaten alive by an alligator. In May 2006, a Miami area woman went out for an evening jog next to a canal and was attacked and eaten by a big gator. What remained of her dismembered body was found by construction workers who notified the authorities. Florida Fish and Wildlife investigators said the gator was about ten feet long. After the gator was killed, the medical examiner found the victim's arms inside its belly.

Exactly one week later, a 23 year old girl on vacation from Tennessee was snorkeling in Juniper Springs when she was attacked and killed by an alligator. On the same date, 130 miles to the south, near St. Petersburg, the body of a 43 year old woman was found in a canal. Bite marks indicated that she too had been attacked by an alligator.

As a word of caution, don't mess with gators. In Florida you're in the gator's habitat...you could end up as an entrée on an alligator's menu.

Town of Doom

St. Joseph, Florida was once called the most wicked city in America. By 1840, the West Florida town had a reputation of gambling, brothels, saloons, fights, murders, and anything else that was anti-social or downright mean. Then punishment arrived in July 1841 when three-quarters of the town's citizens died of yellow fever. Three new cemeteries had to be opened to take care of all the corpses. Still it was not enough to make folks behave themselves. So, in September 1841, a forest fire burned the town to the ground. Residents had hardly rebuilt the town when an 1844 hurricane struck the town and a tidal wave covered it under tons of sand.

The Phantom of Lake George

There is a fading folk story about ghost ship seen in the mists of Lake George. One old commercial fisherman in 1943, described it as, "A sternwheeler, there weren't nobody on board, but on the wheelhouse you could make out the name of the boat, Iris." Strangely, in 1882, a boat by a similar name, Isis, sank at the north end of Lake George.

Post Office Twilight Zone

In April 2006 a postcard sent to Riverside California was returned to Mack McCormick of Deland because it had an incomplete address. Nothing weird about that, except the postcard had been sent in 1956! Exactly where the postcard had been hiding for 50 years is a mystery.

Although he was not the mailer, Mr. McCormick now resides in the house of the person who, in 1956, had sent the card. It was postmarked Deland, Florida but could not have been lost in the local post office because it has moved several times in the past 50 years. Now I can understand how the Postal Service has lost five packages I have mailed over the past six years. Maybe if I'm lucky, my packages will show up fifty years from now.

A Dark Secret

A dark secret from the past was uncovered in the 1970 when workman were repairing pipes beneath the narrow brick street in front of St. Augustine's historic Spanish Hospital. What they found was hundreds of human skeletal parts, legs, arms, feet, hands, and a few complete skeletons. The hospital, which is now a museum located between Aviles and Artillery streets, was used from 1784 until 1821. Historians determined the body parts to be from amputations performed in the hospital. The city declared the strange cemetery of parts to be a historic site and ordered the bones covered-up. The bones are still there, beneath the street, so if you are strolling through this part of the Ancient City just remember what's beneath your feet.

Coral Castle: Florida's Stonehenge

Coral Castle in Homestead, is a must see for folks who like weird places. Coral Castle's mystery is really about its builder, Edward Leedskalnin, who stood only 5 feet tall and weighed a mere 100 pounds. This frail man single handedly built a megalithic marvel out of tons of coral rock as a monument to his lost love.

Ed was born in Riga, Latvia in 1887 and after being jilted by his sixteen year old bride, he came to America. After working as a logger in the Pacific Northwest, he moved to Florida for health reasons and purchased land in Florida City. He began quarrying and carving coral rock and built a huge monument to his lost love, whom he called his "Sweet Sixteen."

Ed worked in totally secrecy and no one knows how he was able to carve, move, and place 1,100 tons of coral blocks without mechanical assistance. Ed claimed to know the secrets that the Egyptians used in building the pyramids. A couple of young boys who spied on his work one night claimed that Ed would hold his hands above the big blocks and levitate them into place. What is most bizarre, is that when Florida City became too crowded in 1936, Ed dismantled and moved the massive structure to Homestead, where today it's a tourist attraction. It was first called Rock Gate Park and the average block weighs 9 tons. When the huge 9 ton gate required repairs in 1986, it took a 50 ton crane to lift it. Yet Ed had placed the gate into position by hand so that the mere touch of a child's finger would open it. In 1951, Ed Leedskalnin took his engineering secret to the grave...a secret that still baffles visitors to Coral Castle.

St. Augustine's Strange Obelisk

There's a strange obelisk in the square behind the Old Government House in St. Augustine. It is a monument to General William Wing Loring, born in 1832, who began his soldier service at age 14 in the Florida militia. Around the base of the tall stone memorial are etched the flags of the United States, the Confederacy, and the Ottoman Province of Egypt. Know as Florida's most unusual general, William Loring served as a general officer in both the U.S. and C.S.A. armies and as a pasha in the Egyptian army. Another unusual fact about General Loring is that he only had one arm, having lost the other one in the Mexican War. He died on December 30, 1886 in New York City, however, his funeral was not held until March 1887 in St. Augustine.

Florida's Deadly Red Tide

This deadly menace, produces a nerve toxin, and is caused by microscopic organisms. It can cover thousands of square miles of sea killing tons of fish and causing severe breathing problems for humans.

Pyramids of Florida

There are two pyramids deep in the Big Cypress Swamp, according to a 1971 article by the Peninsula Archaeological Society. In 1969 amateur archaeologists reported finding two stone structures shaped like pyramids. The stone blocks fitted so precisely that a pocket knife could not be inserted between the cracks. A form of hieroglyphics was observed etched on some of the blocks. One pyramid was 12 feet high and the other about 14 feet tall. Five miles northeast of the site was found a mysterious wall of stacked stones determined to be about seven miles long. While some have tried to link the structures to Atlantis, the origin and purpose has never been determined.

In 1980, a salvage and treasure hunter found what he believed to be a submerged pyramid off the coast of Vero Beach. He described the structure as a flat top pyramid with a flat top, covered with sea weed, with stair-step sides under 100 feet of water. In 1985, a second sighting of this structure was made from an airplane and was reported in several Florida newspapers and in Pursuit magazine. The underwater structure was estimated to be 30 to 40 feet high with each base side being 86 feet and a 20 by 20 feet flat top. In another report the base measurements were estimated to be 100 square feet. It's anybody's guess at whether or not the structure is man-made or a natural formation of coquina rock.

Giant Sink Hole Eats Town

In 1981, a gigantic sinkhole opened up in a Winter Park business district. It began with a small hole but soon grew to more than 300 feet in width and 100 feet deep. The huge sinkhole swallowed a house, a parking lot, a swimming pool, six luxury cars, and a portion of two city streets. The total damage was estimated to be four million dollars.

Frigid Florida in July

The normal July temperature for the Florida surf is 80 degrees. However, on July 30, 1996, swimmers found the Atlantic ocean too cold when the water temperature dropped to 68 degrees. Unusual oceanographic conditions were to blame.

Never Ending Christmas

A living Christmas Tree stays decorated all year in the small town of Christmas, Florida. Each year thousands of holiday cards are mailed from the town's post office just for the unusual postmark. The community is located on east Highway 50 in Orange County and gets its name from Fort Christmas, built in December 1837 during the 2nd Seminole War.

The Case of the Escaped Cobras

According to a couple of articles allegedly from wildlife publications, in 1970, a truck carrying a case of deadly Egyptian cobras wrecked just south of Clewiston. The deadly vipers escaped into the Everglades and have been multiplying ever since. The story is disputed by wildlife authorities and is probably an urban legend...or maybe not.

The Disappearance of the S.S. Marine Sulphur Queen

The S.S. Marine Sulphur Queen, weighing 7240 gross tons, left Beaumont, Texas, on February 2, 1963, bound for Norfolk, Virginia. The huge 504 feet long tanker carried a crew of 39 men and a cargo of 15,269 tons of molten sulphur. The trip was to take the ship around the tip of Florida and up the Eastern Seaboard. Somewhere near the Straits of Florida all communications with the vessel was lost. No S.O.S. calls were made to the Coast Guard. A massive search lasting 16 days was launched involving both surface and air craft. On February 20th, a fog horn and life vest from the ship was found by a Coast Guard patrol. Other than that, the fate of the S.S. Marine Sulphur Queen remains unknown.

Cattle Mutilations

In 1992, a full grown bull was found in Samsula with its head cut off. In 1996, cattle mutilations were reported in Brevard, Orange, and Seminole counties. All of the animals were missing body parts, like an eye, tongue, ears, or tail, which appeared to have been surgically removed. In spite of investigations by the authorities and a 1000 dollar reward offered by the Cattlemen's Association the cases remain mystery.

Lethal Sunken Treasure

There's deadly nerve gas on the ocean floor off Florida's east coast. The Government called it *Operation Chase*, an acronym some say stood for "cut holes and sink 'em."

It all started when the army wanted to dispose of its stock piles of lethal nerve gas. In August 1970, the out-dated Liberty ship Le Baron Russel Briggs was loaded with 418 steel and concrete coffins filled with 12,500 M-55 rockets containing nerve gas. The old ship was scuttled off the coast of South Florida and now lays under 16,000 feet of water. When officials became concerned about the sea pressure imploding the containers, army experts assured everyone that in theory everything was safe. The sea pressure at that depth is about 31-tons-per-square-inch. The next time you swim in the Atlantic, think about the lethal cargo that's still on the ocean floor.

Then there is the legendary WW2 German U-boat that sank off the coast of Tampa. Allegedly this submarine, which some believe is U-boat 166, contains 500 tons of poisonous mercury. Captain Bill Miller wrote about it in his book, *Tampa Triangle*. Researchers argue that there's no reason for mercury to be on board a submarine, but others think the sub was ballasted by mercury. Another theory is the U-boat was carrying a cargo of mercury from Mexico. Mercury is an ingredient in explosives and Mexico was a main source.

A Law Officer's UFO Encounter

It was four in the morning on March 19, 1992, when a Haines City patrolman called his dispatcher to report something very odd. The officer, in a rural area of citrus groves, was watching a green light descending from the early morning sky.

The light moved to his right and soon lit up the interior of the patrol car. The officer reported the light was so brilliant that he had to squint to look at it. He described it as a dome-shaped metallic object about 15 feet wide. The strange craft began following the car at forty miles per hour and soon maneuvered in from of the patrol car. It then hovered about 10 feet above the ground apparently causing the vehicle's radio, ignition, and lights to go dead. Three other patrol cars arrived at the scene to find the officer sitting half out of his police cruiser, cold and shaking. The object had by that time disappeared. The next day the officer underwent a series of physical and psychological tests. It was determined the officer had a high level of credibility and had truly witnessed something unexplainable.

According to the Center for UFO studies in Chicago, what the officer had described was similar to 500 other sightings in their files. The officer remarked, "It was the strangest experience of my life."

Longwood's Inside-Outside House

There's a strange house north of Orlando in the community of Longwood. The weird house started out being built in the 1870s near Boston, Massachusetts for Captain Pierce. In 1873, when the Captain decided to move his family to Florida, he moved everything. His house was dismantled and loaded on an ocean steamer that transported the sections to Jacksonville. The dwelling then began a journey down the St. John's River on a barge to Sanford. From this point it traveled overland by horse drawn wagon to Longwood.

It is known as one of the first pre-fabricated houses in the country, and also one of the most traveled dwellings. The framing is on the outside of the house thus making the exterior the interior...or the interior the exterior...oh well, you get the point. In other words, the place is wrong-side-out. Even the stairway to the second floor was on the outside until Captain Pierce built an inside circular stairway. Oh, yes, the house is still haunted by Brutus, the Captain's dead cat. In recent years, the house was moved again, but this time in a preservation effort by the Central Florida Society for Historic Preservation.

World's Smallest

Carrabelle, Florida, holds claim to the smallest police station; a phone booth! When a new station was built the town kept its original phone booth station as a tourist curiosity. It sits at the intersection of US 98 and County Road 67.

Down in Ochopee, at the opposite end of the state on the Old Tamiami Trail, you'll find America's smallest post office. It's the size of a shed because it was originally a tool shed. Its zip code, 33943, is regular size.

STRANGE FLORIDA II

FLORIDA MARINE GIANTS

These photographs are proof that some very big sea creatures really do inhabit Florida's coastal waters. The giant manta ray, or "devil fish," (top photo) was captured off Cape Canaveral in July 1924. The monster sea turtle was hauled ashore near Daytona in the early 1920s. Both of these harmless "monsters" still live in Florida's ocean waters. The sea turtle is now protected as an endangered species. [*photos courtesy LUTHER'S PUBLISHING and Halifax Historical Society.*]

INDEX

A
Aerial Phenomena, 33
Alien Bodies, 114
Alligators, *gators*, 102, 117
Apparitions, Specters and Spirits, 7

B
Ball of Snakes, 104
Bermuda Triangle, 115
Big Fish, 107
Big Foot, *See Skunk Ape*
Big Tree, 116
Florida's Oldest Living Thing, 116
Bird Nest, World's largest, 113
Black Panther, 27
Bloodsucking Critter
of South Florida, 62
Bone Yard, Daytona, 105

C
Calusa, The Mysterious, 89
Casselberry's Mystery from the sky, 80
Cat Curiosities, 113
Cattle Mutilations, 119
Celestial Railroad, 20
Chuluota Ghost Light, 116
Chupacabra, 62
Christmas, Never Ending, 119
Citrus Tower, 111
Cobras, Case of the Escaped, 119
Coldest Spot in Florida, 109
Confederate Flag, World's Largest, 111
Coral Castle, 118
Curse of Koresh's Tomb, 30

D
Dark Secret, 118
Dead Man's Greeting, Curious tale of, 50
Death from the Sky, 17
Demon of Round Cypress, 116
Devil's Circle, 116
Devine Presence, 113
Dolphin Dialogue, 113

E
Eglin AFB, 43
School built on cemetery, 111
Evil Spirits in Winter Park home, 44
Extraterrestials, 112

F
First Floridians, 24
Flight 19, What happened to, 28
Flight 401, Legend of, 107
Flying Saucer House, 108

Forces of Nature, 63
Fort Bragdon, 106

G
Gondwanaland, 78
Government experiments, exposed, 105
Gravity Defying Hill, 106

H
Halloween Village, 103
Hammerhead shark, 108
Harry Wise, The Great, 52
Herlong Mansion, Haunted, 110

I
I-4 Dead Zone, 21
Inside-Outside House, 120

J
Jaguarundi sightings, 26
Jessup, Morris K., 47

K
Killer Bees, 108

L
Law Officer's UFO Encounter, 120
Legend of Tomokie, 59
Lethal Sunken Treasure, 120
Living Dead, 19
Lion Terrorizes city hall, 103
Lost Confederate Treasure, 85
Lost English Settlement, 113
Lost Tribe, 107

M
Maggie Bell, *The Amazing*, 117
Man Awakes from Sleep, 77
Mastodon Hunt, *Last Great*, 23
Middleburg Meteorite, 112
Mister Greene, 114
Mount Trashmore, Key West, 111
Mystery Beam, Encounter with, 40
Mysterious Creepers, 112
Mystery Hole, Brooksville, 104
Mystery S.O.S. Calls, 110

N
NASA's Moon Tree, 116
Nazis Invade Florida, 116

P
Phantom Buffalo, 102
Phantom Farmer, 104
Phantom, *Lake George*, 117
Pit of Horrors in the Okefenokee, 87
Post Office Twilight Zone, 118
Pyramids of Florida, 119

R
Rattlesnakes, *White*, 111
Record Rain Fall, 110
Red Tide, *Florida's deadly*, 118

S
Sam McMillan, *Horrifying Mystery of*, 60
Sarcophagus in Middle of Street, 110
Scariest Threat, *Florida's*, 92
Schoolhouse disappears, 103
Sea Serpents and Water Monsters, 72
State Seal, Mystery of Florida's, 103
Sinking Florida Feeling, 79
Sink Hole Eats Town, 119
Skull, Voodoo, 108
Skunk Ape, 1
Slithering Secrets, 67
Smallest Police Station, 120
Smallest Post Office, 120
Spanish ship found on Navy base, 105
Spontaneous Human Combustion, 114
Spookhunters, 69
Spook Hill, 106
S.S. Marine Sulphur Queen, 119
Strange Coincidences, 106
Strange Messages from Beyond the Grave 58
Strange Obelisk, *St. Augustine's*, 118
Strange Police Horse Deaths, 115
Strange Sounds, 24
Stuff falling from the sky, 16
Submerged city found, 105
Suicide, Strange Case of, 47

T
The Night Florida Trembled, 84
Thompson, Susan, medium, 44
Tale of Teleportation, 114
Tampa's Dead Zone, 107
Target Rock, 109
Titanic, 14
Torreya Tree, 116
Town of Doom, 117
Tracks on the beach, 18

U
Unidentified Flying Objects, 33
UFO Hill, Strange case of, 38
UFO Crash? Brevard County, 104
Unusual Monument, World's Most, 112

V
Veterans' Train, 111
Volcano, Florida's Lost, 115
Voodoo, 108

W
Wampus Cat, The Elusive, 82
Weird Prophesy, 20
Weird Mail Bag, *Readers' letters*, 95-102
Weird Bicycle Tour, 109
Wild Man, 114
Windover Brain, 113
Wonder House, 108

Y
Yeehaw Junction, 56

Z
Zombie, 19

Special Acknowledgements

The author would like to thank the following contributors who have made this collection of Florida strangeness possible.

Christine Kinlaw-Best, Florida historian

Dr. Warren Browning, anthropologist

Matt Coplan, Profile Racing

Florida State Archives

Dr. Gary Frick, M.D.

Anthony Lopez

Gary Luther, publisher

William Moriaty, Florida author

Scott Marlowe, cryptozoologist

Lisa Sanchez, Weird Florida Fan Club

Owen Sliter, Spookhunters.com

Allen Stringfeld, ufologist

Susan Thompson, medium

Lisa Wojcik, cryptozoologist

About the Author

As a tenth generation Floridian, *Charlie Carlson* has a special interest in the state's lost histories and folklore which he has written about in 14 books and over 300 magazine and newspaper articles. His first book about the Sunshine State's weirdness, titled, *Strange Florida*, [Luther's Publishing] was released in 1997 and became an instant hit with readers. This was followed by contributing articles to *Weird U.S.* [Barnes and Noble, New York, 2004] and his own best seller, *Weird Florida*, [Barnes and Noble, 2005]. In 2005, he published his first novel, *Ashley's Shadow*, [Luthers Publishing], a supernatural, romantic ghost story based on one of Florida's most popular haunted legends. In 2006, he contributed feature stories to a national best seller, titled, *Weird Hauntings*, [Sterling Publishing, New York, 2006]. In 2006, he began work on *Strange Florida II*, a sequel to his original book which includes several subjects dropped from *Weird Florida* by his editors.

Known as *Florida's Master of the Weird*, Charlie Carlson has appeared on hundreds of radio and television programs, in numerous television documentaries, and, in 1999, played a folklore historian on the Sci-Fi Channel in the *Curse of the Blair Witch*.

Charlie Carlson is a charter member of *America's Grand Order of Weird Writers*, www.weirdwriters.com, and has served on the boards of directors of several historical societies. In 2005, he began a statewide lecture tour and currently hosts two presentations for sponsors, his *Weird and Wacky World* and, for outdoor festivals, his tented *Weird and Wacky Sideshow*, an exhibition of oddities and illusions presented in the nostalgic circus style of P.T. Barnum.

The author lives on the east coast of Florida and may be contacted for bookings or interviews through his fan club at weirdflorida@hotmail.com or by writing to: Charlie Carlson Productions, Att: Public Relations, P. O. Box 2684, New Smyrna Beach, Florida, 32170.